Politics, Development and Security in Oceania

Politics, Development and Security in Oceania

Edited by David Hegarty and Darrell Tryon

Studies in State and Society in the Pacific No. 7

Australian
National
University

E PRESS

ANU
E PRESS

Published by ANU E Press
The Australian National University
Canberra ACT 0200, Australia
Email: anuepress@anu.edu.au
This title is also available online at http://epress.anu.edu.au

National Library of Australia Cataloguing-in-Publication entry

Title: Politics, development and security in Oceania / edited by David Hegarty and
                  Darrell Tryon.

ISBN: 9781922144867 (pbk.) 9781922144874 (ebook)

Subjects: Developing island countries.
                  Australia--Foreign relations--Oceania.
                  France--Foreign relations--Oceania.

Other Authors/Contributors:
                  Hegarty, David, 1943-
                  Tryon, Darrell.

Dewey Number: 327.94095

Cover design and layout by ANU E Press

Contents

> Mr Philippe Gomès,
> President of the Government of New Caledonia, 2009-2011

Introduction

   David Hegarty

Oceania and its Inheritance

   Jon Fraenkel

   Jone Baledrokadroka

   Hélène Goiran

   Afamasaga Toleafoa

   Jean-Yves Faberon

   Sémir Al Wardi

Oceania: Current Needs and Challenges

Oceania and its Wider Setting

Preface

French and Australian collaborative research in the humanities and the social sciences in the South Pacific has grown and intensified significantly over the past two decades, beginning with the international symposium *Changing Identities in the Pacific at the Dawn of the Twenty-First Century* held at the Australian Embassy in Paris in 1997, followed in 1999 by a major conference, *Identity in the Pacific*, organised by the French Permanent Secretary for the Pacific, Ambassador Pierre Garrigue-Guyonnaud and held at the Tjibaou Cultural Centre in Noumea. The edited proceedings of this colloquium, generously funded by the French Ministry of Foreign Affairs, constituted the first issue of the *New Pacific Review/ La Nouvelle Revue du Pacifique*, published in 2000 in English and French in a single volume.

In December 2003 a French-Australian symposium, *Pacific Island States Today/ L'État des États*, was held at The Australian National University in Canberra, organised by the Centre for the Contemporary Pacific, Research School of Pacific and Asian Studies. This symposium brought together a wide range of scholars and whose penetrating presentations covered major issues in both the Francophone and Anglophone Pacific.

In August 2004 an international conference, *Les Assises de la Recherche Française dans le Pacifique/ A Review and Evaluation of French Research in the Pacific* was held at the Tjibaou Cultural Centre in Noumea, sponsored by the French Government and the Government of New Caledonia.

In April 2006, another French-government sponsored international symposium, *AGORA* (Ateliers Gouvernance et Recherche Appliquée) was held at IRD (Institut de Recherche pour le Développement), Noumea, New Caledonia, major themes being governance and economic development, again bringing together Francophone and Anglophone scholars from France and the Pacific region.

This was followed in October 2009 by two conjoint Francophone/Anglophone conferences, held at the IRD Centre in Noumea, *Stability, Security and Development in Oceania*, preceded by *AGORA-2,* an international conference on Anglophone research in the humanities and the social sciences in the Francophone Pacific, sponsored by the French Government and the Government of New Caledonia. The first of these conferences was sponsored by the French Fonds Pacifique and the State, Society and Governance Program at The Australian National University. An edited selection of presentations from this symposium constitutes the present volume.

In October 2010 there was another conference held in Noumea, the *École Plurilingue dans les Communautés du Pacifique / Multilingual Schools in the Pacific Communities*, co-organised by the University of New Caledonia, The Australian National University and CREDO (the Centre for Research and Documentation on Oceania).

In March 2011 the Government of New Caledonia and the French Government sponsored a major international conference *Destins des Collectivités politiques d'Océanie/ The Future Destiny of French Pacific States*, co-organised by Jean-Yves Faberon, Viviane Fayaud and Jean-Marc Regnault. This conference was held at IRD Noumea. The French edition of the proceedings appeared at the end of 2011 (Presses Universitaires d'Aix-Marseille), and a selection of the presentations on the future of New Caledonia is in preparation for publication in English at The Australian National University.

To complete the picture of Franco-Australian collaborative research in the humanities and social sciences to date, the French Government Fonds Pacifique and The Australian National University are co-sponsoring an international symposium *Governance, Development and Change in Oceania,* to be held in Canberra at The Australian National University in 2012. The proceedings of that symposium will complement the present volume. For the 2009 and 2012 symposia have been designed to maximise Francophone and Anglophone interaction and intellectual exchange, the first colloquium being held in New Caledonia and the second here in Australia.

It is manifest from the above summary account of collaborative activities, that French and Australian mutual understanding and appreciation have undergone a period of constant and continuous growth for more than a decade now, especially in the fields of governance, social and political change, and economic and social development. Most pleasing, perhaps, has been the marked increase in Francophone and Anglophone Pacific Islander exchanges, backed up by the commitment to collaboration by the metropolitan powers for the development of the Pacific region.

Editors' Note

In the interests of improving accessibility to our Francophone colleagues, an abstract in French is provided at the head of each chapter.

Contributors

Sémir Al Wardi is a Professor of Political Science at the University of French Polynesia, Tahiti, and an analyst of political change in French Territories overseas.

Matthew G. Allen is a Fellow in the State, Society, and Governance in Melanesia program and formerly a Research Fellow, Resource Management in Asia-Pacific Program, College of Asia and the Pacific, The Australian National University.

Jone Baledrokadroka is a former Colonel with 25 years in the Fiji Army having served as Chief of Staff and Land Force Commander. He is researching the role of the Fiji military in ethnic politics towards a PhD at State, Society and Governance in Melanesia Program, College of Asia and the Pacific, The Australian National University, Canberra.

Treva D. Braun is Gender Equality Adviser, Secretariat of the Pacific Community (SPC), Noumea.

James Bunce is a senior researcher in the Joint Standing Committee on Foreign Affairs, Defence and Trade, Parliament House, Canberra, and formerly a doctoral candidate in the Strategic and Defence Studies Centre, College of Asia and the Pacific, The Australian National University.

Asenati Liki Chan Tung is a Lecturer in the School of Government, Development and International Affairs, University of the South Pacific, Suva, Fiji, and formerly Pacific Research Fellow, State, Society and Governance in Melanesia Program, College of Asia and the Pacific, The Australian National University, Canberra.

Jean-Yves Faberon is Honorary Professor of Public Law, Institut de droit d'outre-mer, Paul Cézanne University Aix-Marseille III; Maison de la Mélanésie, Noumea.

Jon Fraenkel is a Professor of Political Science, Victoria University of Wellington, New Zealand. He was Senior Fellow, State, Society and Governance in Melanesia Program, College of Asia and the Pacific, The Australian National University, Canberra, 2006-2012.

Hélène Goiran is a former French military officer, expert on the history of the Fiji military; doctorate in military history and defence studies, University of New Caledonia and University Michel de Montaigne (Bordeaux III).

Philippe Gomès was President of the Government of New Caledonia, 2009-2011.

David Hegarty is a Visiting Fellow in the State, Society and Governance in Melanesia (SSGM) Program, College of Asia and the Pacific, The Australian National University, Canberra. He was Convenor of SSGM 1998-2008, and Associate Professor, Australia and New Zealand School of Government, University of Melbourne, 2010-11.

Henry Ivarature is a political scientist with IDEA (the International Institute for Democracy and Electoral Assistance) based in Canberra and formerly the Regional Governance Adviser at the South Pacific Forum Secretariat in Suva, Fiji.

Rose Maebiru is Human Development Adviser (Youth), Secretariat of the Pacific Community (SPC), Noumea.

Linda Petersen is Manager, Human Development Program, Secretariat of the Pacific Community (SPC), Noumea.

Susana Taua'a is a Senior Lecturer in Geography, Faculty of Arts, National University of Samoa.

Afamasaga Toleafoa is a former Ambassador for Samoa to the European Union in Brussels, a civil society leader, author, consultant and advocate of democracy and governance in Samoa and the Pacific.

Darrell Tryon is Emeritus Professor of Linguistics, College of Asia and the Pacific, The Australian National University, Canberra, and former Deputy Director of the Research School of Pacific and Asian Studies, The Australian National University, 1999-2005.

Acknowledgements

We would like to express our gratitude to the Institut de Recherche pour le Développement (IRD) in Noumea and especially its Director, Gilles Fédière, for their encouragement of collaboration between IRD and The Australian National University, and for hosting the international symposium which gave rise to this book.

In Australia we owe a debt of gratitude to Sue Rider, State, Society and Governance in Melanesia Program for her administrative oversight of the symposium organisation. Our special thanks go to Dr Ewan Johnston whose considerable editorial skills have been indispensable and greatly appreciated.

Tables and figures

Tables

Figures

The Pacific Islands Map

Opening Address to 'Politics, Development and Security in Oceania' International Colloquium, Noumea

Mr Philippe Gomès,
President of the Government of New Caledonia, 2009-2011

In my Inaugural Address on August 31, 2009 I spoke on behalf of the whole government which I have the honour to preside, and, among other things, I said this:

> The sovereignty that we share with the state includes powers regarding international and regional relationships. The Noumea Agreement has not been fully implemented yet and its potential has not been fully tapped in this area. Today we have to speak in the name of this country in the Pacific area.

This goes to show that you are most welcome here in Noumea, New Caledonia, a land where the word is of the essence. Your word, originating in the Pacific, in our neighbour and friend, Australia, carries knowledge of the whole Pacific, and it matters to us. We will listen to it carefully and we will share your insight.

I am particularly keen on research, a field that I was intent on taking care of personally within my government, for research is a nation's intelligence and future, in other words, the promise of New Caledonia. Research is open-mindedness, and we can be only happy to see that you, famous ANU Professors, have chosen to hold your colloquium here this year. Your field covers the French and Francophone Pacific, and you have come to the right place for your study. Our word is at your disposal.

Your conference is taking place here at the same time as our French-speaking Communities' Week. I do not see any contradiction or conflict in this; on the contrary, I am happy to see these two events happen at the same time.

Your bilingual conference shows that the Pacific is not an Anglophone lake but a mare nostrum, as the Latin phrase has it, 'Our Sea', where various waves mix in a common life, and as a result, we can live together.

As you know, on October 6, just a few days ago, France and Australia signed in Canberra an agreement on higher education degree equivalencies, which allows exchanges between our universities, and, obviously, that is of major interest for New Caledonia.

There are only 370 Australian students in France as opposed to 3,000 French people studying in Australia. Dear Professors, tell your students that we are expecting them, that Australians are always welcome in New Caledonia, and this goes for students, and not only because we have the same academic year!

Dear Professors, I see that the precise topic of your conference is 'Stability, Security and Development'. This area of Pacific Studies fits perfectly with the dynamics of present-day New Caledonia and with the policy of my pluralistic and inclusive government.

Of course, we want our country to develop, but we cannot get development by fiat. Development requires an environment which allows our vibrancy to thrive. These conditions are, of course, stability and security. You have perfectly outlined our common problematics in this region.

Security is external security, and the major powers with which you and we are linked unfailingly are the warranty that we most need.

Stability, which includes internal security, is the ideal that we all reach for, and in this undertaking we succeed in varying degrees. Because I do not enjoy your freedom as researchers, I will refrain from expostulating on such and such a neighbouring nation; I will just acknowledge the example of democratic stability that Australia shows in her peaceful parliamentary majority changes.

This model is not the one we have in New Caledonia, for we have chosen to challenge stability by attempting to disconnect it, at least partly, from majoritarian democracy. Our purpose was to constantly seek consensus, and that is a tough proposition. In our country the rift between the two major political groups is a deep one, and as a result, instability seemed inevitable, just as our troubled years have clearly shown; therefore, we resolved to work together toward a more balanced development for our country, for its security and its peace. I'm proud to tell you on behalf of New Caledonia that, so far, we have been successful! New Caledonia has known stability for 20 years now, and my government will continue on the same path.

Dear Australian academic friends, your being here today is proof that you have comprehended this; your having elected to come to Noumea to discuss stability, security and development in the Pacific shows that you have a sense that New Caledonia is a relevant place, a place where all these notions flourish today: we greatly appreciate your coming here, and I thank you very much for it.

I am in no way seeking to show smug optimism and futile complacency. I am perfectly aware that nothing is final, including in New Caledonia, and maybe especially in New Caledonia, where the fire is still smouldering. I know perfectly well that in my country there are too many people who are left behind as far as development is concerned, and they are too obvious a danger for its stability and security. We probably have not found the way; in any case we have not been able to reduce the scope of this problem, and I do not play down its potential for an outburst of political and social violence. As a result, I will stay informed about your research in this area, about the models that are analysed, and about the solutions that are devised and tested. Your proceedings will be not only scientifically valuable; they will also be of great interest to the group of men and women to whom I belong, the men and women who are in the task of building up Oceania day by day.

Thank you, and may your discussions be fruitful!

Introduction

1. A Changing Oceania

David Hegarty

Bilan: Politique, Développement et Sécurité en Océanie

La configuration de la puissance dans la grande région Asie-Pacifique connaît actuellement des changements très importants avec la montée de la Chine comme puissance mondiale. L'influence de cette dernière se fait sentir à travers l'augmentation de l'aide et le développement du commerce et des relations diplomatiques, surtout avec Fidji. L'unité régionale dans le Pacifique connaît quelques tensions, surtout suite au coup d'Etat de Fidji de 2006 : L'Australie, la Nouvelle-Zélande ainsi que les Etats polynésiens et micronésiens sont opposés au régime militaire alors que les Etats mélanésiens continuent à reconnaître son chef, le commodore Bainimarama. Les indicateurs de développement et de gouvernance des pays insulaires sont contrastés mais globalement satisfaisants, la plupart se situant dans une assez large plage autour de la moyenne mondiale. Sur le plan politique, la région a connu à la fois la stabilité et l'instabilité, mais la plupart des petits Etats sont parvenus à « s'en sortir » en cas de crise. La professionnalisation croissante des responsables de l'administration publique, le développement d'organisations au sein de la société civile et leur rôle grandissant dans les politiques publiques et dans leur mise en œuvre, ajoutés à la réaction positive des donateurs en faveur des Etats insulaires, produisent des résultats plus positifs dans les petits Etats. Le besoin d'analyser et de développer les relations entre les Etats insulaires anglophones et francophones d'Océanie est toujours présent.

Asia-Pacific: Power Shifts

As the first decade of the 21st century drew to a close – and morphed into the second – it had become obvious that in the broad Asia-Pacific region dramatic political, strategic and socio-economic change was underway. A 'power shift' was the description applied by strategic affairs specialist, Professor Hugh White of The Australian National University, in which as Asia's 'strategic plates shift' a new Asian power balance arises requiring all states to negotiate a relationship with China. The productivity revolution that is transforming China, White asserts, is 'reordering the world'. Asia and the region will become more contested over the next few decades and the larger powers including Australia will have to reassess defence and security risks – as well as the costs of addressing them.

Former Australian Foreign Minister, Gareth Evans (subsequently head of the International Crisis Group), went further and described these changes in the Asia-Pacific regional power equation as a 'tectonic shift' with repercussions not only regionally, but for the global balance as a whole.

The significance of these developments and their interpretations is contested. Michael Wesley (Head of the Lowy Institute for International Affairs) suggests this does not mean an inevitable direct Chinese challenge to American primacy in the region – nor that China's neighbours will fall immediately into line with Beijing. Wesley's book – which underlines the importance of adding India to the Asia-Pacific equation – analyses the 'new highways of power' across Asia. 'China and India have arrived as major shapers of the how the world works, and their preferences, enthusiasms and aversions will have a strong effect on the choices that other societies face,' he contends. They will be key shapers of globalisation in the 21st century, but they will be acutely sensitive 'to their dependence on the outside world for the oxygen of their development'. Asia will not simply settle into an ordered hierarchy under Chinese leadership – forces from outside the Indo-Pacific will play decisive roles in the evolving region.

Other analysts have seen China's rise as unsettling the established order and prompting a reappraisal of the fundamentals of Asia-Pacific security, yet still providing room to move and scope for creativity for middle powers such as Australia. Former Australian Prime Minister and Foreign Minister, Kevin Rudd, noted a 'strategic uneasiness' accompanying China's rise and suggested the need for an Asia-Pacific regional security dialogue arrangement of some kind. The US government had little doubt about the significance of China's rise and of the need for the West to ensure there was balance at least in the emerging Asia-Pacific strategic equation. President Obama's reference in late 2011 to a 'pivot to Asia' in American strategic thinking and security posture from the Middle East to the Asia Pacific signalled US thinking about that balance.

The Island Pacific

Within the Pacific Islands region itself these 'power shifts' and their geo-strategic and security implications in the broad Asia-Pacific region have not gone unnoticed – nor have they been without some impact. China's rise to international prominence had led also to an increased Chinese official interest and presence in the Pacific Islands region. Chinese diplomacy including official visits, increased aid to the Pacific Island Countries (PICs) and particularly to the Melanesian Spearhead Group, commercial investment and migration activity had increased substantially in the past decade. Lowy Institute analysts estimate that $200m in Chinese grants and soft loans have been made to the PICs: in contrast to USAID allocations of $4m.

A product of a globalising China, this outreach has paralleled China's expansion into Africa and South America (that is, to other developing country regions) in search of trade and commercial opportunities and imports of raw materials for its industrial expansion. China analyst at The Australian National University, Graeme Smith, argues that this expansion is not necessarily state-directed – nor is it likely to be state-controlled. An important element in China's foray into the 'developing world' has been the diminution of its long-standing rivalry with Taiwan.

All the PICs have been impacted to some extent and will continue to be impacted as China extends its reach across the Third World in search of markets, materials and influence. China's exports to the region have increased their market share of all exports to the PICs from 1.5 per cent in 1998 to an estimated 8.5 per cent in 2008. Chinese goods now constitute 11 per cent of Papua New Guinea's imports, while Solomon Islands has rapidly increased its exports to China through sales of timber.

The PICs stand to benefit from a greater range of relatively cheap trade-store goods and building materials; through educational opportunities on offer for PIC university-level students to study in Chinese institutions (Samoa, for example, has over 100 undergraduates currently in Chinese academies); through construction programs such as the delivery of office buildings to Samoa; and from Chinese outbound tourism. For the PICs – and for Papua New Guinea in particular – market and trading opportunities have been expanded. Interestingly, this enhanced Chinese presence has not meant that PICs have had to choose between it and their long-standing regional neighbours, partners and donors. China's rising influence has also had political spin-off, for example, by providing the military regime in Fiji with an opportunity to play the 'China card' to relieve or stymie pressure from Australia and New Zealand for it (Fiji) to return to civilian democratic government.

'Ripple Effect'

In response to China's increasing interest and activity in the Pacific Islands a 'ripple effect' of sorts has occurred. More attention has been paid to the PICs by their 'traditional' partners Australia and New Zealand; but also by the United States, described by one commentator as 'an absent-minded ally' of the Islands. Aware of Fiji's Commodore Bainimarama's interest in China (and his visits there) and also aware that China had not criticised the Bainimarama coup but had in fact increased its aid to Fiji after the coup event, US Secretary for State, Hilary Clinton, held talks in 2010 with Fiji's Foreign Minister Ratu Inoke Kubuabola, canvassing a stronger partnership and dialogue with Fiji and proposing to open a USAID office in Fiji in 2011. US interest in the Pacific Islands was also iterated by Kurt Campbell, US Assistant Secretary of State for East Asia and Pacific Affairs, at a US Congressional hearing in 2010 at which he also spoke of a desire for stronger partnership and dialogue with Fiji. These discussions were not couched in the language of 'threat analysis', but were mildly cautionary in tone and reaffirming of common interests and commitments to liberal democracy, peace and security within the region as a whole. Japan was similarly exercised that Fiji not be pushed closer to China.

Australia's Parliamentary Secretary for Pacific Island Affairs, Richard Marles, in a September 2011 address, 'Why the Pacific matters?', similarly offered affirmations of Australia's commitment and connections to the Islands region – a statement addressed to both Pacific and Australian audiences. While Marles did not explicitly mention China, Australia's clear concern was that Fiji not be pushed into a Chinese embrace. Marles stated:

> We are the Pacific's major security partner. We are the Pacific's major economic partner. We are its largest aid donor – around half of the world's development assistance to the Pacific comes from Australia. We continue to be connected by a deeply rooted network of personal, business, sporting and community ties. Our geography dictates that we have a shared destiny.

Earlier the then Australian Foreign Minister, Stephen Smith, had urged China not to undermine Australian and regional efforts for Fiji to hold elections. The Australian 2020 Summit reported that China had become more visible, more focused economically, but seemed not to know what its own aims were in the PIC region. China had indeed increased its trade and aid to the Pacific; but overt competition with other donors or proselytising on its part had not been apparent. Scholars and foreign policy makers in universities and think tanks across the Pacific continue to grapple with what China's rise means for security and development in the Islands.

The extent to which China's global rise will lead to strategic rivalry between and among the larger powers in the Asia-Pacific region and which may impact the security and well-being of the Pacific Island states remains unclear. Much depends on how an intended 'pivot' in US strategic and security policy from the Middle East to the Asia-Pacific is framed and the extent to which it heightens tensions between the larger powers of the region. The potential for such rivalry may also be limited by the creation of mechanisms for dialogue and accommodation among the region's larger powers.

PIC Economies and Polities

Within the 'Island Pacific' itself changes were also underway – domestically and regionally. Change in the Island Pacific is a product not so much of the geo-politics of the larger extra-regional powers but is essentially set by: continuing concerns within the Island states over the management of economic fragility and the generation of broad-based development; the political and social dynamics within Island polities that are so often the product of local political cultures and generational changes in leadership; and by intra-regional relations between the PICs themselves and between the PICs and their aid and development 'partners'.

The Island groups that constitute the French Pacific Territories – New Caledonia, Wallis and Futuna, and French Polynesia – occupy a somewhat enigmatic position in the broad Pacific Islands community. While clearly 'in and of' the Pacific region, and occupied with their own particular internal dynamics, they are not as yet fully or meaningfully engaged with the 'Anglophone' Island states of the Pacific.

The global economic crisis that shook economies the world over in 2008-09 had impacted adversely upon the PICs. Economies weakened significantly as tourism, agriculture, and manufacturing industries slowed with the fall in global demand. Remittances declined by as much as 20 per cent and the value of the region's public offshore investment funds shrank as international equity prices slumped. As a consequence, government revenues contracted and essential services, maintenance and infrastructure developments were delayed, and jobs were lost. The slowdown across the Islands region was exacerbated by a series of wild storms in early 2009 that disrupted communications and the tourist industry particularly in Fiji, and by the economic and physical impact of the tsunami later that year in Samoa and Tonga.

But the PICs 'navigated the global storm' (the title of an Asian Development Bank publication) and remained in reasonably good shape economically and politically. A briefing paper for the Forum Economic Ministers in mid-2011 expected the Pacific Islands' economies to remain on the path to recovery from the GFC, though with a slow growth for the Islands' economies of approximately 2-3 per cent per annum in the early part of the decade. Were the rapid growth rates for Papua New Guinea and Timor Leste to be factored-in, an overall regional growth rate of 5-6 per cent per annum was forecast.

Improved growth figures in the early part of the decade for the PICs' major trading partners – particularly Australia and New Zealand – were expected to support the recovery of growth rates in the PICs through an increase in tourism, improved remittance flows and infrastructure expenditures. Rising demand for food and other soft commodities especially from China may also have a positive impact for those PICs with fisheries and agriculture exports. Timber exporters – such as Solomon Islands and Papua New Guinea – will also benefit from higher prices for timber products in Asia. The expected decline in timber export incomes for Solomons, as its loggable forests are depleted, may be compensated for by a rise in mining earnings. ADB simulations of long-term growth prospects for the non-mining PICs for the next two decades indicated a yearly growth rate of 1 per cent to 3 per cent. (World Economic Outlook Update, IMF, 2011)

Regional officials and international agencies had noted that an important economic governance lesson had been learned from the GFC crisis experience in that 'policy-based programs' helped sustain the political appetite for reforms, even during difficult times. In the Cook Islands, Samoa, Solomon Islands, and Tonga, extensive SOE and infrastructure governance improvements were implemented during an economic recession and in election years. Even in countries where there were changes in government, commitment to the programs has been sustained pointing to enhanced resolve and confidence in domestic economic management.

Regionalism: Under Stress

The Pacific Islands Forum remains the predominant regional political organisation, but strains within and between the PIC member states have become prominent since the coup in Fiji in 2006. Australia and New Zealand successfully sought the exclusion of Fiji from the Forum because of the coup, but this prompted a reaction from the Melanesian states which embraced the Bainimarama regime and strengthened the sub-regional grouping known as the Melanesian Spearhead Group (MSG). That in turn led not so much to a 'rift' among Forum Island members, but certainly to an increase in the antipathy of Polynesian leaders to their western regional counterparts (and perhaps vice-versa). A new MSG headquarters building in Port Vila had only recently been funded by aid from China.

Doubts subsequently emerged about the effectiveness of the Forum as a regional political agency charged with enhancing collaboration in economic, trade, aid and diplomatic relations with international donors and development agencies and about its ability to build stronger intra-regional cooperation and a higher international profile. The location of the Forum's headquarters in Fiji is a factor in the organisation's decline in potency. While the coup regime remains in power in Fiji a strengthening of the region's political voice is not in prospect. The regionalist effort has thus to some extent become a casualty of the Fiji coup.

At the working level, the *Pacific Plan*, adopted in 2005 for strengthening regional cooperation and integration, has focused largely on making the existing regional organisations more effective; for example on fishing regulation, maritime surveillance, climate change mitigation intervention, regional education systems, strengthening the ombudsman and audit institutions and on development assistance coordination. But the key functional area of greatest moment to the PICs is progress on key regional trade agreements and potentially the integration of markets – an area, however, in which there have been few significant results. And there remain continuing doubts about the viability of the Forum Secretariat's efforts in this direction. Pacific economist Satish Chand has commented that it was the security concerns of the major powers that shaped regionalism – and they still remain important factors – but trade integration is not a significant factor contributing to regionalism today. Pacific Island countries, he suggests, may want to pursue trade liberalisation unilaterally.

The South Pacific Community (SPC), however, with its headquarters in New Caledonia has been a beneficiary of this regional strengthening process with policy coordinating responsibilities for the major technical agencies of the region including the region's fisheries and environmental organisations now falling within its ambit.

PIC Domestic Political Trends

Through the early years of the 21st century, Pacific Island countries experienced degrees of both turbulence and stability. Fiji has been the most conflicted with its history of coups – the most recent occurring in December 2006 with Commodore Frank Bainimarama's seizure of power from a civilian government following a breakdown in power-sharing arrangements between leaders of the country's communally based parties. Bainimarama subsequently consolidated his authority in 2009 by dismissing the Court of Appeal judges (and all the judiciary) who had found his coup illegal, abrogating the constitution, and transferring total control of the country to himself and his military forces for a period of five years. He has proceeded to shake up the institutional fabric of the Fijian polity by challenging both the long-established order of its eastern-based chiefly authority and that of the Methodist Church. The Commodore has held out the prospect of elections in 2014, but the question now remains: is the military ever likely to withdraw from the political scene?

Solomon Islands politics and society has been disturbed dramatically by over a decade-long period of ethnic tension precipitated in the late 1990s on Guadalcanal and which led in its initial stages to conflict, the loss of several hundred lives, considerable damage to property and sharpened antagonism between peoples from the islands of Guadalcanal and Malaita. An intervention by regional forces from the Pacific led by Australian police and military personnel stabilised the situation. While open conflict was contained, the mistrust generated and the disruption to services and to confidence across the nation impacted strongly on the economy and the body politic. Shifting factional alignments within the Parliament and frequent changes of Prime Ministers via Parliamentary ballots, together with the raiding of the country's timber resources through exploitation by 'foreign loggers', have limited the prospect of responsible and reformist government and for the building of an effective state. In fact, it has been suggested that a 'shadow state' of sorts exists in Solomons with influences outside the formal state structure continuing to exercise control over resources and key development decisions.

Papua New Guinea – the largest of the PICs – has a substantial resource base with oil, natural gas, copper and gold deposits, forests and fisheries stocks, all of which provide a solid foundation for long-term income generation and national wealth. Its problems are those of political and economic management, hefty population growth and of service delivery to its six million people across a rugged topography. It has a democratic though fractious political system with security of tenure for coalition governments being problematic – a situation made even more so by a 2010 Supreme Court ruling that allowed MPs to move amongst parties at will. Its rambunctious, 'spoils' and patronage type politics in which parties have little consistent platform or ideology mean that state/public resources are readily squandered. Papua New Guinea's political leadership, however, is undergoing a generational shift and its bureaucracies (central and provincial) are beginning to develop policy and implementation traction which may augur well for future policy-making and administration. Election outcomes in mid-2012 will provide a significant marker for stability or otherwise.

Vanuatu is the more stable of the 'authority-lite' Melanesian states despite having had a history of 'revolving-door' ministerial appointments and fluid (re) placements of senior administrators. It is noteworthy that one of the gurus of 'state-building' theory and practice, Francis Fukuyama, a few years ago, took an interest in Melanesia's conundrum of 'strong societies and weak states' and the relative absence of – and difficulty in establishing – central authority.

Samoa – which gained its independence from New Zealand in 1962 – is the region's most stable polity characterised by a one-party-dominant political system, few changes of government, and an extremely able bureaucracy. It has benefited from the continuance of a bonded, hierarchical political culture; an early history of anti-colonialism; a well-developed education system; a close and continuing relationship with New Zealand; and a diaspora which is diligent in sending remittances to relatives in Samoa. Samoa's domestic critics decry the degree of control exercised by the ruling party (the Human Rights Protection Party), though its civil society is active and informed. The Kingdom of Tonga – unified in the mid-19th century – is transiting gradually from a benign monarchical system to a form of democratic governance. The first ever democratic poll in 2010 produced a reformist-orientated government, though radical change is not on the agenda.

The Micronesian states of Kiribati, Tuvalu, Nauru, the Federated States of Micronesia, and the Republic of the Marshall Islands, along with the small Polynesian state of Tuvalu, are small but generally reasonably stable political entities. But they all face the constraints of distance, small size, small populations and limited resource bases in formulating national development strategies. All are dependent on foreign aid and on remittances from their nationals abroad. National income from, for example, fisheries exploitation has been less momentous that anticipated at independence. Cook Islands and Niue enjoy a special independence in association relationship with New Zealand. Their politics – as with most of the smaller island states – are essentially 'family politics' and rarely do situations arise that threaten their stability.

Indicators of Development and Governance

In attempting to assess the relative strengths, weaknesses and durability or otherwise of states within the international system; to gauge their relative levels of political, economic and human development; and to estimate how well or otherwise a particular state can withstand crises or the threat of state failure, a raft of indicators and indexes have been developed.

Some have proven useful to our analysis of development in the Pacific region – others not. Most offer an interesting guide to how well or otherwise a particular state is progressing relative say to its neighbour – or to similarly-sized states elsewhere in the globe. They are not necessarily analytical tools in themselves, but they are useful to policy makers, governors and civil society organisations within these states in identifying areas of governance, economy and polity that might be supported or strengthened. Donor agencies find them of some value in identifying areas and programs to support. Some of the more regularly used indexes are briefly canvassed below.

The *World Governance Indicators* represent the aggregate views on the quality of governance in countries across the globe drawn from a survey of enterprise, citizen and expert respondents in think tanks and other institutes within each country. Most Pacific Island countries are surveyed for the WGI and their performance can be usefully compared (though with caveats – see below – in mind) on each of the six indicators: *Voice and Accountability*, *Political Stability*, *Government Effectiveness*, *Regulatory Quality*, *Rule of law*, and *Control of corruption*.

There are clear limitations on the utility of these indicators as precise measures of governance within each country and on their direct comparability with others; but they nonetheless provide us with a generalised indication of the state-of-play within PICs and of progress or otherwise towards an ideal-type goal. Papua New Guinea, for example, does reasonably well on the *Voice and Accountability* indicator with a score of 50 per cent; though its scores for the other five indicators are close to the 25 percentile mark. Its scores on the *Corruption* control and the *Rule of Law* indicator are quite low and would appear to be regressing. Solomon Islands, having had a difficult decade marred by an as yet unresolved internal conflict, would appear to have regressed from a mid-way position on all the above indicators to a ranking of 25 per cent or less over the past decade – and especially so in relation to *Government Effectiveness*. Fiji has nose-dived on all six WGI indicators since the coup in 2006; whereas Vanuatu – with the exception of a low *Government Effectiveness* indicator – scores well into the third quartile on all other indicators. Tonga has mid-range third quartile performance scores across all indicators. The clear stand-out countries in terms of governance performance across all indicators are Samoa followed closely by the Cook Islands.

On the *Ease of Doing Business* index created by the World Bank as a guide to private sector conditions and the environment for foreign and national entrepreneurship (and which includes business start-up times, credit availability, taxation regimes and investment protection), of the 24 countries in the Asia-Pacific region many PICs score quite well. Tonga, Samoa, Vanuatu, Solomon Islands and Fiji are placed in the top ten, while Papua New Guinea comes in at 15th, followed by the smaller PIC states with Timor Leste in 24th place at the tail-end of the list. (Singapore is at the top of the Asia-Pacific list).

Pacific Island states – because of their small size and often distant location from the large centres of power and influence in international politics – are often regarded as belonging to the world's weak and fragile sets of states. Fragile states have long been regarded by policy-makers and security analysts in the 'developed' world as: vulnerable to overthrow, to political and economic instability, to 'capture' by unscrupulous neighbours, to be easily 'penetrated' by organised crime and seduced by the blandishments of international criminal organisations; easily led astray by carpet-baggers; more likely to fail because of weak institutions and inexperienced leadership; and therefore likely to be in need of support and 'rescue' by larger powers of the developed world!

The *Failed States Index* published by the ultra-conservative US *Foreign Policy* magazine ranks 60 states across the globe that have prospects of failing: the most likely to fail according to this list is Somalia at number one, and the least likely is Djibouti at number at 60. Only three Pacific states make the list: Timor Leste at number 23, Solomon Islands at number 48, and Papua New Guinea at number 54. Note that these ratings do not predict collapse, but rather attempt to measure vulnerability to collapse or conflict – that is, conflict of sufficient magnitude that would render those state institutions and those embryonic 'forces that bind' to become totally ineffective and/or dissipate.

Perhaps more pertinent to the situation of small Pacific Island states is an assessment of the 'Fragility of Small Island Developing States' produced by Carleton University in Canada's Country Indicators for Foreign Policy Project. It is not a predictive (i.e. of collapse) calculation but rather an index of fragility for small states that in certain severe circumstances may be more prone to collapse. Of the 37 states ranked in this index from 'Least Fragile' to 'Most Fragile', Samoa is ranked 9; FSM 10; Vanuatu 11; Fiji 16; Palau 20; Tonga 21; Papua New Guinea 30; Kiribati 31; Solomon Islands 33; and Timor Leste 35. (The SIDS least fragile small state is Barbados at number 1, while the most fragile is Guinea-Bissau at 37).

The United Nations Development Programme's *Human Development Index* includes all PICs and its 2011 rankings show that all – with the exception of Palau and the Federated States of Micronesia – have risen steadily up the rankings over the last 30 years. Countries are ranked from number 1 (Norway) to number 187 (Congo) on a four-step scale of Human Development: Very High, High, Medium, and Low. None of the PICs feature in the top two rankings of 'Very High' or 'High'. Most PICs inhabit the Medium ranking (as per the table below), while Solomon Islands, Timor Leste and Papua New Guinea are ranked in the 'Low' category.

Table 1: UNDP Human Development Index Rankings 2011

1-47 Very High
(Norway #1 – Barbados #47)
48-94 High
(Uruguay #48 – Tunisia #94)
95-141 Medium
(Jordan #95 – Bhutan #141)
90 Tonga
99 Samoa
100 Fiji
(101 China 101)
116 FSM
122 Kiribati
125 Vanuatu
(134 India)
(135 Ghana)
142-187 Low
(Solomon Islands #142 - Congo #187)
142 Sol Islands
147 Timor Leste
153 Papua New Guinea

Note: Tonga has slipped from a HIGH ranking in 2004 to a MEDIUM ranking in 2011. SI, PNG and TL slipped from the bottom layer of MEDIUM in 2004 to the upper ranks of the LOW category in 2011 (thereby slipping below the Regional Asia-Pacific average).

The anti-corruption agency Transparency International's well-known 'Perception of Corruption Index' ranks the PICs in the following table:

Table 2: Transparency International Perception of Corruption Index 2011

New Zealand = (Rank #1)	
Samoa	69
Vanuatu	77
Kiribati	95
Tonga	95
Solomon Islands	120
Timor Leste	143
Papua New Guinea	154
(Somalia = Rank #182)	

Perhaps of the most utility to PIC governments in addressing their development issues and policies are the UN Millennium Development Goals (MDGs). A 2011 Asian Development Bank workshop on 'The Millennium Development Goals in Pacific Island Countries: Taking Stock, Emerging Issues and the Way Forward', reported that low growth rates, few employment opportunities and subsistence economies for most rural people makes it a difficult proposition for the Pacific region as a whole to make substantial progress in achieving the MDGs by the target date of 2015. Mixed progress has been made, however, across the Pacific Islands region. 'On track' towards achieving the goals are: Cook Islands, Niue, Palau, Samoa and Tonga. Making 'Mixed progress' towards achieving the MDGs are Fiji, Marshall Islands, the Federated States of Micronesia, Solomon Islands, Tuvalu and Vanuatu. 'Off track' in achieving the MDGs are Kiribati, Nauru and Papua New Guinea. The Pacific region overall is on track to achieving the MDGs in the areas of access to primary education, gender equality in education, and reduction of infant and child mortality. Maternal health is a widespread problem though many countries are picking up their performance on that goal.

The GFC has made things more difficult for government expenditure on service delivery. But in the process of helping PIC governments pursue development targets the policy, planning and management effort involved by national bureaucracies has enhanced the effectiveness of national budgeting strategies, of development decision-making and of implementation strategies more generally. In other words the *governance* spin-off from attempting to attain these Goals has been important for PICs.

Themes and Issues

The chapters in this volume canvass political change and development across the Pacific Islands from a variety of perspectives, each contributing to the analysis of a region growing in complexity and in confidence. They fall neatly into three sections: Oceania and its Inheritance; Oceania – Current Needs and Challenges; and Oceania and its Wider Setting.

Oceania and its Inheritance

Political Institutions

Jon Fraenkel opens the volume with a survey of what he regards as the second phase of post independence politics and institutions in the South Pacific, noting – from the mid-1980s – an increasing complexity of domestic and regional issues and a persistent instability confronting leaders and their societies. Despite the hybridisation of political systems – the political engineering and experimentation with power-sharing, decentralisation, and electoral arrangements and the testing of constitutions all of which were intended to settle fractious polities – volatility, he suggests, is likely to persist well into the 21st century. He identifies key 'gaps' in political arrangements – including the absence of popularly-based parties, of women in politics, and, in Fiji's case, of respect for constitutional democratic rule – all indicating that many Pacific countries have yet to reach their post-colonial 'settlements'. Fraenkel book-ends this volume with a chapter discussing the relevance or otherwise of European models of government to Pacific Island states.

Fiji: Which Way?

Interpreting Fijian politics has not proven an easy task. Its polity – divided ethnically, communally and geographically – experienced democratic rule from the time of Fiji's independence in 1970 until a coup in 1987 seemingly irretrievably altered the political landscape. A second coup followed later that year (again led by Rabuka) – then a brief return to civilian rule was punctuated in 2000 (by a George Speight led coup). Elections and a return to parliamentarism followed; but then in 2006 a further coup (led by Commodore Bainimarama) took place. Bainimarama has 'promised' a return to civilian rule by 2014. In his chapter in this volume Jone Baledrokadroka – a former senior officer in the Fiji military and an arch critic of Bainimarama – writes that Fiji entirely deserves the descriptor of a 'coup-prone state'. In the communally bifurcated Fiji there has long been ambivalence towards democracy, and support for it by Fiji's communities over the years has always been conditional.

Baledrokadroka offers an interpretation: in many ways the focus on 'professionalism' in the military and its experience in 'peacekeeping' over many years in the Middle East has led the hierarchy to believe it has a clear 'mandate' or 'obligation' to undertake a 'nation-building' role and to address what it sees as a severe weakness in civilian authority and an ineffectiveness in decision-making structures and patterns. But coup regimes – particularly the most recent – become self-serving. If military officers want political power they should resign their commissions and contest elections, he argues.

Hélène Goiran suggests that there is a degree of inevitability about coup d'etats in Fiji because (a) managing a communally bifurcated society virtually requires the strong arm and discipline that a military force offers, and (b) the continuity of a warrior tradition – built from Chiefly rule within the hierarchically ordered Fijian society and reinforced by battlefield and peacekeeping experience – affords a natural transposition into the political sphere by the military.

Samoa's Story

The Samoan political system, in quite stark contrast to that of Fiji and other PICs, has a police force but no military, holds democratic elections every five years, is built on underlying notions of 'Fa'a Samoa' – or Samoan ways – and has had for the past 30 years a government led by the same political party, the Human Rights Protection Party, which has strong links to leaders at the local level. It is, as former Samoan diplomat Afamasaga Toleafoa writes in Chapter 5, a one-party state with strong executive dominance and one that can be quite authoritarian in its attitude to dissenters and opposition. Toleafoa is concerned about the corruption and loss of integrity that longevity in office can bring. But by the same token Samoa enjoys an enviable reputation in the Pacific region and beyond for stability, improving living standards, and economic management.

Consensus Seeking in New Caledonia

In New Caledonia – after decades of bitter division (including inter-communal violence and bloodshed) and of fraught political and constitutional processes – there is now a positive search for consensus among the Kanak and Francophone peoples of this French Territory. Through power sharing and balancing arrangements, Jean-Eves Faberon suggests, New Caledonians will find over time an identity and common destiny. Faberon eloquently traces: the phases in the 'idea of decolonisation' from the 1950s and the formation of the Union Caledonien – the first anti-colonial political party; the conservative resistance to it as the nickel boom gripped New Caledonia through the 1970s and the substantial in-migration of metropolitan French citizens that followed; as well as the bloodshed that occurred in reaction to the formation and demands of the independentist FLNKS through the 1980s. He is taken by the 'genius' of the Noumea Accord which settled on a gradualist and pluralist power-sharing approach to political change and to limited autonomy and which has helped install a 20-year period of peace and relative consensus. While guardedly optimistic about the future of New Caledonia's power-sharing arrangements, Faberon can offer no guarantee of long-term success.

Political 'Nomadism' in French Polynesia

A perspective on politics in French Polynesia by Sémir El Wardi suggests many similarities and differences in the political styles of the Pacific's island polities. The continuing relationship between colonised and coloniser is quite different from that prevailing in the 'Anglosphere' Pacific – France not having introduced 'Republican' values to its Pacific territories. But patronage style politics stemming from the cultural practice of gift-giving linking constituents to MPs are undoubtedly similar. The 'looting of public resources' of which Al Wardi writes echoes similar themes of 'raiding the state' in polities further west. These personalist and communitarian socio-political type linkages run counter to Weberian rational-legal conceptions of the public good and of 'responsible government'. Political 'nomadism' – floor-crossing and party-switching are familiar across the South Pacific – though less so in Samoa and Fiji. Politics at all levels, Al Wardi asserts, is a 'theatre of persistent conflict' – a point that also resonates well in western Melanesia – though perhaps much less so in the smaller island states of Micronesia.

Oceania: Current Needs and Challenges

Assessing Progress in Development

In assessing development across the South Pacific region one of the best guides – as we have seen above – is the progress or otherwise made towards the achievement of the UN Millennium Development Goals. Pacific Island governments use the MDGs to track and measure their performance particularly on social development progress. Linda Petersen – a long-time development analyst and practitioner in the Pacific – examines the record across the region noting that the target date of 2015 is still some way off and that the cumulative impact of development initiatives will take time to register/show-up in quantitative terms. The record so far is patchy. Progress on MDG 1 (Eradicate Extreme Poverty and Hunger), for example, is not promising – a problem often being the widespread belief in many PICs that social networks, tradition and a strong subsistence base alone will ensure positive futures. For the MDGs relating to health (MDGs 4, 5 and 6) the performance is mixed with some gains in the health status of women and children and in control of communicable diseases. Unfortunately the prospect remains for these positive trends to be reversed. The clear message from the mixed progress to date is that enhanced political and societal commitment will be required for the PICs to meet these social and development targets. Donor analysis – by AusAID in particular – has found that while some PICs have made good progress against and even achieved some MDG targets, the Pacific region as a whole 'still appears to be seriously off track to achieve the MDGs by 2015.'

A Gender Lens

The need to integrate key gender dimensions into all development frameworks and strategies is argued by Treva Braun, a gender specialist and social planner with the South Pacific Community in Noumea. Braun argues for a reframing of the development discourse (and architecture) so that gender equality is considered as fundamental. The imperatives and implications of 'development' are often significantly different for men and women. A gender 'lens' is regrettably absent from definitions of security and development. Were such a 'lens' applied at 'defining moments' in the region's history – as for example with the adoption of the Pacific Plan by the South Pacific Forum in 2005 – Pacific women's concerns for stability and security as well as opportunities for eradicating gender inequality would have been significantly enhanced.

A gendered 'lens' on development also requires greater representation and participation of women within the decision-making apparatuses of Pacific governments. The small numbers of women occupying senior political positions across the Pacific states has been a matter of public record now for some time. The 'list system' of representation in the New Caledonian Assembly does ensure equal gender representation, but that is an exceptional case. Despite some national and donor effort on affirmative action programs for enhanced participation and representation by women over the past decade, the results so far have been disappointing. Excluding the French Pacific, women hold only 3 per cent of the seats in Pacific Parliaments – well below the world average of 18 per cent. Women's representation in Pacific national politics has been estimated at only 50 per cent of that which pertains in the Arab states of the Middle East and North Africa!

But what of women in Pacific public services – hitherto a generally neglected area of research? Asenati Liki Chan Tung's chapter highlights her research on women's upward mobility into senior positions in the Samoan and Solomon Islands bureaucracies – pointing to strong senior bureaucratic representation by women in Samoa and some positive trends emerging at the upper levels in Solomon Islands. The chapter identifies the barriers to upward mobility for women and the attitudinal shifts necessary for further advancement to occur. It also shows a correlation between expanded educational opportunities for girls and an increase in public service participation by women at higher levels. Further research into the teaching, nursing and legal professions will shed light on the status of women in other Pacific agencies of government.

Youth

'YouthQuake' is the startling title of a Discussion Paper produced by the Pacific Institute of Public Policy in 2011. The paper argues that all PICs face serious demographic challenges and particularly so in Melanesia where populations are doubling every 30 years and urban populations are doubling every 17 years. Is this the likely catalyst for radical change? 'Will democracy be sunk by demography?' In this volume Rose Maebiru argues that with an overall population growth rate of 2.2 per cent per annum and the mean age of the Pacific Islands population at 21 years, creative thinking is indeed necessary within the PICs about socialisation, education, employment opportunities and lifestyles for the Pacific's youth. Research on Caribbean youth has shown, for example, that investing in young people – especially through the provision of and encouragement for education – can result in GDP increases of 2 per cent. The South Pacific Community's 'Pacific Youth Strategy 2010' provides some positive messages including a framework for youth development and the managing of generational change in the region. It is, however, an aspirational document that hopes to provide a strategy for youth 'to access integrated educational opportunities, nurture sustainable livelihoods, lead healthier lifestyles, build stronger communities, benefit from effective national and community mechanisms for addressing youth issues, and strengthen their cultural identities'.

Tourism

Tourism has long been regarded as a route to development in the Pacific because of the attractiveness of the South Sea Islands' natural tropical beauty, charm and way of life to tourists from metropolitan countries. Tourism has become vital to most PIC economies: the industry representing 25 per cent of GDP in both Fiji and Samoa; 50 per cent in Cook Islands and 67 per cent in Palau. One tourism pathway – a new niche that has opened relatively recently – is a 'customised' form of tourism focusing on 'authentic' settings and societies. 'Beach Fale' tourism in Samoa is one such example highlighted in Susana Taua'a's analysis of tourism issues in the region.

Rural Development

Agriculture – a most important route to rural and national development and one long neglected by donors and international aid agencies – though certainly not by Pacific farmers – has made a welcome return to the global assistance agenda. Matthew Allen helpfully traverses the changing phases in development theory – from modernisation through structuralism, to post-development and post-structuralist perspectives on rural production. He predicts that those who see hybrid and syncretic approaches and who can capture the localised conceptions of what is a fulfilling holistic approach to rural development will make the most useful contribution to rural political economy across the region.

Oceania and its Wider Setting

Security Tensions?

An overview of regional security issues by James Bunce concludes the regional studies. The security interests of most Pacific Island states align well with those of the region's 'traditional partners' – Australia, France and New Zealand. Australia and New Zealand military forces are engaged in peace building operations (Solomon Islands, Timor Leste), and France has a small continuing military presence in New Caledonia and French Polynesia. Internal security issues are regarded as low-level. The virtual disappearance of the Taiwan-Beijing tension of recent decades has given room for China to take its place as a 'responsible stakeholder' in regional development – and it seems intent (as it has in other parts of the developing world) in providing aid with no strings attached and investing in infrastructure and resource development via its various business enterprises (3,000 or more of which are said to be registered in the Pacific Islands).

Regionalism

Henry Ivarature, political adviser to the South Pacific Forum, reviews the various components of the regional architecture of the Forum aimed at strengthening regional cooperation and integration, that encourage regional dialogue and that seek to support and complement national PIC policies and ambitions. He admits to an apparent regional 'jig-saw puzzle' of institutions and frameworks. The Forum – and all those agencies that work to support the PICs' political and developmental efforts – falls well short of an integrated and authentic model of Pacific regionalism. But perhaps the vision is too big? He sees in the Pacific Plan an attempt to harmonise this regional effort under a jointly-owned 'umbrella'. Its efforts to date, however, have been more productive and credible on the 'political' side of the agenda than they are on the 'economic' side. The Forum is currently dented by political divisions resulting especially from Fiji's departure from constitutional rule and by those PICs which have chosen to support Fiji regardless of the composition and nature of its government. Some might argue though that the Melanesians are helping contain Fiji's wilful 'outriding' behaviour.

Instability *and* Stability: Muddling Through … and Beyond

In assessing the changing 'pattern of islands' in the South Pacific over the decades since the Island states became independent, a key focus has been on the issue of political stability and/or instability. In the history of new states instability has impacted adversely on the prospects for economic and social development and, if severe, leads to social and economic breakdown and the possibility of state failure. In the world of diplomatic and security analysis, it is also argued that in highly unstable situations, new states are liable to penetration or takeover by subversive influences – including criminal organisations or unfriendly states. But the analysis of instability is an imprecise science, both the causes and the outbreak of it being difficult to identify with any certainty. Factionalism is one key driver of instability – yet it is also a precursor to the consolidation of democratic processes and discourse!

Political Strife

A quick survey – from Timor Leste in the west to Tonga in the east – over the last decade shows a number of serious incidences of political strife. Timor has had a difficult transition to independence that included armed resistance to its Indonesian colonisers and then a violent internal conflict between opposing parties (including an assassination attempt on its then President in 2008). Irian Jaya – Indonesia's eastern-most Province – has seen the suppression of a small independence movement over many years including intermittent outbreaks of violence. Papua New Guinea eventually placated an armed rebellion by the Bougainville Province through a form of decentralised political autonomy; but political contestation remains robust and tense, while crime and illegality remain a threat to public order. Solomon Islands experienced a 'coup' against the government by the Malaita Eagle Force in 2000 and although civilian rule was quickly restored and a regional assistance mission (RAMSI) in support of government remains in situ, the country has had an unsettled decade since that time (including riots in Honiara in 2006). Tonga experienced rioting and violent behaviour in 2006 though order was quickly restored. Fiji's coup of 2006 represents the most serious disruption to democratic state authority across the region.

Yet the region is not in constant turmoil and there are many states that have not experienced strife and tumult and in which order – rather than disorder – has generally prevailed. Even those conflicted states referred to above have enjoyed periods of relative calm and (near) normalcy. Vanuatu, despite having had a troubled decolonisation period, has had numerous peaceful changes of government and has remained free of serious political strife since its independence. In fact Vanuatu was named the 'happiest place on earth' by a 'Happy Planet Index' in 2006. Samoa has had four decades or more of effective, trouble free government. The smaller states of Cook Islands, Kiribati, Tuvalu, Nauru and the former American territories of Palau, the Republic of the Marshall Islands and the Federated States of Micronesia have all been free of destabilising tension and political strife.

Muddling Through ... and Beyond

In surveying the changing 'pattern of islands' in the Pacific Island Countries over the past three decades or more, and insofar as one can generalise, perhaps the most useful descriptor of the ways in which PIC governments have managed their political transitions – including their economic development and governance agendas – is that of 'muddling through'. In fact, not only is this concept useful as a descriptor of the PICs' political management style – it could also perhaps be seen at times as close to a conscious strategy on the part of some PIC governments! And over the course of four decades or more of independence across the region, 'muddling through' has shown itself in many ways to be a positive approach – or at least a non-negative approach – to governing.

The term and its usage in political science and public administration derives from a classic article by Charles E Lindblom, 'The Science of "Muddling Through"', published in *Public Administration Review* in the late 1950s. Despite its American origins, it was a concept adapted and used regularly in the late colonial period and early years of independence in classes at the University of Papua New Guinea, administrative colleges and in government workshops to describe the style and processes of the Pacific's transitions to Independence – especially so in Melanesia.

Transferring institutions of state and the building of coherent and regularised bureaucracies in the context of small-scale, multi-ethnic, fissiparous societies with complex inter-relationships and with no bureaucratic tradition to draw from, such as are to be found in Melanesia, was no small task. The processes involved in re-shaping colonial bureaucracies and in framing new policy approaches called not only for adaptation of the familiar but for innovation and the adoption of new directions and approaches in all Pacific countries. The periods of transition to independence and the first decades of that new political and constitutional status were – for Pacific governments of the day – times of adaptation and experimentation, of shifting responsibilities, of partial implementation and of crisis avoidance that often involved reversal of decisions taken earlier.

The Pacific's early post-independence governments and bureaucracies were far from the organised, rational, change management and reform agencies prescribed – and idealised – by donors and international agencies. So 'muddling through' became the default management style and in many ways close to a conscious 'strategy' in many PICs. It was a tactic or method for resisting external 'urgings' to adopt 'models' and 'innovations' that were resented (locally) as an unwarranted intrusion on sovereignty or that were seen, realistically, to be un-implementable given the local PIC context and capacity. It was also often the product of rational judgments made by politicians and bureaucrats about the pace of and capacity for change with knowledge about what would work in the given context and what would not work.

So 'muddling through' has been essentially a positive approach to governance. Perhaps had those forces of both change and inertia so evident in Pacific styles of operation /modus operandi been allowed to play out – there is nothing to suggest that Fiji, for example, would be in any worse socio-economic and political situation than it is currently. The new states of the Pacific have demonstrated considerable resilience, and in many cases, an extraordinary capacity to bounce back from difficulty and to maintain optimism for the future. The continuing professionalisation of public management across the region is building on that tradition. The growth of civil society organisations is also beginning to play a positive role in policy and implementation. Donors are becoming more coherent in their strategies, more attuned to the realities of generating development outcomes in small island states, and are beginning to acknowledge and map progress.

The chapters that follow explore these themes of governance, development and security that signal both continuity and change in the Pacific's pattern of islands.

Selected Readings

AusAID. 2009. 'Tracking development and governance in the Pacific'. Canberra: AusAID (August). Available at http://www.ausaid.gov.au/publications/pdf/track_devgov.pdf

Chand, S. 2010. 'Shaping New Regionalism in the Pacific Islands: Back to the Future?' ADB Working Paper Series on Regional Integration, No. 61 (October). Available at http://aric.adb.org/pdf/workingpaper/WP61_Chand_Shaping_New_Regionalism.pdf

Firth, S. (ed). 2006. *Globalisation and Governance in the Pacific Islands*. Canberra: ANU E Press. Available at http://epress.anu.edu.au?p=55871

Fraenkel, J. 2004. 'The Coming Anarchy in Oceania? A Critique of the 'Africanisation' of the South Pacific Thesis'. *Commonwealth & Comparative Politics*. 42(1) March: 1-34.

Fraenkel, J., and Firth, S. (eds). 2007. *From Election to Coup in Fiji: the 2006 Campaign and its Aftermath*. Canberra: ANU-E Press. Available at http://epress.anu.edu.au?p=54581

Fukuyama, F. 2007-2008. Papers on Melanesia. Available at http://www.sais-jhu.edu/faculty/fukuyama/Melanesia2

Hegarty, D., and Thomas, P. (eds). 2005. 'Effective Development in Papua New Guinea', *Development Bulletin*. 67 (April).

Henningham, S. 1995. The Pacific Island States: Security and Sovereignty in the Post-Cold War World. Hampshire: Macmillan Press.

Huffer, E., and So'o, A. (eds). 2000. *Governance in Samoa*. Canberra: Asia-Pacific Press and Suva: USP Press.

Hughes, A. 1998. *A Different Kind of Voyage*. Manila: ADB.

Kabutaulaka, T. 2008. 'Westminster meets Solomons in the Honiara riots', in S. Dinnen and S. Firth (eds). *Politics and State Building in Solomon Islands*. Canberra: ANU-E Press. Available at http://epress.anu.edu.au?p=78261

Lawson, S. 2006. 'Democracy, Power and Political Culture in the Pacific'. Journal of Pacific Studies. 29(1): 85-108.

Lindblom, C. 1959. 'The Science of "Muddling Through"'. *Public Administration Review*. 19(2): 79-88.

May, R. (ed). 2009. *Policy Making and Implementation: Studies from Papua New Guinea*. Canberra: ANU E Press. Available at http://epress.anu.edu.au?p=78541

McLellan, N. 2011. 'The Region in Review 2010'. *The Contemporary Pacific*. 23(2): 440-454.

Overseas Development Institute. 2011. *Mapping progress; evidence for a new development outlook*. London: ODI Publishing. Available at http://www.developmentprogress.org/sites/default/files/dps_synth_report_-_digital.pdf

Pacific Institute of Public Policy. 2011. 'Youthquake - Will Melanesian democracy be sunk by demography?' Discussion paper No. 17. Port Vila: Pacific Institute of Public Policy. Available at http://www.pacificpolicy.org/publications/discussion-papers/12-discussion-paper-17-youthquake/download

Schoeffel, P. 1997. *Socio-cultural Issues and Economic Development in the Pacific Islands*. Manila: ADB.

Wesley, M. 2011. *There Goes the Neighbourhood. Australia and the Rise of Asia*. Kensington, NSW: UNSW Press.

White, H. 2010. *Power Shift: Australia's Future between Washington and Beijing,* Quarterly Essay 39 (September). Collingwood, Vic.: Black Inc.

Wood, T., and Naidu, V. 2008. 'A Slice of Paradise? The Millennium Development Goals in the Pacific; progress, pitfalls and potential solutions'. Oceania Development Network Working Paper No. 1, Samoa. Available at http://www.gdn-oceania.org/Portals/83/A%20SLICE%20OF%20PARADISE-MDGS%20IN%20THE%20PACIFIC.pdf

Oceania and its Inheritance

2. Post-Colonial Political Institutions in the South Pacific Islands: A Survey

Jon Fraenkel

Vue d'ensemble des Institutions politiques postcoloniales dans le Pacifique Sud insulaire

A partir du milieu des années 80 et jusqu'à la fin des années 90, les nouveaux pays du Pacifique sortaient d'une période postcoloniale marquée au début par l'optimisme et dominée par une génération de dirigeants nationaux à la tête d'un régime autoritaire pour connaître par la suite une période marquée par les difficultés et l'instabilité et qui a connu le coup d'Etat de Fidji de 1987, la guerre civile à Bougainville, le conflit néo-calédonien et l'instabilité gouvernementale au Vanuatu et ailleurs. Dans les pays de la Mélanésie occidentale, cette instabilité a été exacerbée par des pressions exercées par des sociétés minières et des sociétés forestières étrangères. Cette étude retrace l'évolution et explore les complexités des diverses institutions politiques postcoloniales dans le Pacifique Sud à la fois au sein de ces institutions et dans leurs relations entre elles ; elle montre que les questions de science politique classique ont été abordées de façons extrêmement différentes dans la région. On y trouve une gamme de systèmes électoraux comprenant à la fois des régimes présidentiels et des régimes parlementaires ainsi que des situations de forte intégration d'un certain nombre de territoires au sein de puissances métropolitaines. Entre les deux extrêmes de l'indépendance totale et de l'intégration, les îles du Pacifique sont le lieu où l'on trouve un éventail d'arrangements politiques hybrides entre les territoires insulaires et les anciennes puissances coloniales. Cet article examine l'absence de partis politiques disposant d'une base populaire dans le Pacifique, les faibles taux de représentation des femmes et l'expérience acquise par le Pacifique en matière d'accords de partage du pouvoir ; il pose également la question de savoir si la fin de la période de l'état de grâce qui a suivi l'indépendance représente un glissement vers une instabilité permanente ou simplement un intermède précédant une certaine consolidation du pouvoir.

After decolonisation, the new Pacific nations mostly experienced a brief honeymoon period, presided over by a generation of relatively strong national leaders; Fiji's Ratu Sir Kamisese Mara, PNG's Michael Somare, Vanuatu's Walter Lini, Amata Kabua in Marshall Islands, Ieremai Tabai in Kiribati or Nauru's

Hammer de Roburt. The late 1980s and 1990s saw the demise of that initial post-colonial optimism. Fiji witnessed its first coup in 1987, and a year later the Bougainville civil war began in earnest. New Caledonia erupted into conflict in the mid-1980s until tensions were calmed by the 1988 Matignon and then 1998 Noumea Accords. Vanuatu's bipolar party system began to fracture in the late 1980s, and intense government instability reigned across the 1990s. For later de-colonisers, like Tuvalu, the watershed was also later; the two elections of 1993 proved the catalyst for an end to the early era of stability, after which the fall of governments became more frequent (Panapa and Fraenkel 2008). In the Marshall Islands, it was the death of Amata Kabua in 1996 that ended a hitherto unipolar style of government with no genuine opposition, and precipitated the opening of a period of sharper rivalry between the deceased President's successor, Imata Kabua and the opposition UDP led by a commoner, Kessai Note.

In the western Melanesian countries, heightened instability during the 1990s was encouraged by increasing interest from foreign companies in the natural resource extractive sectors. The Solomon Islands government remained reasonably stable until Solomon Mamaloni's second government, when most ministers acquired strong links with logging companies (Frazer 1997: 41). The political links of mining and forestry companies became increasingly important in PNG politics, particularly around election-time. Growing popular discontent with parliamentary processes was indicated by high turnover rates among elected MPs. Issues of corruption became a focal point for the assembly of loose opposition coalitions; the reformist governments that took power in the Solomon Islands under Francis Billy Hilly in 1993 and under Bartholomew Ulufa'alu in 1997 both tried to define themselves through opposition to the 'Mamaloni men' (a reference to backers of the governments of Solomon Mamaloni, 1981-84, 1989-93, 1994-97, which were closely associated with Asian logging companies). Even in Tonga, where the monarchy remained in control, in the 1990s, 'Akilisi Pohiva and the other pro-democracy activists turned from agitation against abuses of office to radical demands for a shift away from royal control over government. Only Samoa remained reasonably stable, as the Human Rights Protection Party (HRPP) saw off challenges from the T☐mua and Pule movement in 1994 and consolidated its grip on state power.

The Pacific Islands region includes entities closely incorporated with the metropolitan powers located around the Pacific Rim, such as Guam (USA), Rapa Nui (Chile) and Tokelau (New Zealand), as well as independent states like Papua New Guinea, Fiji and Kiribati. The region includes countries that achieved independence less than thirty years ago as well as those which are still in the process of adjustment to the post-colonial order. It includes resource-rich territories with strong potential for integration into the world economy alongside chronically resource-poor countries with limited avenues for export-driven economic growth. It includes territories with open access to metropolitan labour markets, and countries without. It includes an extraordinary ethno-linguistic diversity, mostly in Melanesia which alone accounts for one fifth of the world's documented living languages.[1] It includes relatively big nations like Papua New Guinea (6.6 million) alongside tiny micro-states like Niue, which has a population of only 1,500, and minute dependent territories like Pitcairn Island with only 45 inhabitants. Of the 9.7 million people that inhabit the 551.5 thousand Sq km land area of Oceania, just over two thirds are in Papua New Guinea.

Classical political science questions have been addressed in strikingly different ways across the region – whether to accommodate ethnic diversity through unitary, devolved or federal systems; whether to handle conflict through majoritarian or proportional electoral systems and/or through power sharing arrangements and whether to adopt parliamentary or presidential systems or, as in Kiribati and in the autonomous region of Bougainville, some hybrid between the two. Other important questions for the region have been how to meld traditional forms of governance with imported institutions; how to respond to exceptionally low levels of women's representation and how to build states in countries where – for many who live in rural areas and engage largely in subsistence cultivation – the state matters little.

Electoral Systems

Oceania has a history of electoral experimentation. Enthusiasm for preferential voting in the Pacific has been encouraged by Australia's adoption of the alternative vote (AV) for the federal parliament in 1918. Colonially inherited first-past-the-post systems have been ditched in favour of single-member preferential systems in Fiji and Papua New Guinea, although in both cases without the expected results (Fraenkel and Grofman 2006; May 2008). In Fiji, the alleged 'unfairness' of outcomes under the AV system was used to justify coups both in 2000 and 2006. When it was adopted in the mid-1990s, AV was intended to boost the chances of the moderate centrists, and to disadvantage ethnic extremists. Instead, it triggered a sharpening of electoral polarisation. Nauru has a unique simultaneously tallied preferential voting system which oddly resembles the arrangements invented by 19th century French mathematician Jean-Charles de Borda (Reilly 2001). Kiribati uses a two-round system similar to that in mainland France, although unusually in multi-member constituencies. That system permits voters to express preferences, although over two rounds

---

1 Based on data from the US Summer Institute of Linguistics, http://www.ethnologue.com/ethno_docs/distribution. asp?by=area

rather than in a single-round of AV voting.[2] It is also considerably simpler to administer and count than the AV system, even if the need for two elections inevitably raises administrative costs.

List proportional representation (PR) systems are used only in the French territories. Unlike majoritarian systems, list PR systems aim to make the share of seats won by each party roughly equivalent to its share of votes, although there is a 5 per cent threshold below which parties gain no seats at all. By definition, list PR requires multi-member constituencies. New Caledonia, for example, is divided into three constituencies, the south (with 32 seats), the north (with 15) and the Loyalty Islands (with seven) for elections to the 54 member territorial congress. Voters simply tick the ballot paper next to their favoured political party, and the parties submit lists of their candidates in order of preference. After the votes are tallied, electoral officials calculate which members are elected according to each party's share of the vote. In 2004, President Gaston Flosse modified French Polynesia's list PR voting system so as to give a 30 per cent seat bonus to the winning party, thus deliberately removing the system's proportionality. His aim was to give his Tahoeraa Huiraatira Party a stable working majority and to end many years of dependence on coalition government. The result was a crashing defeat for Tahoeraa Huiraatira, and the election instead of pro-independence leader Oscar Temaru. Instead of opening an era of stability, French Polynesia entered a politically chaotic period, with the presidency switching back and forth between the various factions. Paris stepped in to squash Flosse's failed reform in 2007.

Vanuatu is one of the few countries in the world to still use the single non-transferable vote (SNTV) system, alongside Jordan and Afghanistan. In an effort to bind francophone secessionists into the emerging Vanuatu state, British and French colonial authorities agreed on SNTV in the hope of avoiding a clean sweep for Walter Lini's anglophone Vanua'aku Pati (VP). Under SNTV, voters have a single vote, but constituencies have multiple members. Thus, if there is a 40 per cent francophone minority in a three-seat constituency, and if francophones avoid splitting their votes, they should be able to pick up at least one of the three seats. The system achieved its objective reasonably well in the initial elections after independence, when the parties were reasonably disciplined and the contest was a bipolar one between the VP and the francophone Union of Moderate Parties. From the late 1980s, however the francophone/anglophone cleavage faded in significance, and parties splintered (Van Trease 2005). As political parties multiplied, SNTV became less predictable, victor's majorities reduced in size and an increasing number of independent candidates contested.

---

2   AV is often called instant runoff voting in the USA due to this characteristic.

Principles of universal suffrage and voter equality have, in some parts of the Pacific, sat awkwardly alongside traditional systems of authority. In Tonga, the King has not been - as often characterised - an absolutist monarch. Tonga's kings have been bound by the 1875 Constitution. It is the weak powers of parliament that have set Tonga apart from its neighbours. The Prime Minister and Cabinet have been selected directly by the King, and sat in the legislature alongside nine nobles and nine people's representatives. Although there has been universal adult suffrage, there has been no effort to achieve voter equality: the holders of 33 noble titles selected nine noble representatives, while the rest of Tonga's 100,000 people chose nine people's representatives. Commitment to change has been in the air since 2005, oddly preceding the riots that destroyed much of Nuku'alofa in late 2006. In 2005, for the first time one of the people's representatives, Dr Feleti Sevele, became Prime Minister. The King subsequently declined to over-rule Dr Sevele's choice of cabinet ministers.

Upon his coronation in 2008, the new King, George Tupou V, committed to a majority popularly elected parliament. Parliament settled upon a first-past-the-post system and elections to the country's first ever majority popularly elected assembly took place in November 2010. Under the new arrangements, the nine nobles' seats remain, but now together with 17 elected 'people's representatives'. Contrary to expectations that pro-democracy campaigner 'Akilisi Pohiva would assume control, his party gained only 12 of the 17 popularly elected seats. The remaining five independents aligned themselves with the nine nobles to select Noble Tui'vakano as Prime Minister. Although no longer responsible to the King, Tonga retains its tradition of strong centralised government: the Prime Minister is entitled to nominate an additional four members of parliament, and cannot be ousted by a 'no confidence' vote for 18 months after an election.

The principle of universal suffrage was not accepted by the architects of Samoa's 1962 constitution. Initially, both voters and candidates had to be holders of matai titles (a term often misleadingly translated as 'chief', but possibly better translated as 'family head'). A visiting United Nations team in 1959 argued that since there was an internal family decision-making process prior to the award of matai titles, the Samoan system could be regarded as one of 'election at two stages' (So'o and Fraenkel 2005: 335). During the 1980s, that system was widely perceived – within Samoa – to have led to a proliferation of Matai titles, triggered by rival parties exploiting the constitution's incentives to expand their voter bases by awarding titles. In 1990, there were 21,649 such titles, almost double the level a decade earlier. In that same year, the country voted to shift to a universal suffrage, although retaining the matai-only qualification for candidates. The change had several important repercussions for Samoan politics, but it did not halt the multiplication in the number of matai titles. In 1999, over 35,000 matai titles were on the books of the Land and Titles Court (So'o and Fraenkel 2005: 342).

Presidential or Parliamentary Systems

The Pacific's presidential systems are mostly in the north where the US influence exerts greatest sway. Freely associated Palau most closely resembles the US model, with a President and Congress and even a miniature replica of Washington's Capitol building. The Commonwealth of the Northern Marianas, Guam and American Samoa have governors, rather than presidents, but are faithful to the American model in having direct popular elections for the head of government. The Marshall Islands and Nauru depart from the pattern in having 'presidents' that are more like Prime Ministers in the Westminster system; they are elected by parliaments. Kiribati is a unique hybrid since although it has a directly elected President, (i) the nominees for the presidential election are selected through a complex parliamentary ballot, (ii) the president must form his cabinet from within parliament, (iii) the president, despite being directly elected, can be ousted by a no confidence vote within parliament, but doing this precipitates a general dissolution of parliament. Those choices are aimed at lessening the possibility of gridlock between an unpopular President and a hostile parliament, diminishing the likelihood of mid-term removal of the Head of State and giving the head of government a direct popular mandate. As a result, Kiribati has experienced much less political instability than neighbours like Tuvalu and Nauru.

In the Pacific parliamentary systems, government formation can entail a delicate balancing act. In Solomon Islands, forming a cabinet has always entailed a careful harmonising of representation from the most populous island of Malaita with that from Guadalcanal and the Western Province. Oddly, this has at times benefited politicians from none of those three provinces, such as three-time Prime Minister Solomon Mamaloni (from Makira) or 2001-6 Prime Minister Sir Allen Kemakeza (from tiny Savo Island), who could appear to stand above the fray. In Papua New Guinea, it is inconceivable that a cabinet should exclude representatives from the highlands, or Papua or the islands. Even Fiji, which in many respects departs from Melanesian political norms owing to its bipolar indigene-Indian cleavage, cautious inclusion of powerful regions becomes politically astute. When Laisenia Qarase sought to forge a power-sharing government with the Fiji Labour Party in May 2006, he was careful to secure his indigenous Fijian base by drawing in paramount chiefs from the Kubuna, Burebasaga and Tovata confederacies. The neglect of the Tongan-influenced Lau Islands, already suffering from a fading of the former glory associated with the deceased Ratu Mara's years as Prime Minister and then President, proved to be that government's Achilles Heel. The revenge of Mara's descendants, or rather the husbands of his daughters, was to become an important aspect of the coup of December 2006.[3]

---

3   Ratu Epeli Ganilau was not reappointed as a government nominee to the Great Council of Chiefs in 2004 consequently also losing his position as Chair. Ratu Epeli Nailatikau lost his position as Speaker after the May 2006 election and was to become Ambassador to Malaysia, until the 2006 coup intervened. Both men joined the post-2006 coup interim cabinet.

Romantics often criticise the colonial imposition of 'Westminster' and see this as having disturbed traditional styles of political organisation which were, it is claimed, characterised by consensus, and the 'Pacific way'.[4] Yet the cleavages that prevail across the Pacific between government and opposition are not mere reflections of inherited institutions. In the small close-knit micro-states, hostility between the government faction and the opposition leadership can on occasions become far more bitter than in the industrialised mass democracies (even though alliances can also, in other circumstances, become fluid and personality-based, and many opposition leaders will, have some point, served as ministers together in cabinet with those who are now adversaries). Opposition leaders may find themselves out of government for consecutive parliamentary terms, rendering them vulnerable in their home constituencies. Government victories are carried beyond the floor of the parliamentary chamber affecting, for example, opposition leaders' private business interests or the promotion prospects of those in their kin groups. When a chance presents itself to dislodge such governments (either through a no confidence vote or a prime ministerial election), opposition leaders can become desperate, and willing to make deals they would otherwise prefer not to make with wavering opportunists. That sharp rivalry amongst Pacific leaders is not, as often imagined, a mere reflection of colonially inherited institutions can be seen by the regular legal contestation of imposed limits on Prime Ministerial power (for example, Billy Hilly, Solomon Islands, 1993, Saufatu Sopoanga, Tuvalu, 2002 and Serge Vohor, Vanuatu, 2004, to name but a few).

Absence of major ideological cleavages or political parties with a substantial extra-parliamentary membership can give Pacific parliamentarians considerable freedom for manoeuvre. Occupying a ministerial portfolio not only provides a salary and status that is often impossible for a local to equal in the private sector, it also provides access to state funds and state leverage over foreign controlled resource-extractive industries. Particularly in Melanesia, MPs have been known to engage in spectacular changes in affinity as they cross the floor to join government, often justifying this by claiming - probably accurately - that they were not elected to government in order to remain on the opposition benches. Many outside cabinet in PNG have preferred to sit on the 'middle benches' poised between government and opposition, so as to be open to offers of ministerial portfolios but equally accessible to being courted by opposition schemers planning assembly of a new government. Regular no-confidence votes in the Solomon Islands are popularly believed to be money-making schemes: even if they do not succeed, the MPs all round earn large sums of cash as

---

4   A term coined by Fiji's Ratu Sir Kamisese Mara (although it has other claimants), and used to convey a familiar set of contrasts, such as relaxed timekeeping, a preference for leisure over work and consensus over confrontation, felt to distinguish the Pacific from the industrialised societies. Similar ideas are found in the Caribbean and Indian Ocean Islands.

recipients of rival factions' bids for political support. After Vanuatu's 2008 Prime Ministerial election, two MPs were inadvertently heard live on national radio talking about the amounts of cash that had exchanged hands, unaware that the microphone was still turned on (Van Trease 2009).

Pacific parliamentarians, although not constrained by powerful party machines, may nevertheless be pressured by local constituents, wantoks or urban networks. The threat of electoral annihilation haunts Western Melanesian incumbents, who generally experience turnover rates well above 50 per cent. Politicians in Kiribati are intensely sensitive to home island opinion: while debate on government tabled legislation commands slender interest, question-time – when MPs can be heard live on national radio interrogating ministers about matters of local significance – attracts intense interest. Popular engagement in parliamentary processes may be weak, but public interest is strong. When the Marshall Islands Nitijela is in session, most shared taxis running down Majuro's main street will be tuned into the debates. During the 1998-99 struggles between the Kessai Note's United Democratic Party (UDP) and former President Imata Kabua, the public gallery of the Nitijela was packed with onlookers. Jousts between government and opposition leaders in Samoa can likewise grip public attention. Voter turnout is far higher in the Pacific Islands than in North America or Western Europe, and would be higher still if duplicate or deceased voter registrations were deleted from the rolls. Popular engagement with politics is greater than often recognised in the Pacific Islands, even if popular participation in decision-making (e,g. through select committees) is weak and accountability mechanisms work only through the crude 3-5 yearly ditching of incumbents at each general election.

De-colonisation

Close integration of territories with metropolitan powers is a legacy of the colonial experience. Hawaii became the 50th Pacific state in 1959, while other American Pacific territories, Guam, American Samoa, and the Commonwealth of the Northern Marianas (CNMI) are described by the US Supreme Court as having become 'appurtenant to but not a part of the United States' (Underwood 2006: 7). Rapa Nui was annexed in 1888 but only legally absorbed into Chile's Valparaiso Province in 1966. Residence on the island by Chileans is still restricted as is acquisition of property by those not of Rapa Nui descent. By contrast, after West Papua was absorbed into Indonesia with United Nations approval after the 'Act of Free Choice' in 1969, a mixture of spontaneous and sponsored transmigration brought in three quarters of a million people, mainly from the islands of Java and Sulawesi. Integration with a powerful neighbour tends to open the floodgates to settlement, as on Saipan (Commonwealth of the Northern Marianas) where the majority were non-indigenes in 2000, mostly from the Philippines or China.

New Caledonia, French Polynesia and Wallis and Futuna are in law part of the French nation state; all participate in elections for the national assembly and the Presidency. The CFP franc, the currency in all three territories, is pegged to the Euro. In 1958, French President General Charles de Gaulle insisted on the doctrine of the 'one and indivisible republic', and forced voters in French Polynesia to choose between colonial integration or abrupt secession. 64 per cent voted in favour of staying with France. The pro-independence movement was defeated, and after disturbances in Papeete, its leader, Pouvanaa a Oopa, was imprisoned (Henningham 1992: 123-126). The peoples of the French Pacific remain confronted with those stark options, although in modified forms: since 2003 they may opt to become 'territorial collectivities', with considerable autonomy. French Polynesia went a step further by adopting its own autonomy statute. New Caledonia is unique: as a result of the 1998 Noumea Accord, the territory has special legislative powers and a schedule for phased expansion of domestic political control ahead of a referendum on independence between 2014 and 2019. To agree to that accord entailed such a rupture with the doctrine of indivisibility of the Republic that France had to hold a nationwide referendum, the result of which earned New Caledonia a special provision in the constitution (Maclellan 2005: 397).

Of the 16 territories in the world that remain on the United Nations list of non-decolonised territories, the Pacific accounts for five: American Samoa, Guam, New Caledonia, Pitcairn Island and Tokelau. Neither of Tokelau's two referenda (2006 and 2007) on whether to become self-governing achieved the required two-thirds majority, and Pitcairn Island's links with Britain have, if anything, been reinforced by adjudication of child abuses cases by the British Privy Council. American military build up on Guam in the new millennium makes independence less likely, despite longstanding Chamorro disquiet about existing arrangements. Inclusion on, or exclusion from, the UN list can prove highly controversial, with behind-the-scenes manoeuvring at the UN headquarters in New York or Geneva being used to exert leverage towards independence back home. The incentives are clear. In 2008, UN Secretary General Ban Ki-moon urged the world 'to complete the decolonisation process in every one of the remaining 16 Non-Self-Governing Territories'.[5] Pro-independence leader Oscar Temaru, after his initial election as French Polynesia's President in 2004, sought to get his country onto the UN list following the precedent set by New Caledonia in the wake of the 1980s Kanak uprising.

---

5   'Colonisation has no place in Today's World, says Secretary-General', Decolonisation Seminar, 14th May 2008, http://www.un.org/News/Press/docs//2008/sgsm11568.doc.htm

Samoa was the first of the Pacific Island states to secure independence in 1962, and the unique constitutional arrangements chosen at that time (discussed later) have probably contributed to that country's post-colonial stability. Tonga formally became independent in 1970, but here the colonial hand was, for the most part, light. Financial irregularities under King George Tupou II (1893-1918) led the British colonists to demand closer control (Fusitu'a and Rutherford 1977: 180). Britain became preoccupied with Europe during the 1914-18 war, and on its heels the Great Depression enabled Tupou II's more capable successor Queen Salote to preserve Tonga's political autonomy. Fiji's independence was inevitably problematic because of the need to reconcile the competing aspirations of the majority Fiji Indian and minority indigenous Fijian leaders Norton 2004). Ethnic Fijian claims that since the country had been ceded to Queen Victoria by their chiefs in 1874, it should now be returned to those indigenous chiefs were to become a rallying cry of the ethno-nationalists who overthrew elected governments in 1987 and 2000. Fiji Indian claims that the communally based electoral system left as a compromise by the British at independence perpetuated race-based voting were to become a prominent theme of the military-backed interim government that emerged in the wake of Fiji's third coup in December 2006.

Constitutional choices made at independence also had enduring implications elsewhere in the region, in contrast to Africa where initial legal frameworks bequeathed by colonial powers were often torn up and new arrangements adopted (Chazan 1992). Depth of consultation made a difference to the political authority of whatever structures were chosen. Papua New Guinea (1975) and Kiribati (1979) used constitutional conventions for deliberation which left recommendations that had lasting political legitimacy (Macdonald 1982). By contrast, although there was more local consultation than is often appreciated in the Solomon Islands, the 1978 Independence Order dealt with issues of citizenship in ways that pleased the British Colonial Office and swelled the size of the golden handshake, but provided no durable answer to what was to become a perennial issue in Solomon Islands politics: how to balance the powers of the central government against those of the separate islands.[6] The western breakaway movement that emerged in 1978 was echoed by demands for devolution during a constitutional review a decade later, and then again in the wake of the June 2000 coup when many provinces threatened to secede from the nation (Premdas et al 1984; Mamaloni 1988; Fraenkel 2004: 182). In Vanuatu, the Santo rebellion in 1980 was the most severe of the secessionist crises accompanying independence anywhere in the Pacific region; Jimmy Stevens' Vemerana Provisional Government on Santo threatened to break up the emerging state, until the rebellion was halted by the deployment of British,

---

6   For background on the constitution-making process, see Ghai 1983.

French, and Papua New Guinean troops. The only actual case of secession in Oceania was exceptionally peaceful: in 1976, the British Gilbert and Ellice Islands decided to go their separate ways and a few years later became independent as Kiribati (1979) and Tuvalu (1978).[7] Bougainville's decade-long conflict first with Papua New Guinea and then internally is the most severe of the modern-day secessionist disputes. Its peace settlement, like that of the New Caledonian crisis of the 1980s, included a central provision that delayed the decision on independence for at least a decade.[8]

In between the extremes of independence and incorporation, the Pacific Islands are host to a range of hybrid political arrangements between island territories and former colonial rulers. New Zealand experimented with Compacts of Free Association with Niue and the Cook Islands. Palau, the Federated States of Micronesia and the Republic of the Marshall Islands entered Compacts of Free Association with the USA that gave them considerable autonomy (allowing them, unlike Cook Islands and Niue, to join the United Nations), but left the US with 'strategic denial' rights enabling the exclusion of other rival superpowers powers from establishing military bases in that American sphere of influence. As a result of an associated deal, missiles can be fired from Vandenberg air base in California across a 6,760 km arc through the Pacific sky before plunging into the lagoon of Kwajalein Atoll in the Marshall Islands. From there, they can be retrieved and studied by US scientists working at the nearby Ronald Reagan Ballistic Missile Defence Test Site. For this, Kwajalein's chiefs – including former President Imata Kabua, receive substantial rental payments only a fraction of which trickles down to the Ebeye indigenous settlement adjacent to the American base. Negotiations around a new land use agreement for Kwajalein remain an issue of contention between Kwajalein chiefs and the Majuro-based Marshallese government. Washington pragmatically extended its 17th December 2008 deadline for achieving agreement over Kwajalein for a further five years.

For the Marshall Islands and Federated States of Micronesia, the 1986 Compacts of Free Association expired in 2001. They were extended two years before being renewed for a further 20-year period in 2003, although now with greater scrutiny by the U.S. Department of the Interior. Palau commenced its 15-year compact later than its neighbours in 1994, and so the arrangement expired only in 2009. U.S. Secretary of State Hilary Clinton agreed a one-year extension and 'compact review' talks commenced in May 2009. Renewed compacts provide

---

7   The Congress of Micronesia also broke up into Commonwealth of the Northern Marianas, Republic of the Marshall Islands, Palau and Federated States of Micronesia, but the former was always a US-Controlled Trust territory, not an independent state.
8   New Caledonia's 1988 Matignon Accord put off the scheduled independence vote for a decade. However, in 1998, parties signed the Noumea Accord which put the scheduled independence vote back further, to some point between 2014 and 2019. Bougainville's peace agreement provides that there will be a vote on independence at some point between 2015 and 2020.

the US-associated states with sizeable additions to government revenue - US$3.2 billion over the 20 years for FSM and the Marshall Islands. They also give access to costly federal programs, for example in health, education and the U.S. mainland postal service.

Atomic rents kept French Polynesia prosperous for many years. Between 1966 and 1975, 41 atmospheric tests were conducted on the remote atolls of Mururoa and Fangataufa, followed by 137 underground tests ending in 1996, when France signed the Comprehensive Nuclear Test Ban Treaty. French aid then declined, but it still accounts for 35 per cent of French Polynesian GDP. Due to French finance, New Caledonia and French Polynesia easily have the highest income per capita in the Pacific. For the American nuclear-affected islands, independence comes at a price. The Marshall Islands earned global notoriety because of the Bravo nuclear test on Bikini Atoll in 1954. In total, 67 tests were carried out on Bikini and neighbouring Enewetak between 1946 and 1958, the effects of which spread eastwards to Rongelap and Utrik. Washington insists that the US$250 million paid to the Marshallese Nuclear Claims Tribunal under the first compact, and the similar amount paid for federal programs to affected victims, was 'full and final' compensation. The Marshallese government disagrees. MPs representing the nuclear-affected islands have at times made common cause with Kwajalein's chiefs to urge a more belligerent negotiating stance over the new compact and the land use agreement for the Ronald Reagan Ballistic Missile Defence Test Site.

The economic advantages of close integration with a wealthy metropolitan power are everywhere apparent; the independent states are, on average, poorer than those which have been incorporated by powerful neighbours around the Pacific Rim or those that have retained close ties with former colonial powers (Bertram 1999: 114). For many in the French territories, 'free association' arrangements such as those that connect Pacific states to America and New Zealand would be preferable to the controls from Paris, but the conventional French government position, echoing the Gaullist doctrine of 1958, is to insist that post-colonial linkages can only be decided after the territory settles upon independence. Financial incentives thus act as strong deterrents to loosening ties, even if such marked internal inequalities exist that indigenous groups still back political parties that push for independence.

Political Parties and Integrity Legislation

Nowhere in the Pacific Islands have the popularly-based political parties that are so central to conventional western political thinking emerged. Left-right ideological cleavages do not anywhere shape the divide between government and opposition. The only Pacific Island territories with fairly robust political parties are Fiji and New Caledonia, although Vanuatu and French Polynesia have some history of political party organisation.[9] Ever since independence in Fiji, there has been one party that appeals to the vast majority of ethnic Fijians[10] and another that represents the Fiji Indians.[11] The Fijian party has stood little chance in the Indian-dominated constituencies and vice versa. In 1997, when Fiji abandoned the first-past-the-post system in favour of the AV system, politicians were persuaded that adopting this modified majoritarian system would be most likely to encourage multi-ethnic government. That proved false. Over the three elections under AV, the party system polarised, so that by the third election under the system in 2006 one party claimed 80 per cent of the ethnic Fijian vote while the other had over 80 per cent of the Indian vote. Despondency as a result of the failure of the AV system to generate anticipated pro-moderation outcomes helps to explain why former centrist politicians and associated civil society activists sympathised with the military coup of December 2006, even if their choice to do so only legitimised Bainimarama's power grab.

In New Caledonia, issue-based political polarisation has also proved sharp, but not on the ethnic pattern of Fiji. Rivalry in the 1980s between the Front de Libération Nationale Kanak et Socialiste (FLNKS) and the French loyalist Rassemblement pour la Calédonie dans la Republique (RPCR) was intense, but ethnicity was not coterminous with political allegiance. Some indigenous Kanaks backed the RPCR, while the pro-independence parties always obtained at least some support outside their core Melanesian voter base. The Noumea Accord process in New Caledonia may also have served to erode the bipolar divide, in the sense that parties on both sides have fractured politically. Institutional incentives took the heat off the bipolar conflict, and permitted the political emergence of alternative currents of opinion. The territory had long used a closed list proportional representation system, but in the 1998 Noumea Accord supplemented also proportionality in the formation of cabinet through mandatory power-sharing rules. The 1998 deal also devolved power to the provincial assemblies. The contrast between the experience of Fiji and New Caledonia illustrates the perils of using majoritarian systems in bipolar societies with race-based voting.

Few Pacific states have witnessed a strengthening of political party-style organisation. In the Marshall Islands, Kessai Note's UDP administration was elected in 1999 on a 'good governance', accountability and transparency

---

9   For a survey of political parties across the region, see Fraenkel 2006a.

10   From the 1966 election until the 1987 polls, the Alliance Party, in 1992 and 1994 the *Soqosoqo Vakavulewa ni Taukei* (SVT) and from the 2001 polls Laisenia Qarase's *Soqosoqo Duavata ni Lewenivanua*. The exception was the 1999 elections, when the SVT managed only 38% of the Fijian vote, with the remainder split among four other parties.

11   First the National Federation Party and then the Fiji Labour Party.

platform ousting Imata Kabua's government. The UDP government survived the 2003 election, but by 2007 was confronted by a rival party that was backed by Imata Kabua and other leading chiefly families in the Ralik chain, the Aelon Kein Ad (AKA). The AKA struck a deal with Nitijela speaker, and Ratak chief, Litokwa Tomeing, and won the 2007 election. Despite the appearance of an 'evolution' towards political party-style organisation, allegiances remain fluid in the Marshall Islands. The triumph of the 'visionaries' against the 'old guard' in Nauru in 2004 was not accompanied by development of political parties; the reformist's access to political power always depended on courting wavering opportunists with offers of the presidency. In the smaller Pacific states, a hardening of the opposition often entails the formation of a political party but, if successful in obtaining office, the new government will usually prefer to decry political party-style organisation and claim instead to be ruling in the general interest.

Towards the western Pacific, the absence of robust political parties has become a major issue, leading in some countries to ambitious legislation aimed at encouraging the construction of party-based systems. Papua New Guinea's 2001-2 Organic Law on Political Parties and Candidates (OLIPACC) aimed to fast-track the development of strong parties by requiring those who back a Prime Minister after a general election to stick with that choice in any votes of confidence, budgetary votes and votes on constitutional amendments. In an effort to avoid the horse-trading that follows each general election, the party with the largest share of votes is to be given the first opportunity to form a government.

That legislation is widely believed to have ushered in a period of greater stability in PNG; Sir Michael Somare's National Alliance government survived a full 2002-2007 term in office, the first government since independence to have achieved this. Somare also succeeded in getting re-elected for a further term after the general election in 2007, and survived beyond the 18-month grace period that ended in February 2009. Yet there are doubts about this simplistic assessment of the stabilising merits of OLIPPAC. While the Prime Minister remained Somare, deputy prime ministers changed repeatedly over 2002-7, and ministers were regularly reshuffled. Contrary to the rules against floor-crossing, 11 MPs switched sides from government to opposition during the 2002-7 parliament, but none lost their seats as the law said they should do. The Ombudsman - who was in law empowered to act in such cases, if necessary to recommend a forfeit of seats, wisely preferred not to do so. The law proved a toothless tiger, even if in practice floor-crossing did diminish due to the perception of the threat of dismissal. Opposition inside parliament became subdued not so much because of OLIPPAC but because of the presence of a partisan speaker who closed down hostile debate and ruled out of order questions that might embarrass the government. In July 2010, PNG's Supreme Court ruled that key elements of the OLIPPAC violated the freedom of movement provisions in the constitution.[12]

Despite this, the myth of OLIPPAC-engineered stability obtained considerable currency, for there could be little doubt that the political order was more stable than during the chaotic turn-of-the-millennium years (Standish 2000). The more plausible explanation was better handling of the country's second resources boom (Baton et al 2009), and the availability of a good deal more money to grease the political wheels. Other Melanesian countries have been inspired by the PNG experiment, hoping also to discipline their allegedly feckless and unruly backbenchers. Serge Vohor's short-lived 2004 government in Vanuatu wanted to introduce PNG-like 'grace periods', but the court ruled the attempt unconstitutional, and Vohor's government fell to a no confidence challenge. In Solomon Islands, the post 2007 Sikua-led government was assisted by Australian think-tanks in deliberations aimed at adopting legislation inspired by OLIPPAC in PNG (Haywood-Jones 2008).[13] However, several ministers in Dr Sikua's cabinet conspired against the proposed constitutional amendment, which failed to obtain the required two-thirds majority. Those ministers were sacked by Dr Sikua for this act of rebellion, but they re-emerged, holding key portfolios, in the government led by new Prime Minister Danny Philip after the August 2010 election.

In PNG, Solomon Islands and Vanuatu, bills and laws have been ostensibly aimed at beefing up political parties, but in practice at strengthening governments and weakening the opposition. Grace periods during which governments cannot be voted out of office tend to be much more popular than financing a costly political party registration apparatus. Although popular concern centres on the horse-trading prior to Prime Ministerial elections, the rule giving the largest party the first crack at forming a government - by making this a one shot game - generates even greater potential for corruption and instability than the previous arrangements. The risk with 'grace periods', and other forms of restriction on 'no confidence' motions, is that they allow a deeply unpopular government to retain office, and/or that they require the law courts to intervene to control the minutiae of parliamentary conduct.

---

12   Special Reference by Fly River Provincial Executive Council; Re Organic Law on Integrity of Political Parties and Candidates, Supreme Court of Papua New Guinea, 7 July 2010.
13   For a video-recorded debate on these issues between Ben Reilly, Jenny Hayward-Jones, Jon Fraenkel and Nicole George, see Pacific Island Update, Panel on Political Change Across Melanesia, 7 December 2008, available on http://www.crawford.anu.edu.au/media/video/index.php?year=2008&id=156

Women's Representation

Of the nine countries worldwide that have zero women members of parliament, Oceania accounts for five (Solomon Islands, FSM, Nauru, Palau and Tuvalu).[14] Papua New Guinea and the Marshall Islands have only a single female MP. Fiji had eight until Bainimarama dissolved parliament in December 2006. Samoa and Niue have four, Guam, Cook Islands and Kiribati have three, and Vanuatu two women MPs. Male dominance of the political stage occurs not only in the national parliaments, but also in local-level assemblies. Traditional male preponderance in the political sphere, and the conservatism of island societies, are the most frequently heard explanations for inequality in political representation. Yet change is in the air, at least in some parts of the Pacific. In western Melanesia, a growing number of women are now contesting elections. By contrast, in some of the smaller and more remote islands, few women contest and those that do are subjected to extraordinary pressures. In some Pacific Island polities, female leaders prefer to keep out of the male-dominated political world, and to concentrate instead on influencing decisions behind-the-scenes or through civil society activism (McCloud 2002). Increasingly aggressive electoral contests have also diminished women's chances on the campaign trail: in the PNG highlands, for example, candidates need access to large sums of cash to win, and they need large numbers of male campaign backers in order to sustain control over the polling booths and coordinate the process of 'assisted voting' (i.e. the completion of ballot papers en masse by sympathisers).

Temporary special measures have been used to increase the number of women in parliament in the French territories and on Bougainville. The French law on parity has given New Caledonia and French Polynesia close to 50 per cent female members of territorial assemblies. That law has not yielded similar results in the third largest French territory, Wallis and Futuna, where constituencies are smaller and where numerous parties enter the contest. Although the parity law requires parties to lodge lists that alternate men and women, since most 'parties' in Wallis and Futuna obtain only a single member the law does not have the intended effect. Adopting parity laws would have similar results in the other party-less Pacific microstates (Fraenkel 2006b). Where political parties are absent or weak, reserved seats are the only legal measure likely to increase the number of women in parliament. The autonomous region of Bougainville is the sole entity in Oceania to have adopted reserved seats for women. Three of Bougainville's 41 seats are reserved for women. In both Papua New Guinea

---

14   Data from Inter-Parliamentary Union website, http://www.ipu.org/wmn-e/classif.htm The other states with zero women members are Saudi Arabia, Oman, Qatar and Belize. The IPU dataset records only states that are members of the United Nations, not territories like American Samoa and Commonwealth of the Northern Marianas that also have zero female MPs.

and Solomon Islands, increasing numbers of female candidates are contesting elections, and in both countries there are pressures for reserved seats to increase the number of women in parliament.

Although women are poorly represented in Pacific parliaments they tend to be better represented at the top levels of the civil service, where appointments are more likely to be on merit. As of late 2009, Kiribati for example women accounted for only 3 MPs in its 46 member parliament (6.5 per cent), but seven of the fifteen top positions in the I-Kiribati civil service (46 per cent). In Solomon Islands, Nauru and Samoa, the percentage of women in top positions in the ministries is also markedly higher than the share in parliament. The secretaries in the I-Kiribati ministries are, probably uniquely in the Pacific, paid considerable more than parliamentarians. Much of the consultation around new legislation occurs through the ministries, prior to agreement in cabinet and before bills are tabled in parliament. In Kiribati, as in many other Pacific countries, highly qualified women prefer to take positions formulating and implementing policy, rather than going on the election campaign trail or joining male-dominated legislative assemblies. The Kiribati parliament is an assembly open to those over the civil service retirement age of 55, and it is a place where MPs focus largely on constituency matters rather than law-making.

Power-sharing Accords

The Pacific has an interesting but little internationally known experience with mandatory power-sharing accords. Nowhere in the world has witnessed such extensive litigation about mandatory power-sharing rules as Fiji. In the 1997 Fiji constitution, a power-sharing provision required that all parties with 10 per cent or more of seats be proportionally represented in cabinet. The provision was modelled on that in South Africa during the transition from Apartheid, and similar rules were adopted in Northern Ireland as part of the Good Friday agreement in 1998. When Mahendra Chaudhry formed his Labour-led People's Coalition cabinet after the 1999 Fiji election, he proved able to exclude the largest Fijian party, Rabuka's Soqosoqo Vakavulewa ni Taukei, on the grounds that its leaders imposed conditions on cabinet entry that amounted to a decline of the invitation. When Chaudhry's arch-adversary Laisenia Qarase tried to follow that legal precedent after the elections of 2001, the Court of Appeal rejected his efforts as contrary to the 1997 constitution. Qarase appealed, and the cases dragged on until 2004 before the Supreme Court left Qarase's Soqosoqo Duavata ni Lewenivanua party with no option other than to invite Chaudhry's Fiji Labour Party (FLP) into cabinet. Qarase reluctantly complied by offering the FLP a series of token minor portfolios in a cabinet so swollen that his former ministers also retained their portfolios. It was, unsurprisingly after so much legal action, a compromise with the letter but not the spirit of the law. The FLP condemned the expansion in cabinet size as a costly imposition on Fiji's people and criticised the portfolios as trivial. Since a fresh election was anyway looming on the horizon, Chaudhry chose instead to occupy the opposition benches.

After the 2006 election, Qarase complied more wholeheartedly with Fiji's multi-party cabinet rules, drawing nine senior FLP parliamentarians into cabinet, and giving them major portfolios. It proved an enormously popular decision, but Fiji's political leaders again failed to make the arrangements work. Chaudhry stayed out of cabinet, and eventually expelled two of the participating FLP ministers. The short-lived 2006 power-sharing cabinet was the first government since independence to have brought members from country's two largest parties – one representing the Fijians and the other the Fiji Indians – into cabinet (Green 2009). It lasted just seven months before being overthrown by military commander Frank Bainimarama.

In New Caledonia, by contrast, power-sharing provisions agreed as part of the 1998 Noumea Accord worked more smoothly, even if they left the pro-independence parties in a minority. In all post-accord cabinets, the loyalist parties dominated, based on their ascendancy in the more densely populated Southern Province and their ability to gain a minority of seats in the majority Kanak Northern Province. During the initial post-Noumea Accord government, the pro-independence groups regularly took legal action regarding the composition of government. However, after the 2001 assumption of the Presidency by the RPCR's Pierre Frogier, Kanak activist Déwé Gorodé was selected as Vice President, thus meeting one of the major FLNKS demands. The 2004 election saw a fracturing amongst the loyalist parties, with the emergence of Avenir Ensemble, a trend continued at the 2009 election, with further splits this time affecting Avenir Ensemble. Pro-independence parties have also been prone to schisms. The other Noumea Accord provisions of devolution of powers from Paris to Noumea, and a re-balancing of income towards the predominantly Kanak Northern and Loyalty Islands Provinces have helped to encourage the emergence of new alignments also among the Kanak parties.

New Caledonia's arrangements had a more solid foundation than those in Fiji. Provisions for the proportional distribution of ministerial appointments fitted better with New Caledonia's list PR electoral system than with Fiji's majoritarian AV system. Fiji's Westminster-based 1997 constitution was not sufficiently redrafted after the belated inclusion of the 10 per cent rule, and drafters did not fully consider the likely difficulties of a Prime Minister needing to form a coalition government to 'command a majority' on the floor of the house while at the same time being required to form a power-sharing cabinet that includes all the qualifying parties. Whereas Fiji's power-sharing rule generated bipolar incentives for each ethnic group to avoid splits that might entail parties falling below the 10 per cent threshold required for cabinet participation, New Caledonia's rules allowed smaller parties to combine with larger parties to boost cabinet entitlements. New Caledonia's arrangements were considerably assisted by French aid subventions, and by a growing flexibility emanating from Paris as regards which institutions might prove acceptable. Fiji had to tackle its problems alone, with little in the way of helpful advice from supranational institutions or powerful neighbours.

Conclusion: Post-colonial Trends

Does the closing of the post independence honeymoon era represent a shift to permanent volatility, or merely a hiatus before some new leadership consolidation? Efforts by elites to stabilise and regiment the political order have been most ambitious in Papua New Guinea, with OLIPPAC and 'grace periods', but, as we have seen, similar devices are being experimented with in Solomon Islands and have been tried, unsuccessfully, in Vanuatu. Samoa's HRPP is the only political party across the region which has remained in office for close to a quarter of a century, consolidating its control by expanding cabinet size, increasing the parliamentary term to five years, outlawing party switching and creating new sub-ministerial positions for pro-government backbenchers. Solomon Islands and Tuvalu have sought to increase cabinet size, so as to render the executive more resilient to parliamentary challenge. Whether those efforts prove successful, whether they prove harbingers of emergence of more authoritarian political elites or whether the post-independence era's highly contested and fluid styles of politics reassert their influence remains to be seen.

References

Batton, A., Duncan, R., and Guoy, J. 2009. 'Papua New Guinea Economic Survey; From Boom to Gloom?' *Pacific Economic Bulletin*. 24(1): 1-26.

Bertram, G. 1999. 'The MIRAB Model Twelve Years On'. *The Contemporary Pacific*. 11(1): 105-138.

Chazan, N., Mortimer, R.., Ravenhill, J., and Rothchild, D. 1992. *Politics and Society in Contemporary West Africa*, 2nd edn. Boulder, Colorado: Lynne Rienner.

Fraenkel, J. 2004. *The Manipulation of Custom: From Uprising to Intervention in the Solomon Islands*. Wellington: Victoria University Press.

Fraenkel, J. 2006a. 'The Political Consequences of Pacific Island Electoral Laws', in R. Rich, L. Hambly and M. Morgan (eds.), *Political Parties in the Pacific Islands*. Canberra: Pandanus.

Fraenkel, J. 2006b. 'The Impact of Electoral Systems on Women's Representation in Pacific Parliaments', in *A Woman's Place is in the House – the House of Parliament; Research to Advance Women's Political Representation in Forum Island Countries*. Suva: Pacific Islands Forum Secretariat. Available at: http://www.forumsec.org/UserFiles/File/REPORT_2_A_Woman_s_Place_is_in_the_House__the_House_of_Parliament-5.pdf

Fraenkel, J., and Grofman, B. 2006. 'Does the Alternative Vote Foster Moderation in Ethnically Divided Societies? The Case of Fiji'. *Comparative Political Studies*. 39(5): 623-651.

Frazer, I. 1997. 'The Struggle for Control of Solomon Islands Forests', *The Contemporary Pacific*. 9(1): 39-72.

Fusitu'a, E., and Rutherford, N. 1977. 'George Tupou II and the British Protectorate' in N. Rutherford (ed.), *Friendly Islands; A History of Tonga*. Melbourne: Oxford University Press.

Ghai, Y. 1983. 'The Making of the Independence Constitution', in Peter Larmour, (ed), *Solomon Islands Politics*. Suva: University of the South Pacific.

Green, M. 2009. 'Fiji's Short-lived Experiment in Executive Power-Sharing, May – December 2006', State Society and Governance in Melanesia Discussion Paper 2009/2. Canberra: The Australian National University. Avaliable at http://ips.cap.anu.edu.au/ssgm/papers/discussion_papers/09_02_green.pdf

Hayward-Jones, J. 2008. 'Engineering political stability in Solomon Islands'. Lowy Institute Perspective. Available at http://www.lowyinstitute.org/Publication.asp?pid=917

Henningham, S. 1992. *France and the South Pacific; A Contemporary History*. Sydney: Allen and Unwin.

Levine, S. 2009. *Pacific Ways: Government and Politics in the Pacific Islands*. Wellington: Victoria University Press.

Macdonald, B. 1982. *Cinderellas of Empire; Towards a History of Kiribati and Tuvalu*. Canberra: Australian National University Press.

Maclellan, N. 2005. 'From Eloi to Europe: Interactions with the Ballot Box in New Caledonia'. *Commonwealth & Comparative Politics*. 43(3): 394–417.

Mamaloni, S. 1988. *1987 Constitutional Review Committee Report*, vol. 2, Honiara: Government Printer.

May, R. 2008. 'The 2007 Election in Papua New Guinea', State Society and Governance in Melanesia Briefing Note 7, Canberra: The Australian National University. Available at http://ips.cap.anu.edu.au/ssgm/publications/briefing_notes/BriefingNote_The%202007ElectionsInPapuaNewGuinea.pdf

McCloud, A. 2002. 'Where are the Women in Simbu Politics?, *Development Bulletin*. 59: 43-46.

Norton, R. 2004. 'Seldom a transition with such aplomb: from confrontation to conciliation on Fiji's path to independence'. *Journal of Pacific History*. 39(2): 147–62.

Panapa, P., and Fraenkel, J. 2008. 'The Loneliness of the Pro-Government Backbencher and the Precariousness of Simple Majority Rule in Tuvalu', State Society and Governance in Melanesia Discussion Paper 2008/2. Canberra: The Australian National University. Avaliable at http://ips.cap.anu.edu.au/ssgm/papers/discussion_papers/08_02.pdf

Premdas, R., Steeves, J. and Larmour, P. 1984. 'The Western Breakaway Movement in Solomon Islands'. *Pacific Studies*. 7(2): 34–67.

Reilly, B. 2001. 'The Borda count in the real world: the electoral system in the Republic of Nauru', Macmillan Brown Centre for Pacific Studies Working Paper 8. Christchurch: University of Canterbury.

So'o, A., and Fraenkel, J. 2005. 'The Role of Ballot Chiefs and Political parties in Samoa's Shift to Universal Suffrage'. *Commonwealth & Comparative Politics*. 43(3): 333–61.

Standish, B. 2000. 'Papua New Guinea 1999: Crisis of Governance'. Australian Parliamentary Library, Research Paper 4. Canberra: Parliamentary Library, Parliament of Australia.

Underwood, R. 2006. 'Micronesian Political Structures and American Models: lessons taught and lesions learned'. *The Journal of Pacific Studies*. 29(1): 4–24.

Van Trease, H. 2005. 'The Operation of the Single Non-Transferable Vote System'. *Commonwealth & Comparative Politics*. 43(3): 296-332.

Van Trease, H. 2009. 'Vanuatu's 2008 Election – Difficulties of Government Formation in a Fractionalized Setting', State Society and Governance in Melanesia Briefing Note 2009/1, Canberra: The Australian National University. Available at http://ips.cap.anu.edu.au/ssgm/publications/briefing_notes/BriefingNote_Vanuatu_Election.pdf

3. The Military in Post-Colonial Fiji

Jone Baledrokadroka

Les militaires dans les Fidji à l'époque postcoloniale

Les militaires à Fidji sont devenus une institution omniprésente de la politique au sein de l'Etat. Leur rôle traditionnel a fusionné avec un rôle de sécurité humaine politiquement nuancé. L'instabilité politique actuelle à Fidji est liée à l'expansion du rôle des militaires depuis l'indépendance, marquée par un accent trop fort mis sur les activités non fondamentales comme la création d'un Etat, le maintien de l'ordre et la sécurité intérieure. Ceci a eu un effet délétère sur la stabilité politique du pays. Cet article propose une explication de l'intervention des militaires dans la politique à Fidji de façon si continue depuis 1987. Un point de discussion dans ce débat met l'accent sur l'importance de l'héritage colonial et l'image que les militaires ont d'eux-mêmes qui a été encouragée pendant la période coloniale. Un autre montre la faible division du travail dans les Etats-nations émergents et la façon dont ceci peut exacerber les divisions ethniques qui conduisent les militaires à assumer un rôle de médiation et à créer un Etat qui a tendance à connaître des coups d'Etat ou à être un Etat prétorien. D'après de nombreuses personnes, dans les pays nouvellement indépendants, « la réaction négative contre l'incompétence des civils et la corruption » a souvent justifié l'intervention des forces militaires. Le commodore Bainimarama a maintes fois invoqué cette excuse pour justifier son coup d'Etat destiné à réaliser un nettoyage. Cet article affirme que l'intérêt des militaires en tant que corporation tient un rôle de premier plan dans le calcul que fait une élite militaire en faveur de l'intervention et que le nouveau « professionnalisme » militaire dans les pays du Tiers-Monde comme le Brésil, la Birmanie, la Thaïlande, le Nigéria, l'Indonésie et Fidji s'exprime dans la capacité des militaires à assumer un rôle politisé, à tenir les rênes du pouvoir de l'Etat et dominer les institutions de façon provisoire ou permanente.

Introduction

Fiji's military has become an all pervasive institution of politics in the small Pacific island nation state. The military's traditional hard security role has merged with a politically nuanced human security role. The present state of

Fiji's political instability is related to the role expansion of Fiji's military since Independence. The expansion has been marked by an over-emphasis on non-core activities such as nation building, peacekeeping and internal security. This has had a deleterious effect on the political stability of the nation.

Why and how has this development taken place? Since cession in 1874 the patriotic adage of *For God, King and Country* was grafted onto and sat well with Fiji's traditional society. The three central ethos of the British Empire's imperial slogan were integrated into Fijian society as the *Lotu, Vanua kei na Matanitu*. In the 96 years of British rule this slogan underpinned the colony's military service through two world wars and the Malayan Communist emergency campaign in the 1950's. After Independence Fiji's civil military relations pattern was a hybrid between the traditional aristocratic and liberal democratic model (Nordlinger 1977: 11-13). This hybrid pattern cohered well since independence with the ruling Fijian elite in the form of the Alliance party government of Ratu Sir Kamisese Mara.

Upsizing the Military

Since the mid seventies the military was increasingly used by the Alliance government under Ratu Sir Kamisese Mara in a nation building role. The raising of the Trade Training School in 1974, the Engineers Rural Development Unit and the Naval Division in 1975 saw the military increase to over three times its size.

In 1978, with Fiji's first deployment of troops with the United Nations interim forces in Lebanon, peacekeeping became a force determinant. A detachment was sent to Zimbabwe in 1980 and in 1982 another Battalion was raised as part of the Multinational Forces and Observers in Sinai Egypt to monitor the Israeli-Egyptian peace accord. This new role increased numbers to over 2000 regular force soldiers by 1982. All during this expansion period recruitment was always kept at over 95 per cent ethnic Fijian. The huge ethnic recruitment numbers disparity was simply put down to the unappealing nature of soldiering to Indo-Fijian. In retrospect a quota system of recruitment should have been done to even up the ethnic numbers.

Unfortunately this heavily skewed ethnic recruitment only 'reinforced tacit ethnic elitist political association within the institution'. Being overwhelmingly ethnic Fijian the military was always to be a bastion of indigenous political paramountcy. In fact during the March 1977 elections (the second since independence) where the Indian dominated NFP party had won by the slightest majority but were unable to form a government the military was put on alert.

The question still remains today, what would have happened had not the Governor General, Ratu Sir George Cakobau, appointed Ratu Sir Kamisese Mara to form a minority government.

The three major troop number increases were brought about by local and international political expediency rather than in response to any clear defence role. Hence Nation Building; Peacekeeping and Internal Security became the force determinant for the military.

International peacekeeping exposure to the world's hot spots, especially the Middle East, has imbued a confident political mediator mindset amongst Fiji's military officers.

Part of the Political Elite

With the 1987 Rabuka coup many of the senior officers became entwined with the Fijian political elite. Rabuka's coup shattered the Westminster civil-military relations ethos and explicitly unveiled the fragile nature of Fijian democracy since Independence. It seemed the Westminster model only lasted so long as government was made up of the Fijian political elite.

With Bainimarama recently emphasising 'only the military can bring about change' the political role of the military persists. The militarisation of government since is real evidence of this politicised role. Over 40 military officers are still holding important government posts from Prime Minister, Cabinet ministers, Permanent Secretaries and other postings on boards of various statutory bodies.

In a parallel development since 1998 the recruitment of over 2,000 Fiji citizens for service with the British armed forces has been ongoing. This has had significant economic and social implications for Fiji with remittances reaching an all time high of more than F300million in 2005.

The third factor that increased military numbers was the internal security role that evolved out of the 1987 coup. The size of the military reached 3,600 in December of 1988 (Fraenkel, Firth & Lal 2009: 119). The army raised the number of infantry battalions and the number of soldiers in each battalion to 'effectively control' the emergency situation, although many saw that emergency as being one that the RFMF had created in the first place. An elite counter revolutionary warfare unit was formed to protect against government armed insurgency.

As a consequence of executing a supremacist coup in 1987 against a phantom internal security threat, the military in a convoluted way created for itself an internal security role previously the ambit of the Fiji Police Force. Ironically in taking upon itself the IS role, like scores of developing countries in the 1960s and 1970s, Fiji is now a coup-prone state.

Why Coups Happen

In many post-colonial states, civil supremacy under the aegis of democracy is often threatened by the military's colonially-inherited legacies. Often, such societies are troubled by severe schisms of a regional or ethnic character. The military, however, acquires a colonially-induced unifying function. And that given its self image as leading nationalists the military is commonly able to rationalise away or sincerely justify their predatory actions. Since they identify with the nation what is to the advantage of the military is also good for the country. It is almost as if coups promote the national interest.

Western military ethics stress the supremacy of society over the individual, tribe or sub-group, and the importance of order, hierarchy, and division of function in the service of the nation state. Foremost of this military colonial legacy is the principle that the military commander must never allow his military judgement to be warped by political expediency (Huntington 1957: 71). Unfortunately this principle has been compromised as in the Nigeria and Fiji coups with highly professional armies that are drawn from one predominant ethnic group and do not reflect a unified nation. If governments seem captives of those sub-national forces, the incentive for military intervention may become strong.

The degree to which corruption is itself a major cause of military coups is however open to question. Despite its prominence in post coup rationalisations, one might suspect that it is a secondary cause in most cases. Perhaps more significant is military leaders' distaste for the messiness of politics – whether honest or not – and a tendency to blame civilian politicians for failure to meet overly optimistic popular aspirations which would be impossible of fulfilment even by a government of angels (Nye 1967: 422). Again this type of thinking may be the result of the realist and rather simplistic mindset prevalent in military leaders that resorts to coercion in dealing with political evils. For the military view of man is decidedly pessimistic and that the man of the military ethic is essentially the man of Hobbes (Huntington 1957: 63). Bainimarama's 2006 'clean up' or good governance coup rhetoric played to such sweeping justification and an instrumentalist view.

On the other hand military intervention into civilian affairs is not precipitated solely by military groups or elites. Amos Perlmutter found that in most cases civilians turn to the military for political support when civilian political structures and institutions fail or when constitutional means for the conduct of political action are lacking (Perlmutter 1969: 390). The civilians begin to form interventionist coalitions or indoctrinate the military with their political ideologies. Several examples of this process can be found in the Middle East and Latin America and recently in Fiji. Secondly, Perlmutter also found that 'corporatism is a prima facia case for interventionism and that professionalism is only one guarantor of non- intervention' (Perlmutter 1981: 2). This appears to be the case in Fiji prior to the 2006 coup. The commissioning of a security review white paper by the SDL Government in 2003 further undermined the fragile relations with the Military Commander. The paper recommended among others a fifty per cent cut in numbers of the Fiji Military Forces and a change to the selection process for the Commanders position. The Fiji military though a considerably small force consisted of a highly professional officer corps – a credit to its British military legacy. Since independence the traditional aristocratic-liberal democratic pattern of civil military relations worked well enough (Nordlinger 1977: 11-15). However this did not stop the RFMF from overtaking democratically elected governments in 1987, 2000 and 2006. One way to look at the driving forces of military intervention or non-intervention is through Finer's disposition/opportunity theory.

In his disposition and opportunity theory, Finer identifies the disposition of the military elite – which is bound to its corporate and individual interests – as the push factor. The pull factor is the opportunity that the political 'crisis' offers as a key condition for a military political intervention. According to Finer's calculus of intervention the subjective military disposition factor and the objective opportunity factor acting in unison are the most relevant triggers to the likelihood of a coup. The pre-coup interventionist coalitions of Rabuka and the Taukei Movement in 1987, Speight and Nationalist politicians in 2000 and Bainimarama and the Labour Party in 2006 reinforces this point.

Conclusion

One theme in this debate over why coups happen emphasises the importance of the colonial legacy, and the military self-image fostered during the colonial period. Another points to the weak division of labour in emerging nation states and the way in which it may exacerbate ethnic divisions that give rise to the military taking over in a mediator role and creating a coup prone or praetorian state. 'Revulsion against civilian incompetence and corruption', as many have argued, is a frequent justification for intervention by military forces in newly independent states. Commodore Bainimarama has often used this excuse for his 'clean-up coup'.

I have argued that military corporate interest is foremost in a military elite's calculus for intervention. In many Third World countries military 'professionalism' has come to mean not Huntington's old professionalism of external defence, meaning that a professional armed force is one that is subject to civilian authority; but something quite different. The new professionalism in Third World countries such as Brazil, Burma, Thailand, Nigeria, Indonesia and Fiji is expressed in the capacity of the military to assume a politicised role and, either temporarily or permanently, to take the reins of state power and dominate government. Finer takes the argument further in two ways: his disposition and opportunity theory offers an explanation of the push-pull factors that cause the military to intervene in politics; and he suggests an ascending scale of modes of military intervention in politics from working through constitutional channels to overthrowing civilian governments.

In this paper I have endeavoured to explain that the military forces have intervened in Fiji's politics so consistently since 1987 as a result of their non-core-role expansion; the extent to which Fiji exemplifies wider patterns of intervention found elsewhere; the form which intervention has taken at different stages of this story; and the reason for the absolutist character of the intervention that began with the 2006 coup.

References

Fraenkel, J., Firth, S., & Lal, B. 2009. *The 2006 Military Takeover in Fiji: A Coup to End All Coups?* Canberra: ANU E Press.

Huntington, S. 1957. *The Soldier and the State: The Theory and Politics of Civil-Military Relations.* Cambridge: Belknap Press of Harvard University Press.

Nordlinger, E. 1977. *Soldiers in Politics: Military Coups and Governments.* Englewood Cliffs N.J: Prentice Hall.

Nye, J. 1967. 'Corruption and Political Development: A Cost-benefit Analysis'. *American Political Science Review.* 61(2): 417-427.

Perlmutter, A. 1969. 'The Praetorian State and The Praetorian Army. Toward a Taxonomy of Civil Military Relations in Developing Polities'. *Comparative Politics.* 1(3): 382-404.

Perlmutter, A. 1981. *Political Role and Military Leaders.* London: Frank Cass.

4. The Political Roles of the Fiji Military: A Brief History of the Chiefs' Warriors, Heroes of the World Wars, Peacekeepers and Dictators

Hélène Goiran

Les Rôles Politiques des Militaires Fidjiens: brève histoire des Guerriers des Chefs, des Héros des Guerres Mondiales, des Soldats de la Paix et des Dictateurs

L'histoire militaire des Fidji a commencé en même temps que leur Histoire. La société précoloniale était largement fondée sur la guerre et l'art de la faire. L'administration britannique et les missions chrétiennes ont fait cesser les conflits armés mais les Fidjiens, héritiers d'une puissante tradition guerrière, ont cherché à la maintenir. Ils l'ont adaptée et l'ont utilisée pour rétablir puis pour consolider leur pouvoir politique ; d'abord dans le cadre de la colonisation, puis pour préparer l'indépendance et donner à leur pays souverain une place significative sur la scène internationale en participant avec succès à de nombreuses opérations de paix. C'est dans ce cadre qu'ils se sont engagés dans les deux Guerres mondiales, puis dans la Campagne de Malaisie. Depuis 1978, des milliers de soldats fidjiens ont été et sont déployés en permanence sur des théâtres d'opérations extérieurs (Liban, Sinaï, Bosnie, etc.) s'illustrant par leur courage et leur efficacité. Aujourd'hui encore, du fait de leur valeur, et, malgré le coup d'Etat du 5 décembre 2006 et les sanctions internationales décidées contre le gouvernement, l'ONU confie aux militaires fidjiens la protection de ses représentants et de ses installations en Irak. L'armée fidjienne occupe une place prépondérante dans la société et joue un rôle politique majeur, jusqu'à prendre le pouvoir par la force, dans les seuls coups d'Etat militaires de l'Océanie. Ce rôle politique a, sur le plan intérieur, complètement changé d'orientation en une vingtaine d'années. En 1987, les Royal Fiji Military Forces, avec le colonel Rabuka, déclaraient vouloir protéger les intérêts des Mélanésiens menacés par les Indo-Fidjiens. Depuis 2006, les Republic of Fiji Military Forces, solidaires du Commodore Bainimarama, se présentent comme les promoteurs d'un futur Etat multiracial et démocratique, dans lequel chaque citoyen, quelle que soit son origine ethnique, aura les mêmes droits et devoirs. Pourtant, l'armée demeure presque exclusivement constituée de Fidjiens mélanésiens, et les Indo-Fidjiens n'y ont jamais eu leur place.

The Chiefs' Warriors

The military history of Fiji is as ancient as her History. In pre-colonial times, the warriors were the necessary implements of the chiefly power. The Chiefs gained or held authority and influence through the victories of their fighters. War was the natural occupation of men, who were all supposed to fight to protect the community. Some of them were dedicated fighters. Warfare training was a main part of young males' formation. The importance of the social role of the warriors was such that, like the nobles, they were buried with their wives. Moreover, the gods wanted human sacrifice and the vanquished were the usual victims. War and worship were intertwined. Without wars, the offerings could diminish, angering the gods, who could provoke disasters, therefore weakening the power of the chiefs. Frequent wars opposed those who aspired to nobility titles, extended territories, and superior prestige. All men being supposed to the chief's police, thousands of armed men assaulted the enemy groups. But the confrontation was habitually short and the number of casualties was limited, because a symbolic victory was sufficient. Generally, these conflicts were aimed at establishing power, not at exterminating the opponent, who could have been previously an ally, or indeed become one in the future.

Warriors were therefore a major instrument for the chiefs to win and hold power. The leaders who were able to mobilise, train and lead their men into battle could dominate more people on wider zones. The first contacts and exchanges with Westerners introduced firearms and the engagement, in the service of some chiefs, of foreigners whose competences played a major part in the evolution of politics.

> The club was the Fijian warrior's favourite weapon. He had his spears, from ten to fifteen feet long and often richly carved, efficient bows and arrows, and slings for throwing stones; but, although these had each its special use, none approached the club in popularity. Whether his tribe was at war or at peace, he was seldom without it, for until the latter half of last century no Fijian left the precincts of his house unarmed. Whenever he left his village, even to work in his garden, he carried his club on his shoulder; and should he meet a man in the path, the club remained in that position, at the alert, until on friendly recognition both men lowered their weapon in greeting (Derrick 1957).

These weapons themselves could have a political role:

> The Mace of the Fiji House of the Representatives is the former favourite war club that was used in battle by Ratu Seru Cakobau. It is made of a type of hardwood called 'gadi'. He gave it as a gift to Queen Victoria of Great Britain in 1874, when Fiji became part of the British Empire. He named the war club Ai Tutuvi Kuta i Radini Bau (The coverlet of the Queen of Bau).

> The club is beautifully mounted and decorated with emblems of peace, embellished with small silver doves and olive branches.

> The Mace of the Fiji Senate is another war club used by Ratu Seru Cakobau. It was acquired during fighting with the hill tribes in 1874. It is a root stock club called na waka. (http://www.parliament.gov.fj/about/about.aspx?id=hmacehr)

In addition to traditional arms, modern weapons and western strategy enabled certain groups to gain influence over others, and that in a context where it seems that, previously, no group dominated durably and significantly.

This is how, notably, Cakobau, chief of Bau Island and adjacent areas, gained such authority, in the middle of the nineteenth century, as to be considered by the Europeans as the main leader of the entire Fiji archipelago, that is the Tui Viti, the King of Fiji.

In the early 1870s, in Levuka, the Western settlers constituted a government around Cakobau, This Cabinet, and its leader, protected themselves against those who challenged their legitimacy with a 'Royal Army'. This force comprised 1,000 men, organised, trained and used in the western way. It was commanded by a British Officer who had served in the Crimea and in India.

On the cession to the Crown, in 1874, London took over control of the 'Royal Army', and in 1876, the colonial administration renamed it the Armed Native Constabulary but retained its military organisation. The colonial authorities employed the ANC for the 'pacification' of tribes resisting the British presence.

During the same period, the Missions, whose influence had been growing rapidly since the conversion of Cakobau, in 1854, prohibited traditional warfare. Apart from those of the rebellious tribes, the warriors found a new mission by joining the Constabulary or the Police. The ANC was terminated in 1905, having no mission after the 'pacification' and unification of the Fiji Islands under British authority.

The First World War

In 1914, in Fiji, the British settlers and many natives desired to participate in the combat in Europe. For the Fijians, who were now the subjects of the Crown, the engagement was obvious: not to fight for the Queen would have been a shameful and unforgivable breach of the traditions. The Police and all defence-related associations, such as the riflemen, were mobilised, and a Fiji Defence Force was formed.

Approximately seven hundred men of European descent left Fiji for active service with the Allies.

Natives also were eager to join the front, but the British Command refused these coloured men. A few young chiefs, who were studying overseas at the time, succeeded in joining the Maori units.

The famous Ratu Sukuna, rejected because of his race by the British War Office, enlisted in the French Foreign Legion. Seriously wounded in action and highly decorated, he was sent back to Suva as a hero. There, he succeeded in convincing the colonial authority to send a Labour Detachment of about one hundred Fijians to Europe in May 1917.

The Indians in Fiji, at that time, were still indentured labourers. In 1916, their leaders tried to convince the colonial authorities to constitute an Indian platoon. The 32 volunteers were ignored by the government.

The Second World War

After the First World War, in the 1920s, the Defence Force, still composed of indigenous Fijians commanded by Western Officers, was used against striking Indian workers, so creating a feeling of alliance between the Fijians and Europeans against the Indians.

However, the Indian Platoon was at last created within the Fiji Defence Force in 1934 as part of policy of giving Indo-Fijians greater recognition and opportunity to participate in the general life of the Colony.

The platoon was disbanded in 1940. The reason given for this action during a war was shortage of equipment: The real reason was that members of the platoon had asked for equal pay with the Europeans. The New Zealand military authorities (who commanded the Fiji Army at the start of the War) feared that this dissatisfaction could spread to the ethnic Fijians.

When the Second World War began, the Colony already had a Fiji Defence Force. A general mobilisation was ordered. Like twenty years before, the British authorities did not want the natives to be sent to the front.

> However, the jungle skills of Fijian soldiers were notable after a special party of Fiji Commandos was sent to the Solomon Islands for guerrilla operations in support of the Allied Forces in operation there. The party numbered 30 men under the command of Captain D. Williams. They became the first Fijians to go into action in the World War Two. The First Battalion, Fiji Infantry Regiment (1FIR) was assigned to the Island of Bougainville in December 1943. This followed the establishment of a beachhead in Empress Augusta Bay by the United State Marines. The battalion's job on the island was to be forward scouts in support of the United States. The excellent results achieved by the First Battalion, Fiji Infantry Regiment led to a decision to send the Third Battalion, Fiji Infantry Regiment (3FIR) to join the First Battalion in operation in Bougainville. It was in Bougainville that Corporal Sefanaia Sukanaivalu of the Third Battalion, Fiji Infantry Regiment, was posthumously awarded the Victory Cross in June 23, 1944 when a larger and well-concealed enemy force ambushed his platoon. The First Commandos, Fiji Guerrillas went into action on the island of New Georgia in 1943 and were tasked to locate a party of enemy soldiers occupying the island. During this operation the Fijian soldiers suffered their first death in action when Lieutenant B. Masefield was killed after a patrol he was leading was caught in an enemy artillery barrage. The First Commandos were late replaced by the Second Commandos, Fiji Guerrillas on November 25, 1943 (RFMF Website).

Politically and socially, the participation in the Solomon Campaign was of major significance for the Fijian soldiers, who operated with Westerners on the same level. They constituted a consistent group notwithstanding their different origins and were unanimously recognised as valuable servicemen. As a consequence, the Fiji Defence Force was not completely dismantled after the war. Moreover, in 1949, it was officially decided that the Fiji Defence Force would be supported by New Zealand.

The Malayan Campaign

The impression that the Fijian soldiers had left was enduring: in 1951, London wished to deploy a Fiji Battalion in the Malayan Campaign.

World War Two veterans constituted the core of this Fiji Battalion. These men spent four years in the jungle to 'hunt and kill'. The appreciation of the value of the Fijian servicemen as commandos was even superior to those in the Solomon Campaign: in Malaya, the officers were Fijian; London left the Fijians to chose the method of operating, which was shocking. In this war, contact with the enemy was direct; combat close, the environment dreadful. The Fijians were particularly well adapted, and their longstanding warrior tradition led them to the destroy the enemy without hesitation.

Possibly, for some Fijians, the presence of Chinese communists in Malaya could be compared to the presence of Indians in Fiji: unwelcome visitors who had to be chased out. This may explain the enthusiasm of the members of the 'Fiji Batt' to carry out their mission.

During the Malayan Campaign, as well as during the two World Wars, the Fijian units were organised according to the customary hierarchy. The colonial authorities encouraged this structure, which guaranteed loyalty and dedication. Through their commitment, as individuals, the Fijian servicemen gained prestige among their peers. As a community, following their successful overseas engagement, the Fijians gained cohesiveness, in opposition to the Indo-Fijians, who scarcely participated in the wars.

The Defence Force of Sovereign Fiji

After the Malayan Campaign, at the time of the preparation of Fiji's independence, London tried, to no avail, to convince the Fijian representatives that the future State only needed a police force, not an army. Although the Fijians had been impressive combatants, or rather because they had, the British authorities did not want to maintain a significant defence force in Fiji, fearing for the internal security and the safety of the Indian part of the population: the Indians had then become more numerous than the indigenous Fijians.

In 1970, the new sovereign State inherited what remained of the Fiji Defence Force, turned into the Royal Fiji Military Forces, still almost exclusively composed of indigenous Fijians. The first years of independence saw the formation of a Fijian senior staff in the RFMF. Their main mission was to guarantee internal security, by assisting, should it be necessary, the police in maintaining or restoring law and order in accordance with Government decisions. The RFMF also participated in rural development and youth formation mostly in favour of the Fijians.

The command of the RFMF was close to the government. Together, they decided to provide this small army with international experience by appointing it to peacekeeping missions. Without doubt, it was also a long-thinking reflexion that led to the employment of the Fijians' warriors skills as a powerful instrument of international politics for the young Fiji State.

From 1978, a battalion was engaged in the United Nations Force in Lebanon (UNIFIL). From 1982, a second battalion was engaged in the multinational peacekeeping force in Sinai (MFO), under United States command.

Other similar commitments followed, in Zimbabwe-Rhodesia, Sinai, Afghanistan and Pakistan, Iraq and Kuwait, Somalia, Bougainville, East Timor, Solomon Islands. Some of them are still ongoing. So, for more than thirty years, more than 1,000 Fijian men were deployed at the same time in external theatres. Nearly all of them were, and still are, indigenous Fijians.

In total, about 15,000 Fiji men have served in these external operations. This toughened them up, brought their families and the country a substantial income, providing Fiji with international recognition and appreciation, thanks to their professionalism, operational value, bravery and strength. Therefore, until the mid-1980s, a military coup d'état in Fiji was thought to be very unlikely. The submission of the RFMF to the government, the strength of democracy in Fiji, and the multiracial harmony commonly received international acknowledgement and approval. In 1986, Pope John Paul described the country as 'the way the world should be'.

The Indo-Fijians and the Defence Force

Since its establishment, the Fijian military forces have been strong supporters of the long-established customary leaders and the Methodist church. Very early, too, a clear separation (segregation) had been established between the indigenous Fijians and the Indian migrants. The Military Force (whatever its name at the time) was employed to counter their social claim movements.

The RFMF's ceremonial traditions are very Fijian and Christian (yaqona sessions, frequent prayers, etc). There is really no incentive for the Indians to enlist. Their very small number in the RFMF is a consequence of their ethnic identification, religions, interests and aspirations, as well as an outcome of the place accorded to them in Fijian society from the time of the arrival of their ancestors, due to the British colonial authorities, more than one hundred years ago.

Those few Indo-Fijians who join the RFMF, however, have a strong perseverance and motivation.

Some hold important posts as lawyers, doctors or aides-de-camp; and some are part of the higher command and close to the Commander of the Republic of Fiji Military Forces. Colonel Mohammed Aziz, for example, Bainimarama's deputy, has been in command several times during the recent past, while the Commodore was abroad.

A brief history of the Indo-Fijian peoples is important to this narrative. Today, the Republic of the Fiji Islands has a population of 830,000. Nearly 40 per cent of them are Indo-Fijians, mostly born in Fiji to parents themselves born there, and they do not have any connection with India anymore, despite a strong Indian culture.

Their ancestors arrived several generations ago. The movement has been massive: between 1879 and 1916, more than 60,000 Indian indentured labourers, including women and children were transported to Fiji. Many settled there. The 1921 census showed 84,000 Fijians and 60,000 Indians (there were also 12,000 Europeans, Chinese, Rotumans and others).

Nevertheless, they are still called Indians, both commonly and officially, in order to differentiate them from the Indigenous Fijians and the citizens of other origins. The Constitution so establishes four separate electoral rolls, according to the voters' registration as Fijians; Indians; Rotumans; or others.

There are few inter-community marriages, and a small number of Fiji citizens have Fijian and Indian mixed blood. Those who have, belong to one of the communities or to the other, neither to both nor to a real new one of half-caste. This situation is a heritage of the colonial times. The conditions of Independence, in 1970, set up this separation, and therefore the subsequent identification of each Fiji Islander.

Apart from historical and colonial legacy, many characteristics separate the communities, such as religion (the Fijians being Christians and the Indians being Hindus or Muslims), and profession (three quarters of the farmers are Indians, but eighty-three per cent of the land is Fijian-owned).

Until 1987, and the first coup d'état, identities in Fiji seemed plain and clear for everyone. The different communities lived alongside each other without real integration or worrying tension, in what appeared to be a peaceful and prosperous multiethnic and democratic country. The travel agencies successfully sold trips to 'Paradise'.

Nonetheless, the compartmentalised country was built on an unsound foundation, organised by a raced-based Constitution that did not create a common national identity. 'Indigenous Fijians were instilled with fear of dominance and dispossession by Indo-Fijians, and they desired protection of their status as the indigenous people. Indo-Fijians, on the other hand, felt alienated and marginalised, as second class citizens in their own country, the country of their birth' (Bainimarama 2007). And then took place the first military coup d'état to occur in the Pacific.

1987: Colonel Rabuka's Ethno-nationalist Coup d'Etat

In 1987, the general elections saw the defeat of the customary establishment and resulted in the formation, for the first time, of a truly multiracial government under the leadership of Labour's Dr Timothy Bavadra.

In May 1987, Lieutenant Colonel Sitiveni Rabuka, number three in the RFMF hierarchy, and descendant of customary warriors, overthrew the government. His operation was carefully planned and prepared, the RFMF followed him. He declared to have taken action in order to preserve the interest of the Fijians against the Indians. This was the first military coup of the history of Fiji and Oceania. A second one occurred soon after: in September of the same year, Sitiveni Rabuka ousted the government again and declared Fiji a Republic. In 1990 a new constitution was endorsed, establishing the Fijian prominence. Mr Rabuka was made a life member (the only one ever!) of the Great Council of Chiefs, although a commoner, due to the fact that he had carried out his military coup in 1987 in the name of indigenous rights.

For years, the Rabuka government placed Army officers in many posts of responsibilities. The RFMF; henceforth Republic of Fiji Military Forces, greatly grew in strength, equipment, and budget. As a member of a customary warrior clan and a peacekeeping operations hero, Sitiveni Rabuka had charisma and authority in Fiji. He retained political power for more than ten years during which, despite strong international reproof against his regime, Fijian Peacekeepers remained appreciated and welcome in the United Nations' missions.

In 1997, still in power, Sitiveni Rabuka instigated the adoption of a new Constitution, supposed to be considered as progressive. Its provisions maintained some of the Fijians' advantages, but the Indians had significant rights. In 1999, the Labour party won the general elections and its leader, Mahendra Chaudhry, became Prime Minister. Even more than in 1987, access of the Indo-Fijians to political power was a reality. The Melanesian nationalists could not bear it.

2000: The RFMF's Reaction to the Speight Coup d'Etat

In May 2000, George Speight, a half-European businessman, leading an action with members of the Special Forces, took Fiji's Parliament hostage for 56 days. The support of the RFMF was expected, but its Commander, Commodore Bainimarama, backed by the large majority of his men, opposed the coup.

Bainimarama declared martial law, negotiated with the putschists, succeeded in having the hostages released and the weapons returned. Moreover, he had the rebels arrested, and, after only a few weeks gave the power back to civilians. A provisional government was installed, led by Laisenia Qarase. Commodore Bainimarama and his supporters intended to see all the instigators of the coup uncovered and punished. But Qarase and his followers revealed themselves to be in favour of 'Melanesian prominence'. They were maintained in power by the general elections of 2001 and 2006. Despite its racist policies, the Qarase governments were also approved by the international community.

Commodore Bainimarama also stayed in place as Commander RFMF. He too had many supporters, including the President. For years he opposed Qarase and his policy. Despite visible tensions and dissensions within the RFMF, the 'Commodore' remained their legitimate and rightful commander. Steadily, he opposed the government. With him, therefore, the servicemen did the same, refuting what the Commodore and his supporters saw as non-democratic policy. They demanded the abandonment of outdated and unfair provisions that favoured ethnic Fijians and disadvantaged the Indo-Fijian half of the country's population notwithstanding their hundred-year old presence in Fiji.

Since 5 December 2006: the Anti-ethno-nationalist Bainimarama's Coup

On 5 December 2006, through a bloodless coup, Commodore Bainimarama removed the Qarase government. He dissolved the Parliament and, after a few weeks, assumed the title and responsibilities of Prime Minister. He announced and launched anti-corruption campaigns and non-racial government. He admits to having conducted a coup d'état and declared so in front of the United Nations General Assembly. He pledged to organise truly democratic elections for early 2009.

For much of the post-Independence period, the Military Forces in Fiji had been strong supporters of the long-established customary leaders, including by conducting the two coups of 1987 to protect the traditional Melanesian interest. From 2000, under Commodore Bainimarama, the Army completely changed its position, claiming to champion equal rights for all the citizens, contesting the archaic customary power.

Either by supporting or opposing by force the customary chiefs, the elected governments or the putschists, Fijian soldiers have played a major political role. The 'Commodore', without doubt is a military commander who conducted a coup d'état to overthrow a functioning democracy. He has assumed dictatorial power. But my point is that in the historical, social and political context of Fiji, the positions and actions of the 'Commodore' and the RFMF could be said to have historical coherence.

By assuming political and administrative authority they perpetuate, in their own different ways, the ancient role of the pre-colonial warriors. And recent history seems to indicate that there can be a future for Fijian Dictators: after he had lost power in 1999, Brigadier Rabuka did not disappear from the political scene. Quite the opposite: nobody really accused him of having definitively destroyed the peaceful and prosperous Fiji of the 1980s. Neither the local population nor the international community turned their back on him. Not being Prime minister anymore, because he had led the indigenous Fijian government to a severe defeat and paving the way for the country's first Prime minister of ethnic Indian origin, trade unionist Mahendra Chaudhry. Following the polls, Rabuka was elected as chairman of the Great Council of Chiefs. Soon Rabuka resigned from the chairmanship of the Great Council and membership of the Parliament because he had taken up a Commonwealth mission, as the Secretary-General's Special Envoy to Solomon Islands. What better international recognition could he have wished for?

Later, allegations were made against him by former President Ratu Sir Kamisese Mara of complicity in the Fiji coup of 2000. Rabuka was also accused of instigating or supporting the mutiny that took place at Suva's Queen Elizabeth Barracks on 2 November 2000. He was judged 'not guilty'.

References

Bainimarama, V. 2007. Speech to United Nations, cited 'Fiji: Interim PM outlines plans for referendum', Radio Australia (2 October)

Derrick, R. 1957. 'Notes on a Fijian club with a system of classification'. *Journal of the Polynesian Society*. 66(4): 391-395.

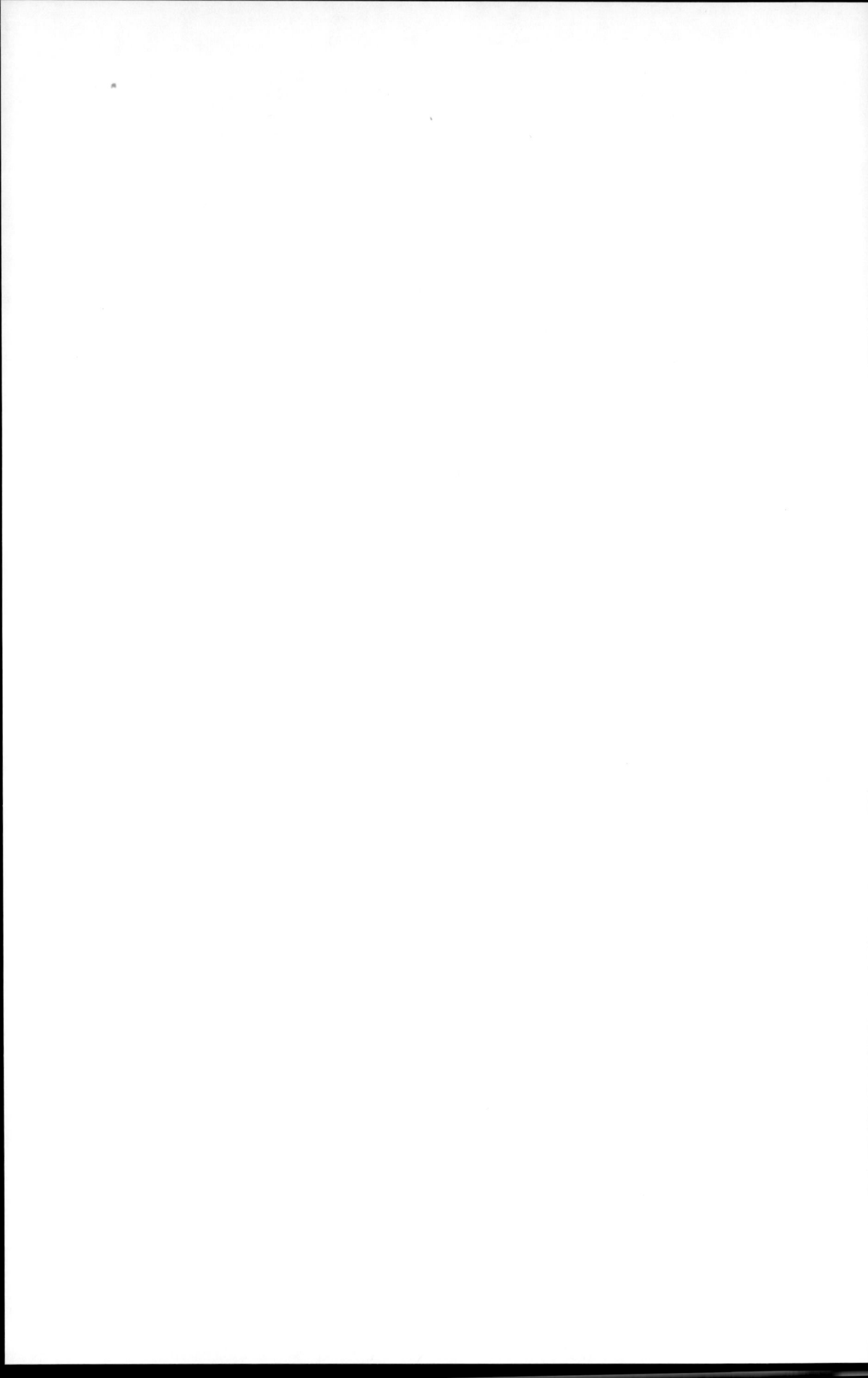

5. One Party State: The Samoan Experience

Afamasaga Toleafoa

Un État avec un parti unique : l'expérience samoane

On fait souvent l'éloge de Samoa pour sa stabilité politique et sociale. Depuis 1985, le pays n'a pas connu de changement de gouvernement et il est gouverné par un parti unique, le Parti de la protection des Droits de l'homme (HRPP), au pouvoir de façon continue. La période n'a connu que deux changements de Premier ministre et le gouvernement HRPP a gouverné avec des majorités écrasantes au Parlement. A un moment où une grande partie de la région connaît l'instabilité politique à des degrés divers sous la forme de coups d'Etat, de gouvernements éphémères et même de la violence et la désobéissance civile, Samoa est perçu par de nombreux observateurs comme un pôle de stabilité et de bonne gouvernance. Mais aujourd'hui, après 26 ans pendant lesquels un seul parti avait le pouvoir, Samoa est en fait un Etat avec un parti unique, avec des conditions actuellement en place pour que le gouvernement actuel reste au pouvoir pendant de nombreuses années encore. Cet article esquisse les forces principales qui ont contribué à la situation en apparence stable de Samoa. Le contenu provient surtout de la chronique hebdomadaire de l'auteur, « Democracy maketh not a democracy—La Démocratie ne fait pas une démocratie » publiée dans le journal local le *Samoa Observer*. Il s'agit d'une série de commentaires sur la politique samoane, notamment le risque que le parti au pouvoir ou l'exécutif accapare le pouvoir politique aux dépens de l'intégrité des institutions démocratiques du pays.

Introduction

Samoa is often lauded for its political and social stability. In fact, since 1985, Samoa has had no change in government with one political party, the Human Rights Protection Party (HRPP), holding office continuously. Only two changes of prime ministers have taken place during that time and the HRPP government has also governed with overwhelmingly large majorities in parliament. At a time when much of the region has experienced varying degrees of political instability in the form of military coups, short lived governments and even violence and civil disobedience, Samoa is seen by many as a beacon of stability and good government.

This chapter sketches the main forces that have contributed to Samoa's seemingly stable political situation. The material is taken mainly from the writer's weekly column 'Democracy maketh not a democracy' in the local Samoa Observer newspaper. This is a series of commentaries on politics in Samoa including the risk of the party in office or the executive accumulating political power to itself at the expense of the integrity of the country's democratic institutions.

After 26 years of one political group, the HRPP party holding office, Samoa is effectively a one party state, with conditions now in place for the present government to remain in office for many more years.

The Samoan Political System

Evolution of Samoa's Modern State System

When Samoa gained political independence as a modern state in 1962, it did so with a Westminster styled democratic constitution with the usual separation of powers between the three branches of government. That constitution had a built-in system of democratic checks and balances that ensures political balance in the system and guards against any one branch assuming excessive power to itself.

Like the rest of the Pacific, Samoa also had its own culture and indigenous forms of political and social organisation. Allowance was made for inclusion of some of these forms in the new modern state system at the initial stage at least and as a transitional measure. But there was an expectation that in time and with increased adoption and understanding of the new democratic practices and forms, some or all of these would be phased out or adapted to suit the democratic substance of and nature of Samoa's modern state system.

During the first twenty or so years following independence, Samoa relied in fact on its existing traditional leadership and forms to usher in and manage the change. In parliament for example and in the absence of political parties, members of parliament continued to follow Samoan traditions and practices on government to the extent that they were not inconsistent with its democratic constitution. Decision making in parliament relied on Samoan consensus practices for example with individual members supporting or opposing as they saw fit government policy. And Samoan concepts and practices of rotation to office as opposed to contesting for office were observed.

These practices would soon change with the emergence of political factions and later political parties with the formation of the Human Rights Protection Party in 1982 followed soon after by the Samoa National Party. And after a short period of changing political fortunes by the two groups, HRPP won office in 1988 and has been in power since. Today, Samoa has a one party political system with HRPP being the only party in parliament.

Changing Samoa's Democratic System of Government

During the long period of HRPP rule, fundamental changes have been made to Samoa's constitution and system of government. The overall impact of these has been to allow the executive to accumulate to itself almost absolute power at the expense of parliament and other democratic institutions. The nature of these changes as such that in the majority of cases, the democratic mechanisms and institutions have remained, but effective control and direction is vested in cabinet. The democratic structure of the system remains, but institutions have been stripped of their independence and power to act on their own as intended in the first place.

Change to Appointment and Powers of the Office of Controller and Chief Auditor

One of the first constitutional offices to suffer that fate was the Office of the Controller and Chief Officer. The independence and protection for the office of Controller and Chief Auditor from political control had been provided through security of tenure mainly. Under Samoa's constitution, once appointed, the holder remained in office till age 60 unless he or she resigns earlier. Removal from office was possible only by a vote in parliament supported by no less than two thirds of the members.

Following an audit report of government operations that heavily criticised government and of a number of cabinet ministers in 1994/5, the then appointee was controversially removed and the appointment provisions in the constitution amended. The term of office was reduced to three years with right of renewable reappointment with cabinet becoming the effective appointment authority. The change was strongly opposed but government had the necessary two-thirds majority to amend the constitution.

Two of the cabinet ministers cited in the Controller and Chief Officer's report were later convicted of the assassination of one of their ministerial colleagues. But unprotected from political control and influence, the office of Controller and Chief Auditor has become just another office of government, answerable directly to cabinet.

Parliamentary Term Extended

Without reference to the electorate, the parliamentary term of office was extended from 3 to 5 years. The change was made retrospectively and adopted by parliament in spite of widespread opposition.

Cabinet Enlarged From Eight to Thirteen Members

Samoa's constitution had set the size of cabinet at eight members. This was extended to thirteen.

Appointment of Under-Secretaries

After the 1991 general elections, the office of Parliamentary Under-Secretary was created. The move was an important part of government's expanding patronage system. It would help to consolidate support for the party in office which would now become a magnet for office seekers. Ten years later, the Under-Secretary post was upgraded to that of Associate Minister. It meant among other things that government was left with no backbenchers as all party members became either cabinet ministers or associate ministers.

Ministerial Committee System

Another part of the patronage system, a ministerial committee system that allowed government members of parliament to reward political supporters through membership of committees was put in place. Committee members were in most cases persons of influence in the village ruling hierarchies. Use of village authorities to control and even subvert the political process is a strong feature of Samoan politics. Village authorities are amongst the main beneficiaries of government's patronage system and strongly support government as well. Ministerial committee members are paid from public funds.

Control of the Public Service

The Special Posts Act 1996 placed the position of heads of government ministries under three year long contracts, renewable on reselection. More significantly, cabinet became the effective appointing authority. The constitutional position of the Public Service Commission as the appointing authority and as a buffer between the political process and public servants was accordingly changed. Subsequently, the public service was placed under direct political control with serious implications for its neutrality and professionalism. In fact, it too became an extension of government's patronage system.

Political Party Rules

During successive HRPP terms in government, party political rules were progressively introduced or amended to regulate the formation and operation of political parties. While such regulation was necessary, cabinet and the ruling party unfortunately had control of the process and therefore determined the outcome. The result is a system that today openly violates fundamental democratic principles of parliament and the rights of members. Political order and stability was given as the justification for these often overly restrictive measures, but this was at a time when the ruling party was entrenched in power commanding two thirds majorities no less.

The arbitrary and partisan nature of the system was demonstrated most recently when the newly formed opposition Tautua party was excluded from parliament in spite of it winning two by-elections. Earlier on when prevented from registering in parliament as a political party, the Tautua party registered instead as an incorporated society in the Companies Registry office using the freedom of association provision of Samoa's constitution. The constitutional freedom of association provision has since been amended to specifically exclude organisations with political aims.

Electoral Process

Samoa's electoral process is directly under cabinet control. As a result, it is the subject of frequent change, often politically motivated in response to the electoral needs of government. An office of the Electoral Commissioner exists. But like other agencies of the state with a part to play in the political process, it too is directly under the control of cabinet. The agency's main functions are to organise the holding of elections. It has no capacity to act independently of political direction with all substantive matters relating to the electoral system remaining under cabinet control.

Understandably, Samoa has a highly politicised electoral system that combines a mishmash of democratic and customary values and practices. In recent years – and to accommodate the wishes of the pro-government politically influential village leaders – customary value systems and practices have been brought back into the system. The result has been loss of clarity and integrity and persistent conflict between traditional values and practices and democratic values and practices.

The Budget System

The budget system has not escaped the reach of cabinet controlling power. Changes made recently in the Unauthorised Expenditure provision take control of public finance further away from parliament.

Un-parliamentary Parliament

With government holding large parliamentary majorities in parliament, Samoa's parliamentary system is directly subservient to executive control and machinations. Partisan interests and continuity in office become the primary motivations and are reflected in the grossly undemocratic approach to parliament's committee system, to the right of members to speak in debate, to the rules and standing orders, and to the timing and frequency of parliament sittings.

In 2004, the Inter-Parliamentary Union conducted an inquiry into the running of Samoa's parliament in response to request from the opposition groups. The inquiry confirmed the un-parliamentary character of Samoa's parliament, but it had no power to change anything and the situation has remained the same. Samoa's parliament is in effect not much more than a rubber stamp and a convenient tool for the party in power.

Other Contributing Factors

Control of Public Media

Control of information inevitably goes hand in hand with undemocratic governments and the situation in Samoa's one party state is no exception. And control of information has been relatively easy to effect because government traditionally must play a prominent part in information dissemination. This is especially true of the more costly television and radio services. Until recently, government owned and controlled Samoa's only television and radio services, together with a well established print media information network.

Direct control of these services has given government in Samoa considerable ability to control and manipulate information for public consumption. Television and radio in particular play a large part in information dissemination because of the underdeveloped state of the print media. Yet, until state television was privatised two years ago, opposition groups were barred access to these services. The ban remained in effect in spite of a successful legal challenge against it.

Access to radio broadcasts of parliamentary debate is a primary source of information for 70 per cent of the electorate for example. It provides both entertainment and valuable learning about government and about the political process. By carefully managing this process, government has been able to control public opinion and political allegiance especially in the less informed and less knowledgeable rural electorates.

Control of the Private Media

Samoa's private media has also been the target of control and manipulation. Samoa has several pieces of media related legislation enacted to control media freedom including access to public funds to pay court costs when public officials take the media to court for defamation of character for instance. The latter provision has been used on several occasions with telling effect on the ability of the media to defend itself in court.

Government's heavy handed approach to media control in the past has in fact turned the Editor of the leading Samoan daily newspaper, the Samoa Observer, into a media celebrity with several international media freedom awards to his credit as a result.

In recent years, the approach has been more subtle with the staff of the Government Information Service taking leadership positions in the national journalists' organisation itself. One outcome of that were the prime minister and deputy prime minister receiving the organisation's 'press freedom persons of the year' award. Financial and other support to media outlets sympathetic to government has also been part of the plan.

Faa-Samoa versus Democratic Government

As in most Pacific states, Samoa had its own system of political and social organisation, Faa-Samoa, the Samoan way, which continues to serve as Samoa's local government system. As a system of government, Faa-Samoa is in most respects diametrically opposite to the values and principles and practices of democratic government.

Unfortunately, little has been done in the intervening years to bring Faa-Samoa, at least at local government level, more into line with the democratic requirements of Samoa's modern state. If anything, the reverse has occurred with village authorities being accorded new powers to influence the outcome of voting.

Village authorities are among the main beneficiaries of government's patronage system, and giving them more say and influence in the electoral system effectively skewers the results in favour of government. According to the prime minister, HRPP owes much of its longevity in office to the support of Samoa's village government leaders.

Conclusion

In Samoa's general elections of March 2011, the present HRPP government was returned with yet another overwhelming large number of parliamentary seats. The party has been in power continuously for going on to thirty years. That is an unusually long period of time to hold power in a functioning democracy.

Samoa cannot be considered as such a functioning democracy. This longevity in power is but the sign of a democracy that is in crisis – as this sketch shows. It is the sign of a system where an unprecedented level of power is now accumulated in the executive through a sustained re-engineering of Samoa's constitution and government systems during the long period of HRPP rule. That power has in turn been put to use to retain office and to perpetuate one political party in government at great cost to the integrity of Samoa's democratic system.

It is too early to say how the system will evolve from here, but the implications for Samoa of it becoming a one party status are becoming more apparent. Power corrupts and the effect on the current leadership of almost thirty years in office is beginning to show. And however the political situation develops after the 2011 elections, Samoa needs to return to democratic government sooner rather than later. But that will require a systematic dismantling of the one party state power structure that exists at present, and a return to the democratic principles and values that underpinned the nation's constitution. It will also require a change in leadership which appears unlikely at present.

6. Instability and Stability in New Caledonia

Jean-Yves Faberon

Instabilité et stabilité en Nouvelle-Calédonie

Le préambule de l'Accord de Nouméa pose un principe de consensus par le biais du partage: «Le passé a été le temps de la colonisation. Le présent est le temps du partage, par le rééquilibrage. L'avenir doit être le temps de l'identité, dans un destin commun ». Si cette déclaration fut approuvée par les électeurs de Nouvelle-Calédonie au scrutin de novembre 1998 avec une majorité de 72%, le chemin vers ce résultat commun a été long. Ce chapitre retrace l'histoire politique de la Nouvelle-Calédonie depuis 1853, dont le point culminant est l'Accord de Nouméa. Celui-ci, prenant en compte le passé colonial, rejette l'hypothèse selon laquelle l'indépendance pourrait intervenir brutalement et met en œuvre un calendrier de partage progressif des compétences en Nouvelle-Calédonie sur une durée de plus de 20 ans.

The preamble to the Noumea Agreement establishes a principle, namely consensus through sharing: 'The past was colonisation time. The present is the time for sharing and reaching a new balance. The future must be the time for an identity, in a common destiny.'

This statement, which is shot through with the spirit of sharing, was approved by voters in New Caledonia in the November 1998 election, with a 72 per cent majority. But the road to this common result has been a long one.

Even before the French landed in New Caledonia, Kanaks were far from being united. Their languages and their customs were different depending upon the area, and for that matter, their 'warrior traditions' are referred to in the Noumea Agreement.

With the arrival of the French, starting on 24 September 1853, the colonisation period started. It shook up the foundations of Kanak society and from a legal standpoint, it lasted over one century. That period was characterised by a very serious rift: the colonial society on the one hand and the indigenous society on the other hand, and they were totally separated, despite some individual exceptions.

With the IVth Republic, the new Constitution, in 1946, put an end to the colonial Empire, and the French Union was substituted for the colonial Empire. The Constitution's preamble abolished colonisation: 'France forgoes any colonial system based upon arbitrariness, France guarantees to all equal access to public employment and to the individual or collective exercise of rights and liberties.' It was not until 1956 that the Defferre law on the future of overseas territories actually implemented the new constitutional provision, and New Caledonia got a new status, through the July 1957 specific executive order.

The year 1953 saw the advent of a unique political organisation advocating a consensual New Caledonia— the Union Calédonienne. The Union Calédonienne's motto was: 'Two colors, one people'. With the 1957 status, this party gave New Caledonia its first Vice-President of the government council. He was a member of Parliament.

This consensus resoundingly translated into overwhelming support for the new French regime, the Vth Republic. General de Gaulle initiated a referendum vote on the new Constitution in September 1958, and the question was whether voters would choose to remain within the French Republic. Now, in New Caledonia at the time, there were more Kanaks than whites, and universal suffrage showed a 98 per cent yes vote.

General De Gaulle's government hardly showed any gratitude to New Caledonia for that almost unanimous vote. The government in Paris chipped away at New Caledonia's self-rule. The State advanced through the 1963 and 1965 Jacquinot laws and the 1969 Billotte laws. One of the Billotte laws dealt with mining regulations, and, precisely, 1969 was the start of a so-called 'Nickel boom', which lasted until 1972. That was an exhilarating growth period for New Caledonia's nickel resources. This unprecedented development operated across the board and impacted all the islands' activities; it attracted numerous groups of people from the motherland and from overseas territories. As a result, Kanaks were now a minority in their own land. They did not reap any profit from the new economic situation. Their country was a source of riches... except for them!

That period clearly coincides with the emergence of the breakaway movement. In 1969, the 'Red Scarves' were created by Nidoïsh Naisseline, the first Kanak to hold a college degree, and in 1971, Elie Poigoune created the '1978 Group'. As a result, in 1973, whites walked out of the Union Calédonienne party. In 1977, the Union Calédonienne joined the breakaway movement. The buzzword at the time was IKS, which means Kanak and Socialist Independence. It created an obstacle to consensus and to the communities' union. The Union Calédonienne's motto, 'one single people', effectively became obsolete.

In September 1975, Jean-Marie Tjibaou, dealing more with the cultural than with the political ground, set up the 'Melanesia 2000' festival. This was to be followed by a more general festival called 'Caledonia 2000', dealing with the whole range of cultures present in New Caledonia. But the time was not ripe for it; the second festival never took place.

From then on, political forces started to line up for battle and not for the compact. Jacques Lafleur created the RPCR in 1978 under Tjibaou's presidency. Each of the two groups had its charismatic leader and was in battle order. The face-off did take place, and the 1980s were the painful and bloody decade: from the assassination of Pierre Declercq, the Union Calédonienne's Secretary General in September 1981, through the 21 deaths at the Ouvea cave in May 1988, to Tjibaou's assassination in 1989.

The 1980s, however, experienced a positive happening, an opportunity to work and be together, and that was the Nainville-les-Roches round table. In July 1983, amidst the conflict, Georges Lemoine, Under Secretary for Overseas Territories, a man who valued dialogue, brought together in Nainville-les-Roches representatives of various New Caledonia political attitudes, some seeking independence, such as Tjibaou, and some opposed to independence, such as Jacques Lafleur, along with representatives from the FNSC, the Federation for a new New Caledonian Society, who advocated a middle road. The meeting also included a representative of customary institutions.

The upshot of that meeting was a brief document containing the gist of the Noumea Accord! A few examples are:

- 'Definitely confirm that colonialism is dead...'
- 'Respect for all ethnic groups'.
- 'The necessity for a specific document with potential for adjustment to new situations...'

The RPCR, eventually, refrained from signing the statement... and this refusal led straight to what history has elected to call New Caledonia 'events'.

During those years, there was bloodshed in New Caledonia. On 24 September 1984, the Front Indépendantiste became the FLNKS, a name that was regarded by its opponents as a call to exclusion. The acronym FLNKS, along with the creation of a 'Provisional new government for the Republic', are clear references to the process that took place in Algeria, and which ended in disaster. So, very quickly, the situation proved to be a long way from the Nainville-les-Roches Declaration.

The status designed by the peace-loving Mr. Lemoine, dated September 6, 1984, was unanimously rejected, as all parties were raring to go, and naturally, tit calls for tat.

The French State appointed Edouard Pisani as government representative, as he seemed to be the right man for the job, since he was a socialist and formerly a long-time Gaullist minister. This political dualism was supposed to allow Pisani to create a link between the two political groups in New Caledonia. The plan he announced, however, and one he announced in a peremptory way, in January 1985, was unanimously rejected. Pisani's failure was as quick as his bursting upon the New Caledonian political scene, and not only did he fail to bring peace; he had to declare a state of emergency.

The rightist government, coming back into office in Paris in 1986, did not fare better in New Caledonia than its predecessor, and for the same reason: it did not act as an honest broker.

That led to the Ouvea massacre in April-May 1988.

Yet, there were history-making events. The new French government, under Michel Rocard, ultimately took an impartial stand, and wanted to solemnly restore peace on that basis. After having a mission called 'Dialogue Mission' analyze the situation on the field, the Prime Minister brought together Lafleur and Tjibaou and had them sign the Matignon Accords. The two partners finally agreed to fight for a common cause. And their gamble was a winner! Since 1988, New Caledonia has been in peace (even though Tjibaou was assassinated), and New Caledonia is on its way to the common destiny.

The genius of the Matignon-Oudinot Accords is that they divided New Caledonia into provinces. They succeeded, like a modern sphinx, in answering the question which had hitherto been left without an answer: How to allow breakaway factions, who are in the minority, to exert some kind of power in a majoritarian democracy? The answer consisted in dividing New Caledonia into three provinces where the respective majorities are different, so that both separatist factions and loyalists could have each a place where they were in the majority and where they could exercise power.

The genius of the Noumea Accord, which puts into perspective all the light and shadow of the past, lies in a gradual and pluralistic process. It is gradual in that it rejects the assumption that independence could occur suddenly, and it implements a schedule for power-sharing in New Caledonia spread over 20 years, one step at a time, so that at the end of the process, potential independence would not be like crossing over an unknown abyss, but only, for the whole population, a last step to add to those that had been taken already, and thus it would avert clashes and surprises.

And the agreement is pluralistic in that it decides—and that is an exception which is the only one of its kind in the world—that New Caledonia would not be governed by a majority government but by a pluralistic government including representatives both of the majority and the minority (an 'opposition' which is in a peculiar situation). At any rate, the government is made up of representatives of separatists and loyalists in a sort of 'mandatory consensus'... This is a huge gamble for a model which is totally out of the ordinary, but it is working in New Caledonia. New Caledonia is now the place where what President N. Sarkozy stated on 22 June 2009 before the French Congress is being verified: 'A democracy where peace has been restored is not a democracy where there is general agreement but a democracy where people listen to each other and respect each other'.

Does that mean that after 20 peaceful and overall consensual years New Caledonia has shaken off its old demons? Of course not. Nobody can assert that the Noumea Accord gamble has been won in any definitive way. This agreement is a compromise between proponents of antagonistic attitudes as to the final relation of the islands to France. It has succeeded in bringing peace and spreading the common destiny mystique, which is a huge accomplishment, but eventually there remains to be seen (which the agreement does not do) whether this common destiny will be within or without France—although, of course, one can still hope for a solution in between, with France. Disagreements are certain to appear again, as in the issue of the definition of the Electorate or that of transfers of powers. People must be aware that when they base their action on a compromise basic document, which is inevitably ambiguous, disagreements are likely and natural. It is always important to face the problems, since by referring to disagreements with a sincere heart, we can make the Accord live on. For, in the final analysis, beyond pluralism and gradualism, beyond the fair memory of the colonial period that we mentioned, beyond the notions of citizenship and power transfer which undeniably make up the spirit of the agreement, what is the Noumea Accord? What gives the key to each of those components is respect for others, tolerance, the will for dialogue, and loyalty; this is the vital force of the Noumea Accord. Now these are components of human nature, and victory is never final on the dark side of human nature. Human nature is also made up of intolerance and the will to power. For this reason, there is no guarantee for success for the Noumea Accord. There simply is none.

7. Democracy in French Polynesia

Sémir Al Wardi

La démocratie en Polynésie française

La Polynésie est une « collectivité d'outre-mer » au sein de la République française. Sa culture politique présente des différences considérables par rapport à celle de la République et l'instabilité politique est l'une de ses caractéristiques principales. En effet, une « collectivité d'outre-mer » est une collectivité « spéciale » surtout parce que, contrairement aux autres collectivités, les lois de la République ne s'y appliquent que rarement, et ce selon le principe de la spécialité législative : par-dessus tout, ce territoire a le droit à l'indépendance. Par conséquent, puisque les anciennes colonies peuvent se séparer de la métropole, la vie politique tourne autour de ce droit à l'indépendance, ce qui inévitablement affecte leurs relations avec la métropole. Ainsi, cette vie politique est marquée par une division entre les indépendantistes et les autonomistes, même si cette division peut changer. La faiblesse idéologique et le nomadisme politique engendrent également l'instabilité politique. En outre, il semblerait que les concepts modernes du pouvoir, les relations entre les compétences nationales et les compétences locales, ne soient pas compris au sein de la société locale, qui semble elle-même assez réticente quand il s'agit d'adopter l'institutionnalisation.

Introduction

Polynesia is an 'overseas community' within the French Republic. French Polynesian political culture differs considerably from that of the Republic and political instability is one of its major characteristics. Indeed, an 'overseas community' is a 'special' community essentially because, unlike the other communities, the laws of the Republic apply to it only rarely, according to the principle of legislative speciality;[1] above all this territory has the right to independence. Therefore since former colonies can break away, political life revolves around this right to independence, which inevitably affects its relations with France. So, political life divides between separatists and autonomists even

---

1   Due to this long-established principle, the laws are not fully applicable in former overseas territories. The law must expressly mention its applicability to a specified territory. As a consequence, overseas territories often become, as Yves Pimont says, 'the forgotten people of healthy reforms'. Worse, the practice of autonomy, in certain cases, even represents a regression compared to metropolitan France.

if this divide can change. Ideological weakness and political nomadism also engender political instability. It would also seem that modern concepts of power, relations between national and local powers, are not understood within the local society, which itself seems to be rather reluctant to embrace institutionalisation.

Polynesia is a Special 'Overseas Community' within the Republic

The involvement of French colonies in national liberation, at the end of the Second World War, led to a new approach to overseas French dependencies in France. From then on, after 1946, there were 'French overseas departments' and 'French overseas territories', and no longer 'French colonies'. The words 'colonies' and even 'empire' were then abandoned forever. This abandonment signified also, the erasure of the reality those very words illustrated, as was the hope of L S Senghor (JORF, Assemblée Nationale Constituante, session of 11 avril 1946: 1729). The change from colony to territorial communities indicates that they fall within the purview of territorial communities, which stipulates that they are administered by elected councils.

'Overseas territories' from this time on consist of citizens and no longer of subjects. It was then that political life came into being in these territories. The minimum bottom line to any democracy, namely democratic representation (the Parliament and/or the executive represents the People and makes decisions on their behalf), the guarantee of public and individual liberties and the presence of one or several oppositions, is real in French Polynesia. The assembly is elected by direct universal suffrage and it is from this assembly that the executive members are chosen. Elections take place according to the rules of the Republic, the oppositions are represented (Tavini/Tahoeraa), and liberties guaranteed normally by the courts.

The Right to Independence

Former colonies, and overseas territories, can become independent by invoking Article 53 of the French Constitution.[2] It is first necessary to consult the populations involved, then to ask the French Parliament to pass a law authorising the secession. In constitutional terms, overseas territories, today 'overseas communities', have enjoyed, as did colonies, 'a permanent right to

---

2   In its decision of 30 December 1975 relative to the Comoros affair, the Constitutional Council states that the provisions of Article 53, 'should be interpreted as being applicable not only if France were to cede a territory to a foreign State or should acquire one from it, but also should a territory cease to belong to the Republic and constitute an independent State or be attached to one'.

independence' (Maestre and Miclo 1987: 1281). The Republic cannot therefore unilaterally declare an 'overseas community' independent. It has the power to decide on and to organise a referendum and even to choose its reading of the referendum (archipelago by archipelago or country-wide reading of the results), only the concerned populations can express their will to leave the Republic or not. The example of Mayotte has demonstrated that if the State wishes to disengage, but the population opposes it, then the territory remains French. On the other hand, if the population, after local elections, expresses a wish for emancipation, then it would seem that France would not oppose it. In other words, the former colonies have the possibility of becoming emancipated.

The Pro-autonomy and Pro-independence Divide

Since they can become emancipated from France, this is becoming a real 'obsession' for French Polynesian politicians. The constant possibility of separating from France has several consequences, the most important of which is to make political elites take sides on the matter of French presence: within (and in which ways) or without France (and again, in which ways); autonomy or independence. The Left/Right political divide does not exist in French Polynesia, only the line between pro-autonomy and pro-independence.

Originally structured around supporters of direct administration by France and proponents of internal autonomy (often labelled independents at the time), in the 1980s this division became a division between pro-autonomy and pro-independence. The French Polynesian political universe is built on this issue. The political game revolves around French presence and the various territorial, or even national, elections are occasions for political parties to proclaim their position relative to the French presence issue. It seems that these are the only two categories in the French Polynesian political field, and the only ones driving ideological confrontations. Yet, the line can be blurred in everyday reality: politicians or voters can swing from one side to the other and back again, and make the divide considerably fuzzier. Even beyond the independence issue, it is the relationship of French Polynesia with France which dominates political thinking.

Unlike what happens in other territories of the French Republic, French Polynesian politicians do not look to the national issues for inspiration. Their indifference to national or 'metropolitan' politics does not mean that they are apolitical but rather that they focus on the local scene, the only one that matters. Therefore, political parties from the French mainland very seldom have a Polynesian extension.

This possibility of emancipation thus triggers a kind of statutory outbidding which has never known any rest since French Polynesians really started participating in political life. Gaston Flosse (2001) said that 'any institutional marking time would bring about, if applied, the death of our autonomy'. French Polynesia has statutes of 1957, 1977, 1984, 1996 and 2004, not counting the amendments of 1991 and 2007 and the major aborted reform of 'overseas countries' in 2000.

One People, One Nation?

France recognises in its Constitution only one people and a single nation. Now, the French Polynesians consider that they are a different people from the French. This feeling strengthened with the granting of autonomy and especially its political symbols. These have been authorised since 1984, namely a flag, a seal, a hymn (Ia Ora o' Tahiti Nui), an Order of Tahiti (the decorations and titles resembling the French Legion of Honour), a protocol and a territorial holiday. Symbolic strength can be added by words such as 'country', 'Tahiti Nui', 'love of our people' and 'love of our country' commonly used in speeches... In fact, the French State is called 'hau farani' (French power) and French Polynesia 'hau fenua' (power of the country). The State is considered, from that time on, as an exogenous and temporary entity.

It is thus the strengthening of national feeling in French Polynesia which has characterised these last twenty years: autonomy and statutory outbidding have strengthened Tahitian nationalism, with the help of political symbols.

Political Instability

According to the Tahitian Academy, the Tahitian word for 'democracy' is 'Hau Manahune' (literally 'the power of the people'). Maco Tevane (2004), the president of the above-mentioned academy specified that "people should be understood as 'common people' (manahune) and that they were to be taken into account in the political system through its access to benefits". The 'ona' (the leaders) had to give some benefits to them.' It is this 'gift and counter-gift', a phrase beloved of anthropologists, which is perhaps at the origin of political patronage. Instability has always existed in Polynesia since the beginning of the political life in 1945. The only exception to this applies to the period 1996-2004, which was marked by a drift towards authoritarianism, with the complicity of the French state.

Ballots Full of Surprises

Electoral results do not always reveal the new holder of power. Last minute alliances and political nomadism can result, as in 2008, in the loser winning, because in fact he became president of French Polynesia with the lowest score. In another scenario the one who wins the elections has no guarantee of holding power till the end of his/her mandate: examples are legion also in the Cook Islands, in Vanuatu, in the Papua New Guinea, in Solomon Islands, etc. In all these islands, elections do not represent a key moment in democratic life but simply one moment among others. We invest a lot of energy in elections, but immediately after the elections have taken place, the various political parties of the opposition constantly look for 'nomads' so as to take back power. In brief, a party which wins the elections can lose power in the days or the months which follow. The political fight does not become diminished after an election and patience, one of the conditions of democracy, does not exist.

Certainly, the proportional voting system has facilitated this instability following the example of the 4th Republic in France. Since 2004, for example, we have had nine presidents of French Polynesia, from two territorial elections, that is an average time in power of about eight months. But, as René Rémond (1991: 392) recalls, under the 4th Republic, 'the same group of men continuously exercises power'. It is the same in French Polynesia with the alternations since 2004. It is the same elected representatives who succeed one another, either alternately or together.

Is it necessary then to simply change the voting system to obtain stability? No, answers Georges Vedel in his Report on governmental instability in 1956 in France. It would only be one palliative among others 'completely powerless to fundamentally change things' (Chevallier 2001: 713).

The proposal, constantly renewed by French Polynesian politicians, to elect the president of French Polynesia by a direct universal suffrage system (Jean-Baptiste Céran Jérusalémy, Gaston Flosse from 1985, Jean Juventin, Gaston Tong Sang) is not a solution. It would change nothing as in terms of instability: a representative elected in a direct universal suffrage system would only be able to be censured with difficulty by a local assembly, making it necessary, from then on, to set up a real Prime Minister who would represent the majority of the aforementioned assembly. The risk of 'cohabitation' is real and the problem is only moved to one side.

Ideological Weakness and Nomadism

Ideological weakness, marked by an economic and social policy common to the various independent or separatist political parties, facilitates political nomadism. Politicians or the electorate can cross from one side to another one and conversely and so considerably blur the divide. French Polynesian elected representatives have often considered that they were free to use their mandate and so to join with any political party after their election. In other words, French Polynesian political culture gives a relative autonomy to elected representatives to negotiate their membership of a party according to their interests and especially to those of their electorate. Alliances even 'against nature' can exist. It is mostly a question of being the closest to public resources to redistribute to one's electorate or even to reactivate political patronage networks. This political nomadism has brought with it a chronic political instability since the beginning of political life in French Polynesia, with the exception of the period 1996 - 2004.

An Emotive Relationship

Democracy is not questioned as such in French Polynesia. Non-violent political instability, which is, let us recall, the hallmark of democracy, is explained by ideological weakness, political nomadism, the voting system and patronage. This latter is aggravated by the gaining of more and more power within the framework of the autonomy: it is this which has provided considerable power to redistribute public resources.

But this is possible only because its relationship to power remains personal even emotive. Can we say that French Polynesia, following the example of the Antilles, 'is the theatre of a persistent conflict – raised in particular by Aimé Césaire – between rational culture, the foundation of modernity, and emotional culture inherited from past...'? (Michalon 2006: 442). It seems indeed that it is an emotive relationship which wins the support of French Polynesians: it is enough to see the difference in the results during the elections between the metua (the guide) and any political fellow party member. Rudy Bambridge (1975), an influential French Polynesian politician, specified to the Secretary of State for French Overseas Departments and Territories, in 1975, that 'in French Polynesia more than elsewhere, politics is based on 'the affection' that the people have for their leaders. They are a sentimental people.'

It is also what explains the undoubted weight of mayors in the compiling of lists for territorial elections: every mayor, supposedly popular because he is one of those responsible for the redistribution of public resources, must be able to bring with him a certain number of votes for the person who heads the list who, once elected, will in his turn redistribute benefactions to the municipalities.

The fundamental consequence of this is the lack of institutionalisation. As emphasised by Max Weber in terms of legal and rational domination, this mode of domination which characterises western democracies leads to the prevention of power being exercised 'as personal privilege' (Braud 1985: 386). The leaders and their administrative departments are subject to the law and the citizens are treated in the same way whatever their affiliation. It is this equality of all in the eyes of the law which is 'central to the new society' (Michalon, in preparation). It is even the pivot of the republican values. However, the emotional link which allows one to acquire a good, even a symbolic one, thanks to personal relationships is in opposition to this equality upon which the State is built. It is the person who is important, not his/her function.

In French Polynesia, the relationship of power is based on this relationship of patronage and on personal exchange. This also explains that the electorate can follow a political leader even if he changes camp several times: it is not a question of things being decided rationally on questions of autonomy or independence, but often just with regard to a person's charisma.

For example, the mayor (Tavana) asks his population to vote for a specific candidate in Presidential elections. The population follows the mayor even if he is not logical, even if the mayor changes sides without explanation every election:[3]

Table 3: First Round of Presidential Election in Papeete

Year	Election of Mayor	Score of socialist candidates		Score of conservative candidates	
1974	F. Mitterrand	F. Mitterrand	45.26%	V. Giscard d'Estaing	30.37%
				J. Chaban Delmas	20.58%
1981	V. Giscard d'Estaing	F. Mitterrand	6.92%	V. Giscard d'Estaing	64.05%
				J. Chirac	24.26%
1988	F. Mitterrand	F. Mitterrand	52.40%	J. Chirac	30.54%
				R. Barre	10.73%
1995	E. Balladur	L. Jospin	12.69%	E. Balladur	33.41%
				J. Chirac	44.02%
2002	J. Chirac	L. Jospin	28.70%	J. Chirac	57.28%
				F. Bayrou	1.21%
2007	N. Sarkozy	S. Royal	39.47%	N. Sarkozy	46.22%
				F. Bayrou	8.24%

---

3   Tables from Jean-Marc Regnault, to appear in « L'hommage à Paul de Deckker ».

Table 4: Second Round of Presidential Election in Mahina

Year	Election of Mayor	Score of socialist candidates		Score of conservative candidates	
1974	F. Mitterrand	F. Mitterrand	52.39%	V. Giscard d'Estaing	25.84%
				J. Chaban Delmas	17.54%
1981	V. Giscard d'Estaing	F. Mitterrand	13.92%	V. Giscard d'Estaing	57.66%
				J. Chirac	21.14%
1988	F. Mitterrand	F. Mitterrand	58.84%	J. Chirac	24.38%
				R. Barre	9.25%
1995	J. Chirac	L. Jospin	13.99%	E. Balladur	22.40%
				J. Chirac	52.17%
2002	L. Jospin	L. Jospin	40.07%	J. Chirac	45.52%
				F. Bayrou	1.07%
2007	N. Sarkozy	tS. Royal	37.83%	N. Sarkozy	44.92%
				F. Bayrou	9.82%

Nomadism is then possible because the divide really has no more meaning. Can we advance the hypothesis according to which only a referendum on self-determination would oblige French Polynesians to depersonalise political concepts? It is not sure, because emotive relations can take over again and the risk can be that the vote is determined with regard to a leader rather than a policy.

Close family and kin ties which we find in French Polynesia and on the other islands of the Pacific, is a serious handicap which hampers social relations. Thierry Michalon (in preparation) notes that for overseas French: 'the request for and the granting of privileges are considered as the normal and legitimate mode of relations with the administration, especially if it is concerns decentralized communities, administered by local elected representatives to whom everyone has affective links'. Once again, French Polynesians do not recognise institutions, but rather recognise people.

Furthermore, this lack of institutionalisation is often due to politicians who draw benefit from it. There would be thus an interest in maintaining this 'emotional' perception of politicians considered as suppliers of services, mostly in a private capacity. In other words, if this perception of power based on emotional links been a part of the Polynesian political culture, the elected representatives are going to maintain this relationship and encourage it so as to prevent the emergence of institutionalisation, for their own electoral benefit. We can again formulate the hypothesis that it is this emotive approach which limits the impact of convictions or gaol sentences: a convicted politician can always pursue his career either by being elected, or even recruited by those in power. A court decision does not seem to have same impact in a society based on personal exchange.

Looting Public Resources?

Ideological weakness is also explained by a different vision of what constitutes the 'common good': it is a question of monopolising public resources for one's clan, one's group, one's party. One threatens to leave the government coalition if the rewards are not considered sufficient. Thierry Michalon (in preparation) explains that 'For these cultures, public institutions are not the place where decisions of general interest are taken and where public utilities are managed, but an unsupervised deposit of wealth to be divided up within the traditional networks of mutual assistance'. Power becomes, according to him, 'something edible'.

The people who French Polynesians call 'Islanders' (elected from outlying archipelagos), have these last few years beaten all records for political allegiance-switching and often broken political majorities, because of 'an insatiable appetite' for the public resources. President Oscar Temaru accuses them: 'I think that there are people who are here for their own personal interest, people there whom we know very well in this country, because they have a business on an island, because their wife is in such and such business, because they want to be a Minister of this or that or would like to become mayor' (Les Nouvelles, 13 October 2009). Moreover, elected representatives have a particular perception of ministries: there are 'technical' ministries and others which are 'political'. It is necessary to understand by 'political ministries', those which allow the establishment of a relationship of patronage and so to spread the linkages over the whole territory. And this is brokered in broad daylight, so that the various political groups, at the time of a governmental coalition, fight over these portfolios. The M.P. Bruno Sandras recognised, for example, regarding a Minister of Postal Services and Sports, that he has an interesting position: 'He has a comfortable portfolio which allows him to play politics for his party...' (Les Nouvelles, 27 January 2006).

Furthermore, there is a socio-economic dimension to power: this latter, thanks to the transfers from the State and to delegated powers, is an inescapable element in the economic and social game. It is this, for example, which distributes jobs, subsidies, diverse authorisations and work to companies: this dominant position has led to what the public prosecutor in Polynesia has called 'a pact of corruption'.

Several Theoretical Approaches

Three theories attract our attention: 'consensual' democracy, the lack of a 'Republic' and the organised chaos.

'Consensual' Democracy

This is the theory advanced by Professor Boumakani (2008: 499 ff.) – Faculty of Law, Brazzaville – according to which, democracy should be consensual in more 'traditional' states and territories. All the decisions are taken in common by consensus. Nevertheless, we can advance that on one hand, political nomadism reduces this possibility and on the other hand, pre-European French Polynesia has never known consensus but was rather a violent society, constantly at war. Furthermore, democracy cannot be consensual because it supposes an opposition of expectations.

The Lack of a Republic

This is a constant subject: the lack of a 'political philosophy' to support democracy. Jean-Marc Regnault underlines that from the beginning of political life, 'the leaders of the RDPT (the Pouvana'a party) are little prepared for the management of public affairs and have thought little about democratic practices' (Tahiti Pacifique Magazine, October 2009, n°222: 36). Since French Polynesian political culture formed only at that time, in the 1950s, quite recently, thinking on this topic has not evolved very much. From then on, the new President of the Territorial Assembly, in 1953, Jean-Baptiste Céran-Jérusalémy 'tried to control everything to muzzle the opposition' (ibid.). Much later, former Minister of Finance Patrick Peaucellier also noted that Gaston Flosse had, in the 1990s, 'acted in such a way that the opposition was essentially abolished' (Tahiti Business n°25, September 2004).

Has there been a misunderstanding of the word 'democracy'? What is lacking is that rather long road towards republican democracy, which derives from the theory of a Social Contract, to consolidate the rights of the individual within the group or the clan, to impose human rights, and so to create a citizen detached from his affiliations (religious, geographical, ethnic, family, clan), to assert the love of equality and finally, with Raymond Aron, to demonstrate that the democracy is not confined only to the political domain but extends to economic development and to the protection of individual liberties (Hadas-Lebel 2002: 217). Liberal democracy, which is our political system, writes Pierre Manent, is 'the fruit of a very long elaboration, a very long distillation, so that it results from all our history, prolongs it and contains it. It is the formula discovered with difficulty thanks to which we have managed to live together in a more or less satisfactory way, us Europeans' (2007: 17). We can maintain that the concepts of 'modern State', of 'Republic' and 'democracy' collide, become confused, in determining modern political life.

Therefore the problem would not be democracy but the absence of this very long process, rather complex, which carried forward this idea and which has, beyond the purely technical aspect of elections, forged a real political philosophy which has in turn made possible the government of the people.

But, in summary can we really blame the French Polynesians for this absence of a democratic philosophy?

First of all, we can wonder why the French Republic has not or not sufficiently introduced its values and principles into French Polynesia. During a session in the National Assembly, the majority and the opposition mutually blamed each other for having neglected the principles of the Republic in French Polynesia (Les Nouvelles de Tahiti, 29 January 2004.). France has not, moreover, introduced its values and principles into its colonies. A point common to all the overseas territories, in the years after the war, there was a demand for more equality and freedom. Philippe Braud (2004: 39) reminds us of the paradox: 'While the assertion of the universalist concept of human rights coincides in time with European expansion in the rest of the world, it has been nevertheless accompanied by extreme violence against native populations'. The absence of a real overseas policy, the constant of the Republic, combined with indifference, is going to keep these territories in zones without rights.

It even made the practice of democracy rather vague: Céran-Jérusalémy and the other French Polynesian politicians ask why France, while asserting democratic principles, arrested Pouvanaa a Oopa who voted 'NO', instead of 'YES', in the referendum of 1958, encouraged demonstrations against some leaders and prohibited them against others, and later, closed its eyes on that 'famous pact of corruption' of Gaston Flosse?

But, we can add also that the French Polynesians did not wish to be assimilated to the Republic but wanted an intermediate solution which allowed them to remain among themselves yet be under the umbrella of France. We can thus note collusion, even unconscious, between the State and French Polynesia in keeping the territory outside the values and the principles of the Republic.

Besides, this type of analysis obliges us to consider ideal political modernisation within a Western-style rationality: little by little, political life has to align itself with developments in metropolitan cities. But can we claim that democracy in France was and is perfect? That France would represent the cursor, the ideal democracy with which overseas territories should align themselves. The recentness of the democratic but unstable regimes of the 3rd and 4th Republic, the affairs of corruption under 3rd Republic, obliges us to be more modest. So, this proposition of the lack of a democratic philosophy remains insufficient.

The Theory of 'Organised Chaos'?

This theory draws attention to the mixture of the democratic principles and the practices proper to these societies. Political analysts, specialists of Africa, noticed that there was in these territories, in fact, an 'instrumentalisation of disorder' (Chabal and Daloz 1999: 177). It is a question of introducing democratic principles and of melding them again into a logic which fits in with the dominant universe of representations: 'registers are multiple even contradictory, without worrying about coherence' (ibid.: 172). Coherence is beyond us: We pass from one register to another according to circumstance. For example, in French Polynesia, political speeches in French and in Tahitian are not the same and involve different registers. Another example, in New Caledonia, Jean-Marie Tjibaou used 'procedures appropriate to every political and social organization' (Mokaddem 2008: 63). We also use honorifics, as opposed to institutionalisation, which imposes the depersonalisation of power, terms such as 'Big man', 'Metua' or even, in Africa, 'Lion'.

We also notice that the systematic research of a 'profit', and thus for a patronage, a reprehensible redistribution in the modern political game, is recognised by the whole population. If a dominant party no longer redistributes enough, it is replaced without compunction. It is moreover at the announcement of an impending fall of government that one of the members of the coalition will hammer the table that the government in power 'is incompetent' and/or 'ineffectual' in the redistribution of jobs or subsidies.

Furthermore, can we believe in 'citizenship', the foundation of democracy, in an essentially communal framework? In other words, community-based and patronage-driven systems are diametrically opposed to the logic 'of individual voters making electoral choices according to programs' (Chabal and Daloz 1999: 176). French Polynesian political parties represent the platform on which a recognised personality stands, much more than on any ideology-bearing organisation. A party serves a man, not a program. This follows a logic which is not anti-democratic but rather one which follows a different line of reasoning. Can we claim, following the example of certain political analysts that 'modernisation' is possible without real 'westernization'? This, they add, 'is not easy to accept for a lot of people' (Chabal and Daloz 1999: 181).

Conclusion

French Polynesian political life thus follows a logic which is to organise this 'disorder', to instrumentalise it for purposes of legitimisation. French Polynesia thus bases its legitimacy on a double approach: democratic legitimacy and redistribution of benefits within a personal relationship.

References

Bambridge, R. 1975. Archives, Letter of 16 April 1975

Boumakani, B. 2008. *La prohibition de la « transhumance politique » des parlementaires. Etudes de cas africains*, Revue française de Droit constitutionnel, n°75.

Braud, P. 1985. *Du pouvoir en général au pouvoir politique en particulier*, in Traité de science politique (sous la dir. Madeleine Grawitz et Jean Leca, vol. 1, PUF.

Braud, P. 2004. *Violences politiques*. coll Essais, Points, éd. du Seuil, Paris.

Chabal, P., and Daloz, J-P. 1999. *L'Afrique est partie! Du désordre comme instrument politique*. Paris: Economica.

Chevallier, J-J. 2001. *Histoire des institutions et des régimes politiques de la France, de 1789 à 1958*. Paris: Armand Colin

Flosse, G. 2001. Speech to the Assembly of French Polynesia. *Les Nouvelles de Tahiti* (19 May)

Hadas-Lebel, Raphaël. 2002. *Les 101 mots de la démocratie française*. Paris: éditions Odile Jacob.

Maestre, J-C., and Miclo, F. 1987. *La Constitution de la République Française*. 2 édition. Paris: Economica

Manent, P. 2007. *Enquête sur la démocratie*. Paris: Gallimard

Michalon, T. 2006. *L'affectivité contre la modernité?* in Michalon, T. (sous la dir.). *Entre assimilation et émancipation, l'outre-mer français dans l'impasse ?* Rennes: éd. Les Perséides.

Michalon, T. (in preparation). Les fondements socio-culturels de l'Etat moderne.

Mokaddem, H. 2008. *Pratique et théorie Kanak de la souveraineté*. Nouvelle-Calédonie: éditions Province Nord

Rémond, R. 1991. *Notre siècle (de 1918 à 1991)*. Paris: Livre de poche, Fayard.

Tevane, M. 2004. Interview (director of the Académie tahitienne), 26 October.

Oceania: Current Needs and Challenges

8. Stability, Security and Development in Oceania: Whose Definitions?

Treva D. Braun

Stabilité, sécurité et développement en Oceanie: Quelles définitions?

Avec le Plan Pacifique qui fête son cinquième anniversaire en 2010 et les Programmes de Pékin et du Pacifique pour l'égalité des sexes qui célèbrent leur quinzième anniversaire, on a une bonne occasion pour réexaminer certaines des définitions sous-jacentes qui continuent à guider le discours dominant sur le développement et de voir comment les approches régionales pourraient être renforcées afin de mieux rendre compte des intérêts à la fois des femmes et des hommes du Pacifique. Les dimensions clés des questions de développement en matière de sexe, telles qu'elles sont exprimées dans les cadres d'égalité existants, peuvent et devraient être intégrées dans tous les cadres et stratégies de développement dominants, y compris le Plan Pacifique. La période est également propice à la création de mécanismes et de processus clairs auxquels doivent adhérer les dirigeants au plus haut niveau en vue de recadrer le discours national et régional et le système institutionnel de façon que des engagements pris il y a longtemps en matière d'égalité des sexes puissent commencer à animer et guider les progrès de la stabilité, de la sécurité et du développement dans la région. Cet article vise en premier lieu à fournir une réflexion sur les limites du discours régional actuel sur ces questions, ensuite à présenter certains aspects de la recherche et les données les plus récentes qui sont de la plus haute importance pour parvenir à des définitions qui tiennent mieux compte de la question des sexes, et troisièmemment à recommander un nouveau modèle régional avec la mise au point de mécanismes de haut niveau acceptés pour appuyer une intégration plus poussée des droits et des voix des femmes dans les processus de développement multisectoriels. Dans cet article, on fait des comparaisons entre le Plan Pacifique en tant que cadre régional principal qui couvre la stabilité, la sécurité et le développement, et les Programmes de Pékin et du Pacifique pour l'Action en tant que cadres principaux qui traitent des dimensions relevant de l'égalité des sexes dans ces mêmes questions. Enfin, cet article présente une critique de l'histoire et de la situation actuelle du Plan Pacifique, avec des propositions pour le renforcer et le consolider.

Introduction

Discussions at the most influential levels in the Pacific on stability, security and development are still heavily skewed towards traditionalist masculine understandings of these terms. High level discussions on development, as reflected in their resulting frameworks and resource allocations, focus on economic and public service delivery models, and stability and security are understood primarily as the absence of public financial and economic uncertainty and public or external threats and conflict. While work in those areas is clearly important, the longstanding and now incontrovertible knowledge is that no discussion on these topics can proceed meaningfully without full attention being paid to more expansive definitions, including those grounded in a full understanding of the often differing perspectives of women and men.[1] 'Development' imperatives and implications are still, often, significantly different for men and women. Similarly, 'stability' and 'security' have both overlapping and divergent meanings for them. Given that women make up half of the population, their definitions in these areas should be driving and informing the development of relevant frameworks and budgets on a fully equal footing.

The aims of this paper are firstly to provide reflections on the limits of the current regional discourse on these topics, secondly to provide some of the latest research and data of critical importance to more gender-responsive definitions, and thirdly to recommend a new regional paradigm including the development of agreed high-level mechanisms to support stronger integration of women's rights and voices into multi-sectoral development processes. The paper makes comparisons between the Pacific Plan as the main regional framework covering stability, security and development and the Beijing and Pacific Platforms for Action as the main policy frameworks addressing the gender dimensions of these same issues. A critique of the history and current status of the Pacific Plan, with suggestions for strengthening and bolstering it, is presented.

With the Pacific Plan marking its fifth anniversary in 2010 and the Beijing and Pacific Platforms for gender equality celebrating their fifteenth anniversary, it is a good time to re-evaluate some of the underlying definitions which continue to guide mainstream development discourse, and to consider how regional approaches might be strengthened to better account for the interests of both Pacific Island women and men.

---

1   Even women and men are far from being homogenous groups with identical issues and experiences, and such categorisations risk the very real limits of essentialism. People's perspectives vary according to age, ethnicity, socio-economic status, rural/urban locale, disability and sexual orientation among others. Even within those categories people are diverse. Nonetheless, there are certain widely shared issues that permit broad-based gender analysis, and this paper will focus on those.

The key gender dimensions of development issues, as expressed in existing gender equality frameworks, can and should be integrated into all mainstream development frameworks and strategies, including the Pacific Plan. The time is also ripe for the development of clear mechanisms and processes, to be endorsed by leaders at the highest levels, for reframing the national and regional discourse and institutional architecture so that long-standing commitments to gender equality can begin to systematically inform and guide the advancement of stability, security and development in the region.

Defining Moments

It is vital to the effectiveness of any dialogue or process that those involved in it, and those impacted by it, have a common and complete understanding of the underlying definitions of the issue under discussion. Many, however, are begun without any opportunity for preliminary agreement on terminology. Further, discussion topics and their definitions often become presumed truths set for a wider group by a smaller and more powerful group, particularly where there has been an advance filtering by virtue of an agenda setting process. This is certainly the case with discussions on development, stability and security, where those setting the agenda, namely those in senior decision-making positions in government and in bilateral and multi-lateral donor and development agencies, are also the ones deciding upon or making assumptions about the basic underlying definitions from which all further discussions flow. Unless those definitions are accurate and inclusive, the entire dialogue and its outcomes can be highly problematic for certain groups.

The Pacific Plan (Pacific Islands Forum Secretariat 2005a) – the main regional framework addressing stability, security and development – provides a useful illustration of the problems that can arise from incomplete definition-setting processes.[2]

The identification of 'regional priorities' for the Pacific was the first of many definition-setting processes over the course of the Pacific Plan's development from which the voices of Pacific Island women and regional gender equality experts were largely excluded. An Eminent Persons Group (EPG),[3] appointed

---

2   It is not the intention of this paper to undertake a comprehensive analysis of the Pacific Plan, though it is clear that the Plan urgently requires revision based on a comprehensive gender and human rights analysis to make it responsive to concerns widely expressed by Pacific women's groups. The Plan's weaknesses from a gender perspective have been the subject of earlier scholarly commentary (Huffer 2006). These and other critical inputs have scarcely been taken up to date.

3   The EPG was comprised of Sir Julius Chan (former Prime Minister of Papua New Guinea), Bob Cotton (former Australia High Commissioner to New Zealand and special envoy to Papua New Guinea), Dr Langi Kavaliku (Pro-Chancellor of the University of the South Pacific and a former Deputy Prime Minister of Tonga), Teburoro Tito (former President of Kiribati), and Maiava Iulai Toma (Samoa Ombudsman and former Ambassador to the United Nations).

to review the Pacific Islands Forum and make recommendations for addressing 'key regional issues', recommended defining the four priorities of the Forum as economic growth, sustainable development, governance and security, and these subsequently became the four pillars of the Pacific Plan adopted by the Pacific Islands Forum Leaders. As such, the Pacific Plan as endorsed provides that its objective is to 'enhance and stimulate economic growth, sustainable development, good governance and security for Pacific countries through regionalism.'

While the EPG laudably recommended that the Forum 'address the low participation of women in all levels of decision-making processes and structures,'[4] it did not seek to ensure (and the Forum did not require) that the very decision-making structures that were already in existence or about to be launched in furtherance of the elaboration of the Pacific Plan were gender balanced or had the relevant gender expertise, and most of the relevant bodies were either exclusively or predominantly constituted by men.

A Task Force was charged with developing the Pacific Plan based on terms of reference which themselves constituted a definition-setting exercise. The terms of reference instructed the Task Force to consider strategies for better regional cooperation 'taking into account the broader international environment and agreements in which the Forum members participate' and identified two international development frameworks as being of primary importance: the 2002 World Summit on Sustainable Development and the 2000 Millennium Declaration (Pacific Islands Forum Secretariat 2005b: para 4). While both of those contain some gender equality language, neither provides a comprehensive and transformative agenda for rectifying gender inequalities across the development spectrum, in keeping with human rights principles, in the way that the World Conference on Women and its Declaration and Platform for Action – which all Forum Island Countries endorsed – did in Beijing in 1995 (United Nations 1996). One wonders whether the Beijing Platform for Action (BPA) might have been considered one of the defining international agreements of primary importance for the elaboration of the Pacific Plan – a regional framework in support of 'peace, harmony, security and economic prosperity for all Pacific people'[5] – had women participated on an equal footing in setting the regional priorities and drafting the terms of reference, and if it had been what the Pacific Plan might look like today. Instead, the Pacific Plan terms of reference only briefly recognised the 'importance of women and gender'.

---

4   As well as the reduction and elimination of domestic violence, and the improvement of women's literacy and health status.

5   The Forum Leaders' 'Vision' as expressed during the 6 April 2004 Auckland Retreat which set the development of the Pacific Plan in motion begins: 'Leaders believe the Pacific region can, should and will be a region of peace, harmony, security and economic prosperity, so that all of its people can live free and worthwhile lives.'

Perhaps the most defining of the background papers which informed the Pacific Plan's development is an Asian Development Bank and Commonwealth Secretariat joint report analyzing issues and possibilities for achieving the Leaders' Vision based on a series of working papers (Asian Development Bank and Commonwealth Secretariat 2005). Of the eighteen working papers that fed into that joint report, not one is dedicated to the options and benefits that regionalism could present for eradicating gender inequality in the Pacific, and with the exception of a paper on bulk petroleum procurement which links energy efficiencies with social improvements including achievement of the Millennium Development Goals (Morris 2005), none even mentions gender or uses basic sex disaggregation within its thematic topic. Rather, they focus on gender-blind infrastructure and sectoral cost-benefit analyses.

The gap is glaring. For instance, whereas several quantitative assessments were conducted on issues ranging from telecommunications deregulation (McMaster 2005) to the economic cost of governance failure in four Pacific countries (Duncan 2005), and despite recognition in the main body of the joint report that discrimination against women in employment is widespread (Asian Development Bank and Commonwealth Secretariat 2005: 29), there was no assessment done of the economic cost of systemic sex discrimination and the potential benefits to the region of its eradication. As will be discussed below, within two years of the endorsement of the Pacific Plan such a study for the Asia-Pacific region as a whole estimated billions of dollars in losses each year due to discrimination against women and girls in education and the labor force alone. Similarly, the fisheries sector analysis fails to mention much less address the issue of prostitution of women and children on foreign fishing vessels in Pacific waters. Not surprisingly, these and other issues which are disproportionately women's concerns remain severely under-addressed in the Pacific Plan and in other mainstream Pacific development spheres.

The concerns and priorities specific to the female half of the Pacific population were largely left to public consultations, discussions that were premised on a document the parameters of which had been defined without gender or human rights analysis or women's meaningful involvement. Pacific women and gender experts had neither agenda-setting nor priority-balancing influence. They were merely one of many interest groups or 'non-state actors' – alongside youth, the disabled etc. – the inputs of which those in control of the agenda and of determining the relative importance of various submissions could accept or reject.[6] This is partly the fault of skewed leadership structures in the Pacific,

---

6   Indeed, among the submissions and recommendations of gender experts including the Regional Rights Resource Team, UNIFEM Australia and a joint submission by the Fiji Ministry of Women, Social Welfare and Poverty Alleviation on behalf of a number of women's organisations, virtually all were apparently rejected.

and partly that of insufficient planning processes. Among others, consultations were criticised for being rushed, leaving little time for meaningful input and analysis (Huffer 2006: 161).

Unsurprisingly, the failure of the Pacific Plan to properly address women's issues, as will be discussed below, flows directly from this series of oversights. Unfortunately, few if any of the weaknesses have been rectified in the processes that have taken place during the first five years of the Plan's existence. Encouragingly, however, the Pacific Plan is a 'living document' which has the potential for immediate and high impact improvement.

Towards More Inclusive Definitions

The definitions and underlying assumptions in the Pacific Plan and other key frameworks, including most national development strategies in the region, about what constitutes stability, security and development, as well as the delineation and prioritisation of necessary initiatives in these areas, are largely gender blind. For these frameworks to acquire legitimacy as being relevant and responsive to Pacific Island women, they arguably require a wholesale re-drafting through a wholly reconstituted design process.

However, even if one is limited to working within the existing frameworks, a number of substantive improvements are possible. For instance, the BPA and its regional counterpart, the Pacific Platform for Action on Advancement of Women and Gender Equality (PPA) which was first adopted at a Pacific Ministerial Meeting on Women in 1994 as part of the regional preparations for the Fourth World Conference on Women and subsequently revised in 2004 – both versions pre-dating the adoption of the Pacific Plan – address identical issues as the Pacific Plan but from a very different angle (Secretariat of the Pacific Community 2005). That angle is a critical piece, roughly half the size, of the regional development puzzle.

However, among all of the Pacific Plan's initiatives for 'immediate implementation between 2006-2008', for 'agreement in principle' and for 'further analysis', there was no direct reference to implementation of the BPA or PPA.[7] This contrasts with the multitude of references in the Plan to the need to develop and implement other regional strategies and action plans such as the Pacific Islands Energy Policy and Strategic Action Plan, the Pacific Regional Action Plan on Sustainable Water Management, the Pacific Climate Change Framework,

7   The December 2004 draft of the Pacific Plan included within the Sustainable Development goal the following 'medium-term benefit': 'Specialised support provided to help Pacific governments take the implementation of CEDAW, the Beijing Platform for Action and the Pacific Platform for Action further.' This was later removed.

the Pacific Disaster Risk Reduction and Disaster Management Framework for Action, the Forum Principles on Regional Transport Services, the HIV and STI Strategy, and the Regional Digital Strategy.

The BPA and PPA are extensive, transformative and cross-cutting policy frameworks informed and guided by international human rights law on the right to non-discrimination on grounds of sex. Their implementation, however, has been extremely weak in the Pacific (Secretariat of the Pacific Community 2010a). Among the barriers to better implementation are that they have not had the engagement of political leaders, they are mere calls for action rather than agreements for action, they remain the purview of highly marginalised women's departments despite their expansive, multi-sectoral application, and while they support the implementation of legally binding instruments such as the UN Convention on the Elimination of all forms of Discrimination Against Women (CEDAW)[8] they have no high level accountability. Activities under them have been uneven at best, and progress has been largely disappointing.

As such, an integration of the key thematic recommendations of the BPA and PPA into the corresponding thematic areas of the Pacific Plan, and the parallel development of clear regional multi-sectoral strategies for achieving gender equality commitments, would bring gender concerns into the mainstream and onto a more level playing field with other areas of priority concern in the region. These measures could go a long way towards overcoming both the gender deficiencies of the Pacific Plan and the lack of movement on the BPA, PPA and CEDAW.

A few non-exhaustive examples will be discussed below. Several of them do not fit neatly into just one of the pillars or strategic objectives of the Pacific Plan. They are intended here as illustrations of the history and current status of regional development paradigms from a gender perspective and of potential avenues for shifting those paradigms, all of which would require more detailed analysis and discussion if and when the Leaders take up the call to gender mainstream the Pacific Plan and develop the necessary mechanisms and strategies.

---

8   In force throughout the Pacific with the exception of Nauru, Palau, Tonga and the American territories of American Samoa, Commonwealth of Northern Mariana Islands and Guam.

Stability and Security

Security is defined in the Pacific Plan as 'the stable and safe social (or human) and political conditions necessary for, and reflective of, good governance and sustainable development for the achievement of economic growth.'[9]

The ADB-Commonwealth Secretariat joint report's first working paper notes that 'security is no longer viewed in the narrow sense of merely defending a state from external or internal threats of a military nature. Rather, it is now realised that security is closely linked with generating conditions that free people from fear and misery arising from various causes' (Hassall 2005: 1). It establishes that while questions about security had been considered in a number of earlier Pacific Islands Forum documents the term was not fully defined in any of them, though the range of examples given from those documents makes it clear that 'security' carried a presumed definition limited to internal or external threats of a public nature such as natural disasters, threats to national integrity, and ethnic or social tension.

Despite the working paper's urging that security issues were most likely to arise from internal issues such as land pressures, economic disparities and ethnic division and that as such 'security responses must be re-oriented to meet … internal threats rather than external ones' (Hassall 2005: 4), there is no mention of the need to address the range of gender-specific internal security concerns. For most women, the biggest human security risks come from within their borders, communities and often their own home. Yet these security issues which are of particular and heightened daily concern to women, and which have been the subject of countless international and regional research and lobbying efforts, did not register as key causes of the 'fear and misery' from which any security framework ought to free people. In the end, the joint report, while acknowledging that security has become a multifaceted concept, expressly elected to focus on 'those aspects of security that relate to dedicated law and order institutions—e.g., police, military, border enforcement, customs, and intelligence services—as well as the more dramatic manifestations of insecurity—e.g., terrorism, transnational crime, civil conflict, secessionist movements, and domestic political instability' (Secretariat of the Pacific Community 2005: 170). It viewed broader 'comprehensive' or 'human' security issues as falling within the other pillars of the Pacific Plan.

---

9   It is curious and perhaps telling that security in the Pacific Plan is linked specifically to an end goal of 'the achievement of economic growth' rather than being an end in itself.

The result is that security remains traditionally and narrowly defined in the Pacific Plan. Its single strategic objective is 'improved political and social conditions for stability and safety', with the enumerated security initiatives focusing on maritime, aviation, border and bio-security issues.

Among the stability and security concerns specific to or disproportionately faced by Pacific women are lack or erosion of land and housing rights, personal economic insecurity, and lack of basic physical security, none of which are directly addressed as key initiative areas in the Pacific Plan.

Land and housing insecurity is a major and growing concern for many Pacific Island women. Examples vary from the Tongan extreme where women are not legally allowed to own or inherit land to traditionally matrilineal land systems such as those in the Republic of Marshall Islands, Solomon Islands and Vanuatu where women's traditional ownership of land in complementary systems of custodianship and decision-making with men has increasingly been eroded due to the introduction of the cash economy, large scale extractive industries, and women's exclusion from modern decision-making bodies including land authorities (Stege, et al. 2008). In many Pacific contexts, women do not enjoy equal housing rights.

The need to ensure women's equal access to land and other resources, and avenues for doing so, are expressed in the BPA (Strategic Objectives A.1-A.4). It recognises that women's poverty is directly related to lack of access to land ownership and inheritance and recommends legal and administrative reforms to protect women's land rights. At their 2008 meeting in Niue, Forum Leaders directed that land be considered as an emerging region-wide priority, yet made no mention of women's specific land insecurity issues, citing only 'migration, urbanisation, increasing numbers of disenfranchised youth, and population displacement caused by climate change and natural disasters' among the list of land-related security concerns (Pacific Islands Forum Secretariat 2008: 14-15). The meeting communiqué did, however, attach guiding principles in respect of land management and conflict minimisation, which include provision that consensus-based solutions to land conflict should include strengthening of customary and formal institutions and decision-making processes that, among others, 'reflect principles of gender equity', and that processes for clarifying customary land tenure would be consistent with CEDAW for those countries that have ratified it (Pacific Islands Forum Secretariat 2008: 19).

Economic insecurity is another major issue disproportionately affecting women in the Pacific Islands region. In virtually all countries and territories, women's access to and participation in the labor market is still significantly lower than men's, as is their participation in wage employment in the non-agricultural sector, as illustrated in Figures 1 and 2.

Sex disaggregated labor force data on wages are not systematically collected in the Pacific and need prioritisation, however estimations show that even for women earning an income their earning power is a fraction of that of men (see Figure 3).

This structural inequality is exacerbated for women in situations of economic downturn, as they typically suffer the greatest adverse impact of generalised economic insecurity including under the present global financial crisis.

Figure 1: Labour Force Participation Rate

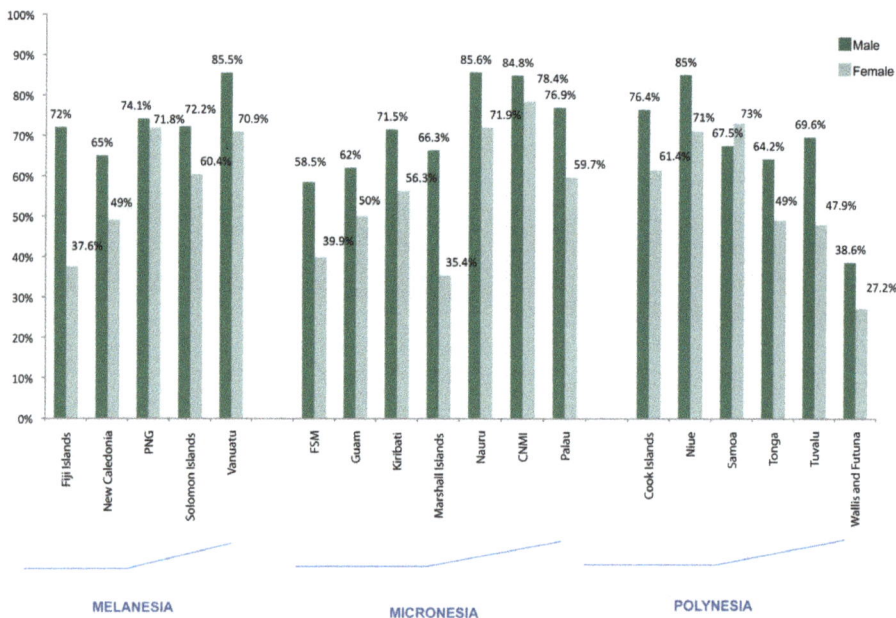

Source: SPC PRISM.

Economic imperatives for Pacific women as expressed in the PPA include attention to women's contributions to the informal sector, equal opportunity of men and women in employment, better collection and analysis of gender specific labor force and economic data, and women's participation in income generating activities in rural areas and disadvantaged households (Secretariat of the Pacific Community 2005: paras 89-90). Poverty eradication priorities include provision of government-sponsored social schemes for male and female wage earners in the private sector and enhancements to financial literacy at the community level (Ibid: paras 91-94). The BPA also draws the link between women's poor economic status and their risk of sexual exploitation (Strategic Objectives A.1-A.4), a common and increasing security risk for both women and girls in the region (see UNICEF, UNESCAP and ECPAT 2006).

Figure 2: Share of Females and Males in Wage Employment in the Non-agricultural Sector

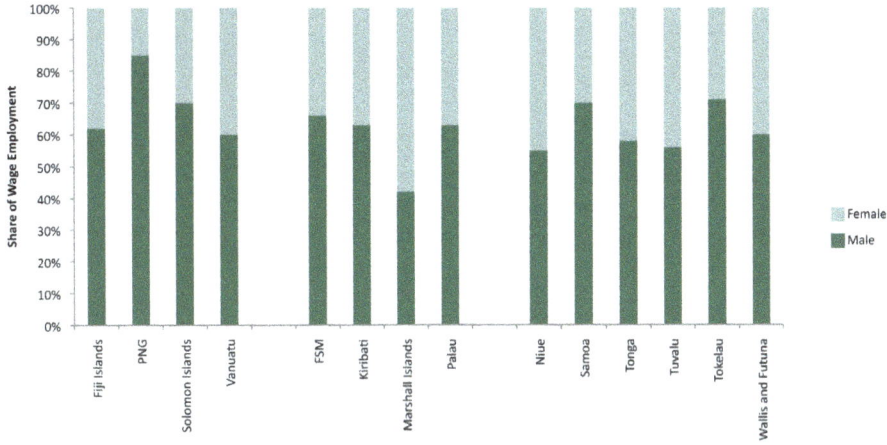

Source: SPC PRISM.

Figure 3: Ratio of Estimated Female to Male Earned Income

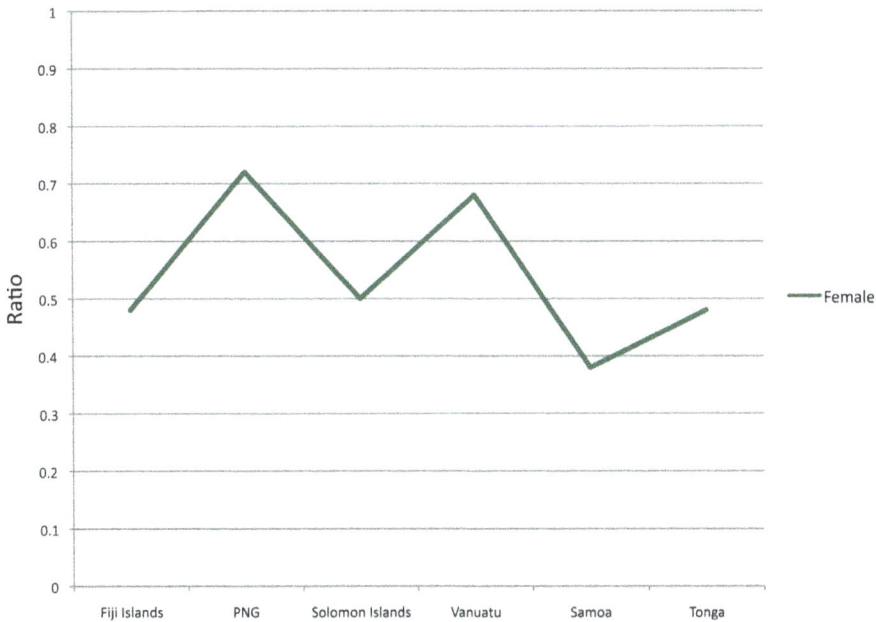

Source: UNDP Human Development Report 2007–2008, pp. 330–33.

Personal physical security in the home and community is a serious daily issue for many Pacific women, and one that is still largely unaddressed. For many, it is the police and military themselves who present a major security risk (see Human Rights Watch 2006). For more still, violence in the home presents the single biggest risk to physical security. Domestic violence in some countries in this region is occurring at among the highest rates in the world, much more frequently than any public conflict or external security threat. Three countries, one per sub-region, have conducted national level surveys using a globally comparable World Health Organization survey methodology: Samoa (Secretariat of the Pacific Community, United Nations Population Fund, and Government of Samoa 2006), Solomon Islands (Secretariat of the Pacific Community and Government of Solomon Islands 2009) and Kiribati (Secretariat of the Pacific Community and Government of Kiribati 2010). Demographic and health surveys in the region are also starting to ask questions about the safety of women at the household level (Secretariat of the Pacific Community and Government of Republic of Marshall Islands 2008; Secretariat of the Pacific Community and Government of Tuvalu 2009). The results show that up to two thirds of women experience physical and/or sexual violence by an intimate partner in their lifetime (see Figure 4). Up to 60 per cent experience physical violence,[10] up to 55 per cent experience sexual violence, and as many as half have experienced forced intercourse. Between 20-40 per cent of women aged 15-49 in Kiribati and Solomon Islands reported having been sexually abused before the age of 15. Many women suffer beatings by their partners during pregnancy putting not only the mother's but also the child's health and safety at risk. The national surveys show that the violence suffered by these women is more likely to be severe violence such as punching, kicking or having a weapon used against them, rather than more moderate forms of violence.

These issues are all compounded by the lack of legal protection in many Pacific Island countries. For example, at least three countries have no constitutional prohibition on sex discrimination, almost none have comprehensive domestic violence legislation, none have comprehensive integrated legislation covering all forms of violence against women, and marital rape is not criminalised in several countries. Even when legislation is in place it is often very poorly enforced. Virtually no strategies, policies and action plans to eliminate violence against women exist in the region.

---

10   Between 50-70 per cent (and usually much closer to the 70 per cent mark) of both men and women surveyed agree with at least one 'justification' for such violence, and the most common justifications are things like 'disobedience', 'unfaithfulness' and 'neglect of household duties', indicating a very high socialisation of both inequality between women and men in the household (women are expected to 'obey' their husbands rather than being equal partners) and of violence as a means for resolving disputes. This socialisation is reflective of the longstanding unequal power relations between men and women and is a mechanism by which women are kept in a subordinate position compared with men.

Figure 4: Prevalence of Lifetime Physical and/or Sexual Violence by an Intimate Partner, Among Ever-partnered Women

Global WHO comparisons

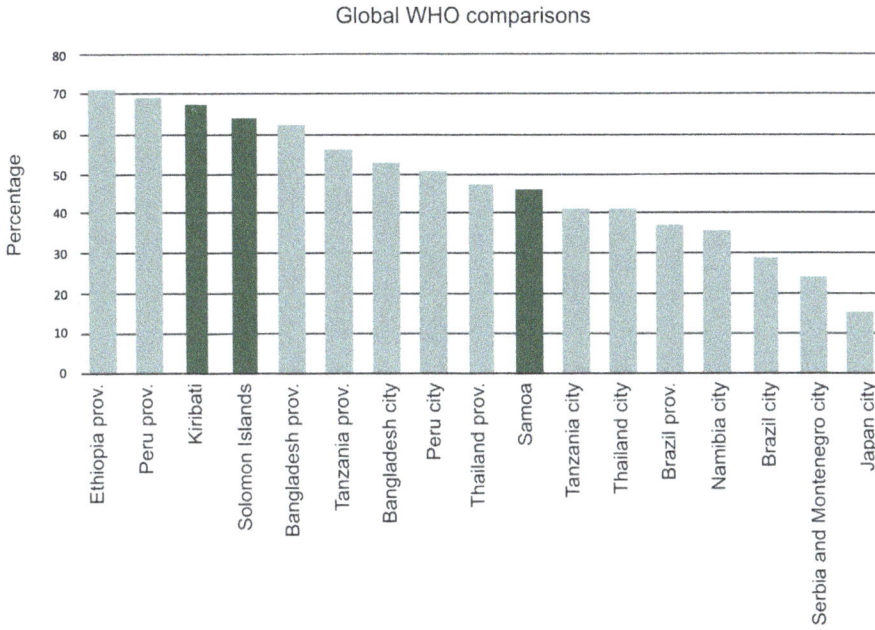

Sources: World Health Organization, WHO Multi-country Study on Women's Health and Domestic Violence against Women: Initial results on prevalence, health outcomes and women's responses (2005); SPC, UNFPA, Government of Samoa, The Samoa Family Health and Safety Study, 2007; SPC and Government of Solomon Islands, Solomon Islands Family Health and Safety Study, 2009; SPC and Government of Kiribati, Kiribati Family Health and Safety Study, forthcoming.

In addition to the significant personal security risk and high social costs of violence against women, the financial cost to Pacific Island economies is staggering. The Reserve Bank of Fiji estimated that violence against women costs the Fijian economy between FJD300-500 million per year, which at the low end amounts to seven per cent of GDP (Jalal 2010). Those estimates are higher still if opportunity costs are considered.

Despite all of this, the only mention in the Pacific Plan of violence against women is in one of several 'milestones' for Security Initiative 13.3 ('Strengthen law enforcement training, coordination and attachments'), namely through regional training courses on family, domestic, gender and sexual violence. All other areas of security are addressed through specific initiatives containing robust language such as 'develop and implement strategies and associated legislation' (for maritime and aviation security) with a clear milestone of having legislation developed by 2008; 'implement the Pacific Islands Regional Security Technical Cooperation Strategy' (in respect of border security, including for transnational crime and bio-security); and 'develop and implement policies and plans' (in relation to biosecurity, urbanisation and mitigating natural disasters). If women's physical security risks had been on an equal footing perhaps they would not have been limited to a milestone of training courses but would have had clear initiatives for the enactment of appropriate legislation by a fixed target date and the development of strategies, policies and plans to eliminate all forms of violence against women.

The unique security issues faced by women are squarely addressed in both the BPA and the PPA. The BPA acknowledges that acts or threats of violence against women 'instil fear and insecurity in women's lives and are obstacles to the achievement of equality and for development and peace' (BPA, Critical Area of Concern D: Violence against Women: para 117). In keeping with human rights standards, both frameworks address violence against women in both the private and public spheres including in conflict situations, and provide recommended strategies for eradicating it (Secretariat of the Pacific Community 2005: paras 49-56 and 113-121).

Many Pacific women also experience high physical security risk as a result of poor sexual and reproductive health and rights. Eleven out of 21 Pacific Island countries and territories are ranked as being in either a high or very high reproductive risk category (Family Planning International 2009). Key causes include low contraceptive prevalence rates, high teenage fertility rates, increasing rates of sexually transmitted infections including HIV, poor access to antenatal care, poor access to emergency obstetric care, and restrictive abortion legislation, all of which contribute to poor maternal health and often to maternity related deaths. Underpinning the risk are various persistent forms of discrimination against women (Secretariat of the Pacific Community 2009). The BPA and PPA outline the major contributing factors to maternal risk, including social determinants, and the necessary measures for ensuring women's physical reproductive security (Secretariat of the Pacific Community 2005: paras 73, 79; BPA, Strategic Objectives C.1-C.5).

All of this should be informing both the definition and prioritisation of core regional security issues under the Pacific Plan and the elaboration of comprehensive initiatives to be agreed by Forum Leaders. However, while the EPG report recommended that the Forum address the reduction and elimination of domestic violence and the improvement of women's health status, neither of these made it into the Pacific Plan as priority objectives. Indeed, none of the gender specific security concerns of women made it in under any of the four pillars.

Certain issues such as violence against women are gaining some attention amongst regional leaders. For instance, recently the Forum Regional Security Committee – the principal forum for setting the regional security agenda – has given a slot on the 'day two' agenda (when 'soft' human security issues are discussed) to women, peace and security issues including domestic violence. It has yet to appear on the main agenda where 'core' security issues are discussed, demonstrating the continued resistance to seeing women's security as a core regional concern. At the 2009 Pacific Islands Forum meeting, Forum Leaders acknowledged that 'sexual and gender-based violence (SGBV) is now widely recognised as a risk to human security and a potential destabilising factor for communities and societies alike' (Pacific Islands Forum Secretariat 2009, para 63) It was described as a 'sensitive issue in most Pacific cultures' that required 'national ownership' (Ibid.: paras 63-64). The meeting communiqué stops short of prioritising the elimination of violence against women as a core regional security concern. This contrasts with the outcomes of other thematic discussions such as disability, on which Leaders agreed that a Regional Disability Strategy should be considered (Ibid.: paras 33-34), and on Influenza A (H1N1) in respect of which they called for a 'more coordinated regional approach' in part due to how stretched national health administrations are and the limits that has on their ability to respond independently with any great effect (Ibid.: para 24), a situation that is certainly mirrored in national departments for women.

The key structural problem, of course, is that even when gender issues get on high-level agendas, they get there in an ad hoc and uncertain way through women's rights advocates biting at the heels of existing structures and frameworks that are not designed to take proper account of women's issues in the first instance. As such, women continue to be an afterthought, entering via the side door a dialogue that got underway with a set of presumed definitions well before they arrived.

Several of these obstacles could be overcome by explicitly integrating the gender-specific security issues discussed above into the security pillar of the Pacific Plan as core regional security issues. Parallel with that, a set of agreed regional processes could provide for, among others, standardised enhancements to data collection including wage gap and gender-based violence data; the development of model legislation including to criminalise and punish all forms of violence against women, to protect women's reproductive health rights, to ensure equal employment opportunities and social benefits, and to guarantee women's land and housing rights; and the elaboration of more cost-effective regional campaigns to create awareness of women's unique security concerns.

Governance

Good governance and sustainable development form part of the Pacific Plan definition of security, both of the former being pre-conditions for and results of the latter. Good governance is defined as 'the transparent, accountable and equitable management of all resources. Good governance is a prerequisite for sustainable development and economic growth.'

Women's lack of voice and influence in governance structures is a major concern in the region, calling into question the legitimacy of virtually all resource management and other governance processes from an accountability and equity perspective. Although small advances are being made, women are still excluded or restricted in their access to most decision making structures across the micro, meso and macro levels from the household and customary and religious institutions to local and national government and regional organisations. For example, the Pacific Islands region has the worst record for gender-balanced parliaments anywhere in the world. As Figure 5 shows, Pacific Island countries as a whole stayed stagnant between 1995 and 2008 with an average of only 2.5 per cent of seats in national parliaments held by women.

Figure 5: World and Regional Averages of Women in Parliaments, 1995–2008

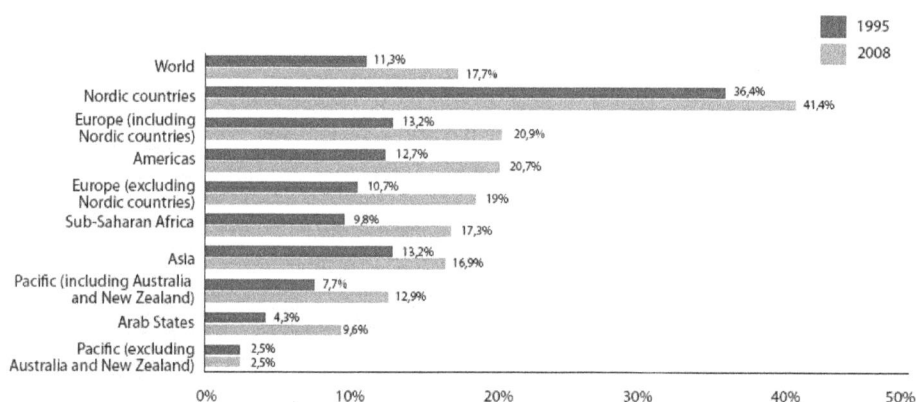

Source: Inter-Parliamentary Union, Equality in Politics: A Survey of Women and Men in Parliaments, 2008, p. 15.

By 2009, the Pacific Islands countries had inched up to an average of 4.2 per cent of seats held by women, still coming in at less than half that of the Arab states.[11] The notable exception in the region has been the French territories.[12] While France's parity law seems to have done little to bring greater gender balance

---

11 The figures for Fiji are based on the 2006 Parliament, prior to the December 2006 military coup. To date there is still no democratically elected government in Fiji.

12 The French, American, New Zealand and British territories in the Pacific are not included in the regional or international women in parliament statistics since they are not sovereign nations. Figure 6 however illustrates the data for all Pacific Island national and territorial legislatures.

in the national legislature,[13] it helped New Caledonia's Congress and French Polynesia's Assembly achieve 43 and 56 per cent, respectively, of seats held by women as of 2009 (see Figure 6).

Figure 6: Number of Seats Held in National and Territorial Legislatures in the Pacific Islands (Male/Female), October 2009

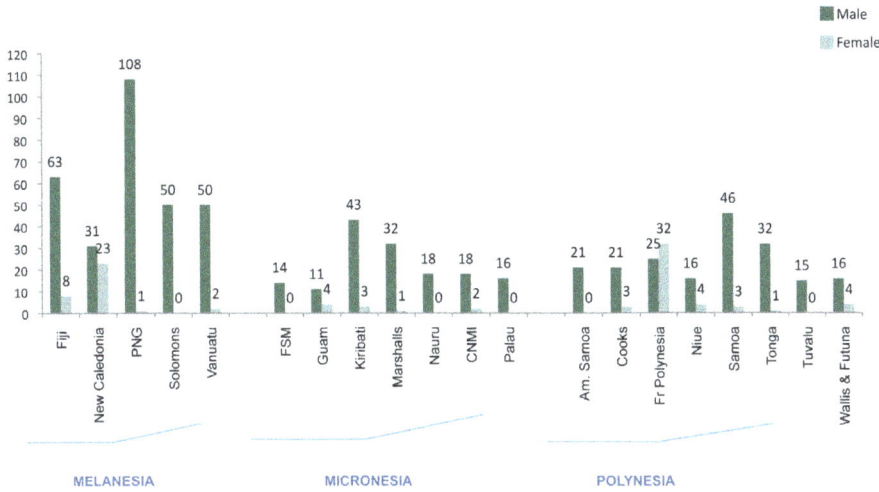

Sources: United Nations Development Programme and Pacific Islands Forum Secretarial, *Utilising Temporary Special Measures to Promote Gender Balance in Pacific legislatures; A Guide to Options,* 2008; Secretariat of the Pacific Community government focal points.

At the household level, while women in some countries such as Samoa and Cook Islands fare much better, many others in the region still have diminished decision-making control over issues ranging from household finances and health care to how to spend their social time (Secretariat of the Pacific Community 2010). In some countries and territories customary leadership is restricted to men, while in others there is greater though still imperfect balance. As noted earlier, women's strong traditional role in land ownership and decision-making in matrilineal societies is being eroded and is in urgent need of protection and strengthening. Religious institutions are heavily skewed towards male leadership and decision-making. The highest levels of decision-making in regional organisations like the

---

13 The 2000 French law on parity requires political parties to have 50 per cent of each sex on their list of candidates, alternating the names of male and female candidates, to increase the likelihood of gender balance in elected positions. In certain cases it is merely a disincentive approach, with political parties who do not comply simply being subject to a fine. Many wealthy parties in France have chosen to pay the fine rather than comply with the object and purpose of the law.

Pacific Islands Forum Secretariat (PIFS), the Secretariat of the Pacific Community (SPC) and other Council of Regional Organisations in the Pacific (CROP) agencies are heavily male dominated.[14]

These are just a few examples of the range of governance and decision-making spheres that directly impact women's lives but in which they lack equal (and in some cases any) voice and influence, and which presumably contributed to the EPG's recommendation that 'the Forum needs to acknowledge and encourage the participation of women in decision-making at all levels'.

The Pacific Plan, however, was eventually restricted to an initiative to develop 'a strategy to support participatory democracy and consultative decision-making (including NSAs, youth, women and disabled), and electoral processes'. This is a significantly watered down approach which not only lumps women in with minors and civil society, it reinforces the faulty yet tenacious notion that provided women are consulted governance systems will be equitable and accountable to them. The Pacific Plan also makes no reference to the broader range of decision-making levels to which women have no or unequal access.

The 2007 Vava'u Decisions which outlined Pacific Plan priorities for the ensuing twelve months included only a single gender-specific agreement (under 'governance'), namely to 'explore ways to enhance participation, particularly by women, in decision-making processes and institutions, and in particular parliamentary processes' (Pacific Islands Forum Secretariat 2007: 14). However, in the 2008 Pacific Plan Annual Progress Report, in which extensive detail is provided on key achievements over the reporting period and anticipated progress in the following reporting period, there is no mention of any achievements or anticipated progress on this issue. Similarly, the 2009 Annual Progress Report is completely silent on gender and women's issues, including under the governance priorities (see See Pacific Plan progress reports at http://www.pacificplan.org/). While work in support of women in parliament is being done in the region including through PIFS, it is not registering as a priority for Forum or regional leaders nor is it being highlighted in Pacific Plan annual reporting processes.

The BPA and PPA provide practical frameworks for transforming decision-making structures at all levels including the political, judicial, private sector, community and household levels. They recognise the need to consider attitudinal, cultural and religious factors surrounding the political advancement of women, and to enhance those practices which are supportive while removing with urgency those which disadvantage women. Recommended strategies include improving the collection and monitoring of data on women and men in decision-making at all levels, promoting shared responsibility for household and parental duties to

---

14 A 2007 stocktake of the implementation by CROP agencies of the CROP Gender Strategy (1998, revised 2005) found very little progress by CROP agencies in adhering to their gender commitments.

eliminate women's time disadvantage, providing leadership training for women, taking positive action to build a critical mass of women leaders in strategic decision-making positions, and aiming for gender balance in the composition of delegations to regional and international forums (Secretariat of the Pacific Community 2005: paras 42-48; BPA, Strategic Objectives G.1 and G.2).

Integration of these types of strategies into the Pacific Plan initiatives would provide a pathway to the 'transparent, accountable and equitable' governance that is sought in the region. Further, a set of high-level agreed processes could include, among others, the establishment of a Regional Centre for Women in Leadership; support for and enhancement of undergraduate and postgraduate level gender studies programs;[15] agreements on region-wide targets for gender balanced decision-making structures at all levels including in local and national governments and regional inter-governmental bodies, based on international standards; and the development of strategies for ensuring women's decision-making and leadership within customary, religious, community and household spheres across the region.

Development

Sustainable development is defined in the Pacific Plan as:

> [T]he integration and mutual reinforcement between the three pillars of economic development, social development, and environment conservation (where conservation is defined as wise use, including protection, in some circumstances). Essential requirements for sustainable development include active stakeholder participation, poverty eradication, changing unsustainable patterns of production and consumption and managing and conserving the natural resource base for economic and social development, while maintaining the underlying ecological processes.

The Plan's eight strategic objectives under this pillar include poverty reduction and improved gender equality. However, unlike all of the other strategic objectives which have clearly defined initiatives for their achievement, neither Strategic Objective 4 (Reduced Poverty) nor 8 (Improved Gender Equality) have any initiatives attached. Rather, according to the crafters of the Pacific Plan, '[o]ther regional initiatives contribute to [them] and will be monitored and evaluated for their contribution to achieving [them]'. The document is silent on

---

15 This has been on the gender agenda for many years. Encouragingly, the University of the South Pacific is now embarking on a new initiative to introduce a gender studies programme. This initiative will need to be strongly supported to ensure long-term viability.

which specific initiatives will contribute to reducing poverty and how, and the 'other regional initiatives' listed as contributing to Improved Gender Equality do not include any under Economic Growth and only one peripherally under Security.[16] Further, as stated earlier, unlike other initiatives which expressly reference the need for implementation of relevant existing regional strategies and plans of action, there is no reference in the gender equality objective, nor anywhere else within the Sustainable Development goal, to implementation of the BPA or PPA. Both of these frameworks contain clear recommendations to governments for achieving gender equality, including a number of gender-responsive economic, social and environmental development strategies of direct application to any meaningful interpretation of the Pacific Plan definition of sustainable development.

It is perhaps reflective of the continued low political attention that is given to national and international commitments to gender equality that it was seen as being the eventual result of, rather than a condition precedent to, achievement of the other regional initiatives of the Pacific Plan. International analysis confirms the reverse to be true, and yet there is little practical understanding or application of the need for systematic gender and human rights analysis, budgeting and mainstreaming at the outset and through the course of all development and governance processes and frameworks in the Pacific. At the national level, women's issues are typically restricted to social sectors, usually with a social welfare or service delivery approach, rather than mainstreamed across the full range of government policy making and programming based on a human rights and gender transformative approach (Secretariat of the Pacific Community 2010a). Also reflective of the low attention given to women's issues at the highest levels, since the 2007 Vava'u Decisions and through to the 2009 Annual Progress Report gender equality as a strategic objective is not included within annual priority areas, has not been reported on, and has had no specific initiatives developed for its achievement.

The PPA and BPA, on the other hand, had as their raison d'être the elaboration of comprehensive analyses of and recommendations for achieving gender equality. If the drafters of the Pacific Plan were unclear on potential implementation strategies on Strategic Objective 8, they had only to reference these ten-year old (at the time) frameworks for inspiration. According to the BPA, for instance, the twelve 'critical areas of concern' for gender equality are: the persistent and increasing burden of poverty on women; inequalities and inadequacies in and unequal access to education and training; inequalities and inadequacies in and

---

16   Initiative 13.3 relating to the strengthening of law enforcement includes regional training on 'family, domestic, gender and sexual violence' and human rights. Among others, there is no mention of the need for comprehensive legislation on gender-specific security concerns, full inclusion of women in peace and security institutions and processes including police forces, or holistic measures to eliminate gender-based violence.

unequal access to health care and related services; violence against women; the effects of armed or other kinds of conflict on women, including those living under foreign occupation; inequality in economic structures and policies, in all forms of productive activities and in access to resources; inequality between men and women in the sharing of power and decision-making at all levels; insufficient mechanisms at all levels to promote the advancement of women; lack of respect for and inadequate promotion and protection of the human rights of women; stereotyping of women and inequality in women's access to and participation in all communication systems, especially in the media; gender inequalities in the management of natural resources and in the safeguarding of the environment; and persistent discrimination against and violation of the rights of the girl child (United Nations 1996).

The PPA, which provides the regional perspective on the above critical areas as well as emerging areas of concern, notes that a pressing issue in the region is the failure of governments to provide adequate resources to women's departments. National budget allocations specifically targeted to women's affairs were found to range between 0.002 and 1 per cent (Secretariat of the Pacific Community 2005: para 28), often just enough to fund a women's affairs desk. Further, despite the cross-cutting nature of gender it is rarely treated as such in any practical sense, and women's departments are rarely included in the various sectoral meetings which have clear relevance from a gender perspective. It is no surprise that these government departments are completely unable to implement any of the BPA and PPA strategic objectives with those meagre resources and siloed government structures. The PPA goes on to recognise that the government budget is the single most important policy tool of government, mirroring in financial terms the importance governments place on different issues, and notes the poor performance throughout the region in formulating gender-responsive budgets (Ibid.: paras 29-31). Based on these findings, it provides specific strategic recommendations for governments including on appropriate staffing, resourcing and situating of national government offices for women and gender equality (Ibid.: paras 36-37).

Regional organisations, which play a major role in many aspects of the Pacific Plan's implementation, are characterised by the same barriers of inadequate institutional architecture and low attention given to gender equality commitments. Out of ten CROP agencies, only two have full-time gender positions in their staffing structure. PIFS has only one full-time position dedicated to gender issues. The organisation elected not to fill the more senior Gender Issues Adviser position that has been vacant since 2006, and as of 2009 it has taken that position out of its organisational structure altogether. Until very recently, SPC similarly has had only one permanent, dedicated gender position, although as of 2008 the Pacific Regional Rights Resource Team which focuses on human rights including women's human rights became a programme under SPC and the Human Development Programme is in the process of expanding its gender equality unit. None of the other CROP agencies have gender experts among their staff. Within the work of PIFS and SPC, gender equality as a cross-cutting issue is often given tokenistic attention, with no processes in place to ensure gender expertise informs high level planning, programming and budgeting decisions across sectors.

This marginalisation of national and regional institutional structures is a major obstacle to the achievement of national, regional and international commitments to gender equality including under the Pacific Plan.

Given the number of commonalities throughout the region on gender equality issues, and in light of how stretched women's departments in national governments are, a regional approach to complement and strengthen national efforts is necessary. Several of the BPA and PPA critical areas of concern need to be integrated as clear initiatives under the Gender Equality strategic objective of the Pacific Plan. At the same time, a set of agreed, high-level, multi-sectoral processes and mechanisms could, among others, seek to: significantly enhance national and regional institutions for the achievement of gender equality including through increased staffing and financial resources; develop minimum agreed standards and benchmarks for gender and human rights mainstreaming and gender budgeting within government; establish processes and timeframes for mainstreaming gender and human rights into other existing regional and national frameworks and strategies including sectoral strategies and national development strategies; develop and implement standardised multi-sectoral gender and human rights analysis tools; establish thematic sectoral working groups to develop best practices for gender-responsive law- and policy-making and programming; strengthen processes for achieving full compliance with the CROP Gender Strategy; and create regional platforms at the highest levels for monitoring and evaluating progress on gender equality and measuring the gender performance and accountability of leaders and regional institutions. A regional human rights body will also be critical for promoting and protecting women's human rights in the region, including a dedicated special mechanism on gender equality such as a special rapporteur or expert working group, as has been used with success in other regions, for example the work of the African Commission on Human and Peoples' Rights' special rapporteur on the rights of women in Africa.[17]

---

17   This special mechanism has been in place since 1998 and has been responsible for the development of a Protocol to the African Charter on Human and Peoples' Rights on the Rights of Women in Africa and for significant work with individual countries and populations on advancing women's rights. See http://www. achpr.org/english/_info/index_women_en.html

Economic Growth

Economic growth is defined in the Pacific Plan as 'sustainable, pro-poor growth'. That is promising on its face since we know that sustainable growth and development require the participation by and accrual of benefits to both women and men, and that poverty is disproportionately experienced by females. However, the economic growth aspects of the Pacific Plan are completely gender blind. The initiatives for immediate implementation included expanding and integrating trade markets, developing an ecosystem-based fishery management framework, developing strategies for bulk petroleum purchase, enhancing regional transport services, implementing a regional digital strategy and supporting private sector mechanisms. Issues for agreement in principle or further analysis were limited to tourism and bulk purchasing of pharmaceuticals.

Not a single economic growth initiative relates to women's access to and participation in the economy, despite the region's poor performance in this area as illustrated earlier. No gender economic analysis was commissioned among the eighteen ADB-Commonwealth Secretariat working papers or otherwise. In contrast, the need for better gender specific labor force data, protection and promotion of women's employment rights and attention to the differential impacts of trade liberalisation on men and women, among others, is identified in the BPA (Strategic Objectives F1-F6) and PPA (Secretariat of the Pacific Community 2005: section D and paras 95-98). The BPA recognises that macroeconomic policies focus almost exclusively on the formal sector, fail to take into account their differential impact on women and men, and need rethinking and reform based on proper gender analysis (Strategic Objectives A.1-A.4). It also recommends that governments restructure and target the allocation of public expenditures to promote women's economic opportunities (Strategic Objective A.1).

A 2007 UNESCAP Social and Economic Survey of Asia and the Pacific found that the region as a whole loses an estimated US $42-$47 billion per year because of restrictions on women's access to employment opportunities and a further $16-$30 billion per year from gender gaps in education (UN Economic and Social Commission for Asia and the Pacific 2007). While women's right to equal access to economic participation is an end in itself and not something to be seen from a purely instrumentalist perspective, this kind of detailed analysis of the economic costs of gender inequality specifically in the Pacific Islands region should be initiated by regional leaders as part of any economic growth discussion, alongside full analysis of the particular barriers women face in accessing the economy and what women see as appropriate pathways to full economic empowerment.

Certain gender aspects need to be mainstreamed into the Pacific Plan text, such as a requirement to conduct a systematic gender analysis of trade related initiatives within the current trade agenda. A set of agreed regional processes could also help address some of the major gender deficiencies, for instance by agreeing on modalities for ensuring that analyses of women's economic rights and empowerment inform all regional economic discussions, including at Forum Economic Ministers Meetings.

Conclusion

Gender equality continues to be highly ghettoised despite its centrality to stability, security and development in the Pacific Islands region. Women's issues are at best being given tokenistic attention across much of the region, which is harmful not only to the female half of the population but to development and governance effectiveness overall. They are largely left to be dealt with by severely under-resourced and poorly placed 'gender desks' despite their primary and cross-cutting nature across the stability, security and development spectra, and despite the multiple development benefits that could accrue to the region as a whole if they were put front and centre on all high level agendas.

Squeezing neglected gender issues into pre-determined definitions and frameworks after the fact is a frustrating exercise. Going forward, regional discourse, frameworks and resource allocations need to be developed not just in consultation with women's groups but by women participating equally from the outset, in structures that they have helped conceptualise and which are free from longstanding systemic gender barriers. As a matter of priority, existing national and regional structures and processes relating to stability, security and development need to be re-conceptualised so as to ensure men's and women's needs, perspectives and human rights are equally accounted for from the outset. Women can no longer be required to chase at the heels of andocentric structures and processes that are simply not designed to reflect their different situation or address their specific concerns and aspirations.

In the interim, major gains could be achieved in this region by integrating existing, comprehensive gender equality frameworks such as the BPA and PPA into the Pacific Plan and other national and regional stability, security and development frameworks. Those gender equality frameworks address all of the same issues as the Pacific Plan (and most national development strategies) but from the perspective of women. They are the result of intensive regional and international consultation and discussion amongst gender and human rights experts within government women's departments, international agencies and civil society. Given that the Pacific Plan lacks the requisite gender perspective, and that the BPA and PPA lack the requisite multi-sectoral ownership, accountability and resourcing, a marriage of the frameworks would provide for a more comprehensive and inclusive regional development platform going forward.

As part of that integration, national and regional leaders should consider endorsing the development of a set of agreed regional processes for strengthening national and regional mechanisms for gender equality. Such processes should be heavily informed and guided by the BPA and PPA along with other legal and policy frameworks such as CEDAW and the CROP Gender Strategy, and should contain clear timeframes and methods for coordination. In light of the cross-sectoral nature of gender issues, implementation and monitoring of the agreed processes should rest with a high-level, multi-sectoral collectivity.

These steps should be prioritised as part of the next Pacific Plan review. With the fifteenth anniversary of the PPA and BPA now upon us, and the Pacific Plan marking its fifth anniversary, 2010 would be a good time to work, and celebrate, together.

References

Asian Development Bank and Commonwealth Secretariat. 2005. *Toward a New Pacific Regionalism: An Asian Development Bank-Commonwealth Secretariat Joint Report to the Pacific Islands Forum Secretariat*. Volume 2. Available at http://www.adb.org/Documents/Reports/Pacific-Regionalism/default.asp

Duncan, R. 2005. 'Quantitative Assessment of the Cost of Governance Failure in Fiji Islands, Nauru, Papua New Guinea, and Solomon Islands', Working Paper 3. Asian Development Bank and Commonwealth Secretariat. *Toward a New Pacific Regionalism*. Volume 3: Working Papers. Available at http://www.adb.org/sites/default/files/pacific-regionalism-vol3.pdf

Family Planning International. 2009. *A Measure of the Future: Women's Sexual and Reproductive Risk Index for the Pacific 2009*. Wellington.

Hassall, G. 2005. 'An Assessment of the Scope for Regional Cooperation, Integration and Collective Provision on Security Issues', Working Paper 1. Asian Development Bank and Commonwealth Secretariat. *Toward a New Pacific Regionalism*. Volume 3: Working Papers. Available at http://www.adb.org/sites/default/files/pacific-regionalism-vol3.pdf

Human Rights Watch. 2006. *Still Making Their Own Rules: Ongoing Impunity for Police Beatings, Rape, and Torture in Papua New Guinea*. Volume 18, No. 13(C) (October).

Huffer, E. 2006. 'The Pacific Plan: A Political and Cultural Critique' in J. Bryant-Tokalau and I. Frazer (eds), *Redefining the Pacific? Regionalism Past, Present and Future*. Aldershot: Ashgate.

Jalal, I. 2010. *Gender Equity in Justice Systems of the Pacific Island Countries & Territories: Implications for human development*. Asia-Pacific Human Development Report Background Papers Series 2010/14.

McMaster, J. 2005. 'Costs and Benefits of Deregulating Telecommunication Markets in the Pacific'. Working Paper 15. Asian Development Bank and Commonwealth Secretariat. *Toward a New Pacific Regionalism*. Volume 3: Working Papers. Available at http://www.adb.org/sites/default/files/pacific-regionalism-vol3.pdf

Morris, J. 2005. 'Small Island States Bulk Procurement of Petroleum Products: Feasibility Study'. Working Paper 13. Asian Development Bank and Commonwealth Secretariat. *Toward a New Pacific Regionalism*. Volume 3: Working Papers. Available at http://www.adb.org/sites/default/files/pacific-regionalism-vol3.pdf

Pacific Islands Forum Secretariat. 2005a. *The Pacific Plan for Strengthening Regional Cooperation and Integration* (revised 2007).

Pacific Islands Forum Secretariat. 2005b. *The Pacific Plan Background Papers, Background Paper 1*: Pacific Plan Task Force Terms of Reference.

Pacific Islands Forum Secretariat. 2007. *Thirty-eighth Pacific Islands Forum Communiqué*. Nuku'alofa, Tonga, 16-17 October 2007, Annex A: Vava'u Decisions on the Pacific Plan. Available at http://www.forumsec.org.fj/resources/uploads/attachments/documents/2007%20Forum%20Communique,%20Vava%27u,%20Tonga,%2016-17%20Oct.pdf

Pacific Islands Forum Secretariat. 2008. *Thirty-ninth Pacific Islands Forum Communiqué*. Alofi, Niue, 19 - 20 August 2008. Available at http://www.forumsec.org/_resources/article/files/FINAL%202008%20Communique.pdf

Pacific Islands Forum Secretariat. 2009. *Fortieth Pacific Islands Forum Communiqué*. Cairns, Australia 5 - 6 August 2009. Available at http://www.forumsec.org.fj/pages.cfm/newsroom/press-statements/2009/final-communique-of-40th-pacific-islands-forum-cairns.html

Secretariat of the Pacific Community. 2005. *Revised Pacific Platform for Action on Advancement of Women and Gender Equality 2005 to 2015: A Regional Charter*. Noumea, New Caledonia.

Secretariat of the Pacific Community. 2009. *Ensuring approaches to maternal health in the Pacific are evidence-based, human rights- and human development-based and multi-sectoral*, Submission to the New Zealand Parliamentarians Group on Population and Development Open Hearing on Maternal Health in the Pacific, 21 September 2009.

Secretariat of the Pacific Community. 2010a. *Beijing +15: Review of progress in implementing the Beijing Platform for Action in Pacific Island countries and territories*. Noumea, New Caledonia.

Secretariat of the Pacific Community. 2010b. *Transforming Power Relations: Equal status of women and men at the family level in the Pacific*. Advocacy brief. Available at http://www.spc.int/hdp/index.php?option=com_docman&task=cat_view&gid=58&Itemid=44

Secretariat of the Pacific Community and Government of Kiribati. 2010. *Kiribati Family Health and Support Study: a study on violence against women and children*. Noumea, New Caledonia.

Secretariat of the Pacific Community and Government of Republic of Marshall Islands. 2008. *Marshall Islands Demographic and Health Survey 2007*. Noumea, New Caledonia.

Secretariat of the Pacific Community and Government of Solomon Islands. 2009. *Solomon Islands Family Health and Safety Study: a study on violence against women and children*. Noumea, New Caledonia.

Secretariat of the Pacific Community and Government of Tuvalu. 2009. *Tuvalu Demographic and Health Survey 2007*. Noumea, New Caledonia.

Secretariat of the Pacific Community, United Nations Population Fund, and Government of Samoa. 2006. *The Samoa Family Health and Safety Study*. Noumea, New Caledonia.

Stege, K., et al., *Land and Women: The Matrilineal Factor. The cases of Republic of Marshall Islands, Solomon Islands and Vanuatu*, Pacific Islands Forum Secretariat, Suva, 2008.

UNICEF, UNESCAP and ECPAT. 2006. *Commercial Sexual Exploitation of Children (CSEC) and Child Sexual Abuse (CSA) in the Pacific: A Regional Report*. UNICEF Pacific. Suva.

United Nations. 1996. *Report of the Fourth World Conference on Women, Beijing, 4-15 September 1995*. UN Doc. A/CONF.177/20/Rev.1.

United Nations Economic and Social Commission for Asia and the Pacific. 2007. *Economic and Social Survey of Asia and the Pacific* 2007. *Surging Ahead in Uncertain Times.* New York: United Nations.

9. Millennium Development Goals and the Pacific

Linda Petersen

Le Pacifique et les objectifs de développement du millénaire – mise à jour 2009

Cet article présente une vue d'ensemble du rapport de 2004 sur les Objectifs de développement du millénaire (ODM) établie par le Secrétariat de la Communauté du Pacifique (CPS) et le Programme des Nations unies pour le développement (PNUD). Ce rapport constitue une référence utile pour mesurer le dévcloppement dans la région du Pacifique insulaire par rapport aux Objectifs de développement du millénaire et aux indicateurs et objectifs qui leur sont associés. Il couvre 15 pays insulaires du Pacifique et donne des indications à la fois sur les pays individuellement et sur la perspective d'ensemble de la région quant aux réalisations des ODM en 2004 avec quelques projections de progrès à l'horizon 2015. On constate que sur la période de six ans, un certain nombre de questions ont influencé les progrès ou constitué une menace pour la réussite du programme et on conclut que les gouvernements des îles du Pacifique doivent changer leur façon de gérer et d'utiliser les ressources ainsi que la façon de présenter les rapports relatifs à celles-ci. Ces ressources ne sont pas utilisées de façon aussi efficace qu'elles le pourraient et en outre elles ne bénéficient pas à ceux qui en ont le plus besoin, à savoir le nombre croissant de pauvres et de démunis dans nos pays, y compris ceux qui, dans les zones rurales et les îles excentrées, ne disposent pas de services et qui n'ont pas les occasions de gagner leur vie et de parvenir au bien-être. Pour qu'un changement intervienne, les gouvernements doivent concentrer leurs efforts sur la façon de faire parvenir ces ressources et ces services à ces personnes. Ceci devrait être une priorité. Les pays doivent mettre en pratique leur engagement politique et leur détermination afin d'accomplir cette tâche dans leur contexte propre en consultant leur population et les acteurs du développement.

Introduction

Since signing up to and endorsing the Millennium Declaration in 2000, Pacific island countries have – some more than others – used the Millennium Development Goals (MDG) as a measure of development progress both at national and regional level. United Nations development agencies working in the Pacific have been the main driving force for using the MDG to measure and track development progress in the Pacific but more recently, there has been a stronger push from the larger metropolitan Pacific countries towards this approach, in particular Australia.

This brief paper provides an overview of the regional MDG 2004 report compiled by the Secretariat of the Pacific Community (SPC) and the United Nations Development Program (UNDP) which provided a useful baseline for measuring development in the Pacific island region against the Millennium Development Goals and their associated indicators and targets (Secretariat of the Pacific Community 2004). It covered 15 Pacific island nations and provided both an individual country and overall regional perspective on MDG achievements in 2004 with some projections of progress to 2015.

Since then most countries have produced an initial MDG report and many have integrated MDG targets and indicators into their national development plans. A few countries have gone as far as to begin to assess what it will cost to achieve the MDG by 2015. There have also been subsequent regional assessments most recently by the Australian Government, in the August 2009 AusAID report, *Tracking development and governance in the Pacific*. This paper will also comment on where we are today six years on and provide some reflection on some of the issues influencing progress or threatening success.

The Millennium Development Goals

The global focus on the MDG has often overshadowed the Millennium Declaration which provides the glue that binds the goals together. The Declaration while recognising the role of individual countries and societies in achieving the MDG, puts emphasis on collective responsibility, principles of human dignity, equality and equity, the duty and the responsibility of leaders to all the worlds' people especially the most vulnerable and particular children and future generations. The Declaration is a commitment to the right to development, to peace and security, gender equality, the eradication of many dimensions of poverty and sustainable human development for all of the world's people. If each goal is mapped against this overall vision for countries and the world it becomes easier to understand and appreciate that they all linked in one way or another.

The Millennium Development Goals – the eight goals with their respective targets and indicators – present a challenge to the world to accelerate the pace of development while testing political commitment. For developing countries achievement demands policy reforms and strengthened governance while for the developing world new aid commitments, equitable trading rules and debt relief through mobilising stronger partnerships and resource; initiating pro-poor policy reforms, institutional change and budget allocations; and improve monitoring of social indicators.

The Pacific Islands Regional Millennium Development Goals Report, 2004, SPC/UNDP

The report was endorsed by Forum Economic Ministers and a product of the UN/CROP MDG working group which was formed in 2004 to assist with the integration of the MDG into Pacific island country development goals and strategies. It was intended to supplement national reports being prepared by countries as part of the first comprehensive review of MDG progress conducted the UN. The report was produced in consultation and with the participation of countries. The findings are summarised below.

Millennium Development Goal 1: Halving Hunger and Poverty

At the time poverty related data was found to be incomplete but suggested that poverty was increasing in a number of countries. When this data is combined with data on participatory poverty and hardships assessments carried out by ADB and the UNDP, the picture is of a significant and growing problem and one that calls into question the view that Pacific islanders because of their social networks, traditions and subsistence lifestyle are protected from poverty. Data on hunger was similarly found to be incomplete but indicated that a significant proportion of children are undernourished and that prevalence of underweight children is relatively constant or increasing in at least four Pacific island countries (PICs).

The report found that poverty reduction is clearly of relevance to the Pacific and data needs to be complete and support analysis of differences between countries. It also needs to address the non-economic aspects of hardship in order to take into account subsistence and traditional resources and social networks which are so important for many Pacific islanders. In relation to hunger there is a need to develop additional indicators and gather information on family settings and hence the causes of childhood malnutrition.

Millennium Development Goal 2: Achieving Universal Primary Education

The goal of achieving universal primary education measured in terms of enrolment was reported as being reached or on the way to be achieved in many Pacific island countries. But the challenge of providing universal primary education that effectively addresses both individual and societal needs remains and is growing. There is growing evidence from across the region that a large number of youth leave school without the adequate life skills and are unable to either further their education or gain employment. Contributing problems include alienation of poor performing students and poor financial support for basic education. Despite the commitment of Ministers of Education to improving all aspects of the quality of education and ensuring excellence for all, progress towards this goal is not measured effectively through existing MDG education related indicators.

The report recommended the development of alternative indicators for the Pacific to measure the proportion of pupils who start grade 1 and reach grade 6 which is the primary school completion rate in the Pacific, in addition to developing key indicators to capture quality and relevance of education. It is not clear whether this is in fact being done. However, there is the opportunity at regional level for new education frameworks such as revisions to the Forum Education Ministers Action Plan to be developed with these recommendations in mind in order to better measure improvements in educational outcomes such as essential life skills and success in providing skills required for employment and livelihood in the traditional subsistence economy.

Millennium Development Goal 3: Promote Gender Equality and Empower Women

Significant achievements have been made in some PICS with respect to gaining equal access to educational opportunities for women, and the importance of gender issues and equality are now widely recognised in the region, and increasingly reflected in policy documents. Despite this progress serious challenges remain. Females are distinctly underrepresented in many PICs at one or more educational levels. Census data on literacy levels indicates relative gender equality, but the measure used is not rigorous, and more discerning indicators are needed to accurately measure literacy levels and gender differences. Data on women's representation in the non-agricultural sector of the labor market showed increases in women's share in some PICs, but country specific research suggests women continue to be at a significant disadvantage in terms of wages, working conditions and overall opportunities. Women were severely underrepresented in national parliaments across the Pacific, holding and average of 5.5 per cent of seats at the time. Today the Pacific (excluding Australia and New Zealand) has the lowest levels of female representation in parliaments when compared to other regions of the world.

Recommendations around Goal 3 included: to improve gender related analysis of the education sector; and the need to adopt indicators that measure literacy in its broadest sense, and in ways that are relevant to PICs, e.g. basic legal literacy and business literacy; to develop indicators that measure both the participation and relative status of women in the labor market; and encouraged countries to include additional indicators to parliamentary representation in order to measure the relative status of women in other areas of decision making such as the local government level or in the public service.

Moving beyond policy level successes (which may have gone backwards since 2004 as indicated by recent country indications in the Beijing +15 review process) the need for further research and evidence to gauge the effect of inequality on broader development progress was highlighted in order to enable analysis that can identify where assistance should be targeted. SPC is pursuing work in this area and is working with six countries to assess the capacity of governments to mainstream gender in all aspects of national development. Other work has started to improve the compilation and use of gender statistics in national planning and development processes; and there are plans to research the cost to governments of neglecting targeted investment in gender equality. There have been many other initiatives both regional and bilateral aimed at improving various dimensions of gender equality at country level with support from UNIFEM (United Nations Fund for Women), UNFPA (United Nations Population Fund), and the Government of Australia in particular. Major focus has been in the areas of governance and women's legal and human rights – women's political representation and violence against women.

Millennium Development Goal 4: Reduce Child Mortality

The findings in 2004 stated that children's health status in the region has improved significantly from the 1960s as a consequence of health programs focusing on maternal and child health, much the same as the 2009 report and under –five mortality rates are below the average for all developing countries therefore the targets may not be applicable to all PICs. However, child and infant mortality and overall health remain serious issues in all PICs as evidenced by significant rates of underweight children. The report noted significant under reporting of infant deaths in some PICs, and highly variable rates in countries with small populations, in addition to highlighting the need for disaggregated data that will allow analysis of sub-national differences and determination of various causes of infant and child mortality. Recommendations included the need to enhance cooperation between the health sector and national statistics offices to improve coverage and accuracy of statistics relating to infant, child and maternal health and mortality and for increased support for nutrition programs focusing on infants, mothers and children especially in countries with high malnutrition and high infant mortality.

Millennium Development Goal 5: Improve Maternal Health

Again, the 2004 report notes that maternal health status has improved significantly in the recent decades and figures for the Pacific island region are below the average for developing countries (440 per 100,000 live births) and all except Solomon Islands and Papua New Guinea are below the average for the Asia Pacific region (110). Despite these improvements, maternal health remains a serious concern across the region. Leading causes of maternal death were similar to those reported globally: postpartum hemorrhage, preeclampsia, obstructed labor, puerperal sepsis, and complications of unsafe abortion. Important indirect causes include anemia and malaria (the latter in PNG and Solomon Islands.) Improving the level of obstetric care is a priority in all PICs, in addition actions need to be taken to expand overall access to health care during pregnancy and childbirth, and to improve pre-natal care standards. Early first visits for medical checks during pregnancy and regular ongoing health care thereafter are important in ensuring the health of both mothers and children.

Maternal health in all PICs will also benefit from strategies that focus on: improving nutrition for women and girls (including prevention of micronutrient deficiencies and anemia), combating infectious and non-communicable diseases, addressing reproductive health needs, and addressing violence against women.

In relation to tracking maternal health indicators, recommendations included the need for other process indicators to measure progress in providing obstetric care, and maternal health more generally. Information requirements and issues included: common definitions to measure the proportion of deliveries with skilled attendants trained in the delivery of emergency obstetric care (EmOC); indicators of the number of facilities offering EmOC and their geographic distribution within each PIC; indicators for the percentage of women with complications treated in EmOC facilities, and for caesarean section and fatality rates; age specific fertility rates e.g. rate of teenage pregnancy; rate of births in private clinics as opposed to public hospitals or health centers; nos. of overseas referrals; data regarding the percentage of women attending antenatal care at least once during pregnancy, percentage of women receiving postnatal care, and the percentage of anemic women (antenatal and postnatal care are important to monitor birth weight and complications during pregnancies).

Other recommendations included: the undertaking of a regional needs assessment relating to maternal mortality and morbidity (with assessment of emergency obstetric facilities), and systems instituted to perform maternal and perinatal reviews; training of health practitioners and health service providers (including midwives and traditional and village birth attendants) in the utilisation of evidence-based obstetrical protocols and guidelines relating to delivery care; raising awareness of attendants on the importance of birth and death registration (as required under the Convention on the Rights of the Child) and of the importance of early (and regular) pre-natal care visits. In addition to training there is a need for the development and upgrading of infrastructure, particularly in rural areas (including communications, medical facilities and equipment), and provision of adequate supplies.

Millennium Development Goal 6: Combat HIV/AIDS, Malaria and Other Diseases

It is commonly known that the Pacific faces a 'double burden' of infectious and non-communicable disease (NCD) which impacts on the health of individual and populations and has the potential to significantly affect broader social and economic development as well. Addressing them is critical to development progress.

In relation to HIV/AIDS, although prevalence was low (outside of PNG) when compared to global levels, levels of infection were of serious concern and there was a real risk of substantial and rapid increase. Data was unavailable for a number of indicators e.g. condom use rate of the contraceptive prevalence rate; condom use at last high risk sex; no. of children orphaned by HIV/AIDS. Recommendations included: (i) working with NSOs and Ministries of Health to select HIV related indicators (such as access to affordable drugs) that are relevant at regional and national level for which data will be available; and (ii) coordinate the effort across HIV programs for data comparability. This is being addressed through new and ongoing regional programs addressing HIV.

Malaria is a significant disease burden in the Papua New Guinea, Solomon Islands and Vanuatu where it is endemic but reliable data on either incidence or prevalence was not available. Additional indicators should be adopted that will allow a more accurate assessment of progress. This issue is beginning to be addressed through support from the Global Fund. Again, NSOs and Ministries of Health need to work together to select relevant indicators and ensure that data is available as part of this process.

Tuberculosis (TB) is a serious health problem in a number of countries and there is increasing concern over the emergence of multi-drug resistant TB, and co-infection with AIDS. Although the Directly Observed Treatment Short Course (DOTS) strategy has been widely implemented across the Pacific, access to DOTS is not universal in all PICs. As a result an important indicator to monitor is the population accessible to DOTS. Recommendations include: to adopt an additional TB indicator measuring the proportion of the population with access to health centers that use the DOTS strategy; and increase efforts to limit the spread of drug resistant TB.

Given the prevalence of NCDs in the Pacific the report recommended that PICs develop NCD targets and indicators under Target 8 of this goal even though they are not monitored globally. Relevance of monitoring specific NCDs and NCD risk factors will vary from country to country and implemented through national NCD plans supported by WHO and the SPC.

Millennium Development Goal 7: Ensure Environmental Sustainability

In summary there has been no systematic effort to monitor the state of the environment despite a number of reviews. Consequently, the ability to effectively monitor environmental changes is weak. Data from which environmental change may be monitored and on which management decisions can be based is scarce, with time series information generally not available.

The 2004 report noted that deforestation continuing at an unsustainable rate and a lack of up to date information prevents any comprehensive assessment of the status of different forest types and land uses important to PICTs. Protected areas have expanded in size and number but again the data not accurate on their status, the use of traditional cultural practices to protect marine and land resources – these may not be included in internationally accepted protected area definitions; threats to biodiversity affect many species or habitats generally and cannot be effectively addressed through protected area designation.

Global warming and climate change are very important issues for PICs and the region is committed to reducing carbon dioxide emissions per capita, which are already typically well below the average for Asia and Oceania. All PICs have committed to phasing out the use of ozone-depleting substances by the end of 2005, and to increasing the use of alternative energy sources. The sustainability of biomass resources is recognised to be an important issue, particularly because only 30 per cent of the region's population has access to electricity. The Pacific Islands Energy Policy and Plan recognises the fundamental importance of access to energy for economic and social development, but also the need to ensure that energy use and resource development is undertaken in a way that is compatible with the special needs and circumstances of PICs.

Access to safe water is vital for health and human development. The data quoted in the report is part of a significant body of evidence that indicates sustainability of water resources is a significant and increasing problem in much of the region as a consequence of drought, population growth, increasing water demand for tourism, agriculture and industry, and aging water systems. The problems are not new. Many of these issues were identified as concerns over 20 years ago. Nevertheless, comprehensive, comparable data to evaluate access to fresh water on a regional basis are scarce. In many PICs, knowledge about the type, extent and sustainable yields of surface and groundwater resources is very limited. This is true even on islands where water shortages occur as s result of demand exceeding supply during drought periods. Problems in the knowledge base include: a lack of baseline water resource assessments; insufficient regular monitoring of water resources; limited analysis and interpretation of water resources data for planning and design of water resources development projects, and for management of catchments.

Access to basic sanitation that serves to protect human health and environmental quality (including water resource quality) is of vital importance for both human health and development making the target of proportion of urban population with access to improved sanitation and the associated indicator very relevant for PICs. Inadequate sanitation systems currently have a significant impact on water quality and human health in many PICs, making collection and analysis of relevant sanitation related data a high priority.

In general the report found it difficult to make an assessment of progress towards Goal 7 targets from existing quantitative data. Data are not uniformly available and not of consistent quality. In a number of cases modifications are needed to the standard indicator definitions (and/or changes needed to the indicators themselves),if a meaningful assessment is to be made. There is strong political will within the region to environmental sustainability and good regional cooperation in all areas covered under this goal as evidenced by the various regional frameworks and action plans. Relevant regional environmental priorities not mentioned in the MDG which need to be included are: solid waste management and sea level rise.

Millennium Development Goal 8: Develop a Global Partnership for Development

It is clear that the primary challenge for PICs in achieving the MDGs lies in securing the necessary extent of external support through overseas development assistance, foreign direct investment, trade and development partnerships. ODA has been relatively high for most PICS given their small populations. Cost of aid delivery is high due to the dispersed and geographic nature of the region. The 2004 report noted the declining levels of ODA from Australia and New Zealand, FDI declines as a result of inefficient bureaucracies, the high cost of doing business, inconsistent policies, poor access to land and a lack of skills in the investment promotion area. The situation with respect to ODA, FDI and trade in the Pacific highlights the need for ongoing dialogue regarding the provision of development support to the region. Recommendations included: the need to conduct research on aid effectiveness in the Pacific; strengthening civil society partnerships in the delivery of aid particularly in targeting the poor and vulnerable groups; the need for both donors and countries to focus on capacity building and to support policies and reforms that enhance the quality and responsiveness of development institutions; further the need to rely on country mechanisms in the provision on aid; to pool resources and to develop common reporting and accountability standards.

Conclusion

The 2004 report demonstrated that substantial progress had been made against certain indicators and the Pacific region will meet some MDG targets. It also showed that the Pacific region compares relatively favorably to other regions in a number of areas – particularly in education and health. Although, progress varied greatly across the region and even within countries, the progress that has been made towards some goals clearly illustrated the efforts by the region's people, governments and development partners have resulted in positive development outcomes. However, much greater efforts is needed if the Pacific is to achieve the MDGs by 2015 and in some areas such as health there is a real risk that the some of the region's gains could be reversed.

So where are we in 2009, five years later and as we approach 2015? The Australian government's recent report on *Tracking development and governance in the Pacific* provides an update on MDG progress in the Pacific which in short, shows that not much has changed but sets the alarm bells ringing that the Pacific as a region is unlikely to meet the MDGs by 2015.

Rising poverty is more evident; chronic hunger and poor nutrition persists; economic growth was good but concentrated in a few countries with the global recession affecting all countries and reducing opportunities for gains from this growth. The gains had not necessarily led to a reduction in poverty. Despite high levels of children entering the school system there are still serious concerns for the numbers of children out of school and not completing primary school. Gender equality improvements are mixed with women's participation in political decision-making still very low throughout the region. Reports of very high levels of gender based violence in some countries indicate that gender inequality is prevalent at the very core of societies in the Pacific and needs to be addressed as a fundamental development issue. Despite progress in combating Malaria, the health MDGs need serious attention with NCDs now the leading cause of death in 8 countries in the region, and only three countries on track to reduce maternal mortality by three-quarters in 2015. Improved service provision continues to be high priority as while addressing the social determinants of these health situations through education, in particular of girls and women and through the empowerment of women and communities. Environmental threats are intensifying and issues such as climate change have the potential to affect progress in achieving the other MDG. All strategies to adapt and mitigate the effects of climate change on the health and wellbeing of Pacific island people must be designed, planned and implemented with involvement of the people who are most affected, including women and young people.

What Needs to Change in Order For Us to Get Back on Track?

The most critical change needs to come in the way that Pacific island country governments manage, use and report on resources acknowledging that many countries are already making significant investments in their own development. However, the region's track record on MDG progress, makes it clear that these resources are not being used as effectively as they could be nor are they benefiting those who need them the most – the growing numbers of poor and disadvantaged in our countries including those lacking services and opportunities for livelihood and wellbeing in the rural and outer island areas. Governments need to focus on getting resources and services to these people if there is to be change. This must be the priority. Tracking MDG progress through these regional and country reviews provides valuable direction on what to do and how to go about doing it. Countries must follow through on their political commitment and resolve to do this within their country context in consultation with their people and development actors.

References

Secretariat of the Pacific Community. 2004. *Pacific Islands Regional Millennium Development Goals Report 2004*. Noumea, New Caledonia.

10. Leading the March for Gender Equality? Women Leaders in the Public Services of Samoa and Solomon Islands

Asenati Liki Chan Tung

Ouvrent-elles la voie à l'égalité des sexes? Les dirigeants féminins dans les services publics de Samoa et des Îles Salomon

La notion de « femmes aux postes de direction » est au centre des travaux pour promouvoir l'égalité des sexes dans la région Pacifique depuis deux décennies. Une grande partie de ces travaux a suivi les efforts effectués à l'échelle de la planète pour accroître le pourcentage de femmes dans les assemblées parlementaires. Plus spécifiquement, les efforts faits par des groupes de femmes dans les sociétés civiles du Pacifique se sont concentrés sur la promotion de certaines politiques, stratégies et formations en vue de la participation des femmes à la vie politique. Cependant, cette insistance a dans une large mesure détourné l'attention des autres domaines des institutions, à savoir le secteur public, où les femmes occupent des postes de direction importants. La nomination de femmes à des postes gouvernementaux de premier plan comme titulaires de portefeuilles ou à la tête de subdivisions ministérielles constitue une évolution récente dans les secteurs publics dans le Pacifique. Pourtant, on connaît peu de choses sur l'importance du nombre des postes de direction attribués aux femmes dans ces domaines et sur ses conséquences sur l'objectif global d'égalité des sexes comme point central du développement. Cet article étudie le lien entre la présence accrue de femmes aux postes de direction dans les services publics et la valorisation de la cause des femmes en général. Plus particulièrement, il pose la question de savoir quel effet la présence des dirigeants féminins au gouvernement produit sur le statut ou la situation des femmes dans la société. Les résultats de la recherche à Samoa et aux Îles Salomon indiquent que si l'amélioration aux niveaux les plus élevés peut ne pas forcément refléter le développement au niveau de la société dans son ensemble, le changement dans les attitudes au niveau de la population et au niveau du gouvernement est d'une importance capitale pour un changement effectif et efficace de politique en matière d'égalité des sexes. La première partie étudie la situation actuelle des femmes aux postes de direction dans les services publics dans les deux pays ; la deuxième examine les conséquences de la situation actuelle sur l'amélioration de la situation des femmes et l'article se termine en insistant sur la nécessité, dans la recherche sur l'égalité des sexes, d'intégrer tous les éléments et tous les secteurs impliqués en vue d'une connaissance plus équilibrée de la condition des femmes dans les îles du Pacifique.

Introduction

'Women in leadership' has been a focus of gender-equality advocacy work in the Pacific region over the last two decades. Much of this work has followed a global push for a higher participation of women in parliaments. Efforts by Pacific women's civil society groups especially have concentrated on policy advocacy, strategies and training for women's political participation. This emphasis however has to a large extent sidelined attention to other arenas of government, namely the public sector, where women's leadership is also prominent. Women's appointment to senior government positions such as heads of ministries or divisions within ministries has been a recent development in Pacific public sectors (Maetala and Pollard 2009; Liki 2010). Yet, not much is known about the extent of women's leadership there nor about its implications for the overall objective of gender equality as a development focus.

This paper examines the link between having more women leaders in the public service and the enhancement of women's cause in general. Specifically, it asks the question: To what extent do women leaders in government impact on the status of women in society? The paper is based on research conducted in Samoa and Solomon Islands in 2009 and 2010 which identified patterns of women's ascension to public sector leadership. In the Solomon Islands the position of head of a government ministry is referred to as Permanent Secretary (PS). The Samoan equivalent (or near equivalent) of this title is Chief Executive Officer (CEO). I use the term 'women leaders' to refer to women in these senior positions as well as those in deputy, assistantship or managerial levels. Results from research indicate that improvement at the upper levels may not necessarily reflect development at the broader societal level. Attitudinal change at the levels of community and government is central to effective policy change towards gender equality. The first part of the paper surveys the current status of women's leadership in the public services of the two countries. The second part discusses the implications of the current situation for women's advancement. The paper concludes by emphasising the need for analysis on gender equality to be more inclusive of all elements and sectors involved for a more balanced understanding of Pacific Island women's condition.

Women in Higher Places

Despite certain political and sociocultural variations, one factor that parallels Samoa and Solomon Islands is the noticeable rise of women to decision-making levels in government. It is also a notable factor that these women are highly qualified in terms of tertiary educational training and the qualifications they hold. Women's appointment to public service leadership of the two countries is a recent phenomenon, yet an important one for two reasons. First, never before in the respective histories of their public services has been a sharp increase in the number of women appointed to senior executive positions. Second, whether this phenomenon echoes transition at the broader society level is a complex matter and would merit further research. A general picture of the situation of women leaders in government is provided here. An emerging trend is that there are certainly more women in senior positions today than was the situation 10 or 15 years ago. Statistics indicate that in the Solomon Islands, 6 of the 24 government ministries are headed by women. In Samoa 6 of 18 ministries and 8 of 13 government corporations have women CEOs.

The research focus on Samoa and Solomon Islands was to understand the current status of women's leadership in the public service. The study objective was to understand the socioeconomic, cultural and political reasons behind the absence of women in senior Public Service positions. A field visit was undertaken to elicit concrete responses from the women and men in government. Two research tools were employed for data gathering: a survey questionnaire and interviews. The findings indicate an improvement in women's participation in senior and mid-level government jobs pointing to a possible beginning of a new trend for women and leadership in this sector for both countries.

Of the 24 government ministries in the Solomon Islands, five are headed by women. The Office of the National Legislative Assembly is directed also by a woman with another woman as her deputy. Of these six senior women, two have been in these positions since 2002. Two were appointed within the last two years and the other two within the last eighteen months. A sharp increase in the number of women appointed to mid-level positions is a feature of the last ten years. This trend corresponds with a growing number of older public servants and younger women completing tertiary training overseas. Typical positions occupied by these women include Deputy Permanent Secretary, Registrar, Principal Officers, Directors of Divisions within Ministries, Managers or Supervisors of sections. For the newer cohort of women graduates the major fields of study are general bachelor degrees with majors in management, sociology, accounting, biology and education, and a few in law, dentistry and medicine. A significant number obtained their diploma and certificates from Solomon Island College of Higher Education. About 60 per cent of the women graduated with degrees from the University of the South Pacific in Fiji and Vanuatu, and the rest from tertiary institutions in either Papua New Guinea, Australia or New Zealand.

It is likely that the total figure for this younger cohort of graduates is higher. There are many women who do not work for the public service. Kathleen Lega, for example, graduated with a Bachelor of Pharmacy from the University of Otago, New Zealand, in 2005 and now runs her own business, *Le Pharmacy*, in Honiara. Phyllis Maike, graduated with a Masters of Arts in Planning from the University of Hawai'i in 2004 and now operates her consultancy firm, *Positive Development Limited*. Others like Linda Au, Dr. Joanna Daiwo, Dr. Alice Pollard, Hazel Lulei and Nairie Alamu are employed in either private companies, regional organisations (USP, FFA, SPC and RAMSI) or para-public organisations (NPF, Central Bank and SICHE). Many more women reside in the outer islands operating small family businesses or working in tourist resorts. Indeed, a more thorough survey would locate and confirm the exact count for this group of women graduates.

In Samoa, the number of women in top positions in government ministries is indeed a new thing for the country. Although women did head government departments in the past, appointments were sporadic. Most of those women were wives or daughters of politicians, business people, and church leaders. Today, it is a very different situation with women from different socioeconomic backgrounds making up part of Samoa's pool of the highly qualified.

A combination of factors has contributed to the growing number of women in top government positions. These include: (i) an established cohort of highly qualified women; (ii) international pressure through conventions on the enhancement of women's status; and (iii) the country's accommodating political climate. All these influences happen to emerge at the same time and the right time too. Public Sector Reform in Samoa began in the mid-1990s, and it was basically driven by the three women Chief Executive Officers at the time. Respectively they headed the Public Service Commission, the Ministry of Finance and the Ministry of Women's Affairs. All of these women have graduate degrees.

Broader Implications for Women's Advancement

We need to situate the emerging trends for the two countries in the context of sociocultural and political processes. There is also a need to adopt a more holistic perspective on the improved status of women based not only on the outcome of women's participation in leadership roles in the public arena but also in their leadership at the community and village levels.

An interesting finding from a recent study by Zubrinich and Haley (2009) indicates that for some Pacific women, despite their being senior public servants and involved in decision-making processes in government, they continue to experience problems of domestic violence from jealous husbands, barriers to job promotions and study opportunities, and sexual harassment in the work place. These experiences obviously cannot be seen in the statistics that we have about the women's ascension to government leadership.

Given these problems, we cannot completely claim women's leadership participation as sufficient indicators of the enhancement of women's status. We need to consider more seriously the question of whether high numbers are a condition for policy change. Increasing women's presence in government leadership (and political positions, for that matter) may help highlight gender demands and lead to greater political unity among women. But what is primarily important for the advancement of gender policies is strong advocacy and co-ordination by those who aim for changes in gender relations. Attention must therefore be paid also to other areas or groups that work on increasing awareness campaign on gender equality. These include local women's church or village groups and NGOs.

Domestic violence and VAW are acute social and development issues in the Solomon Islands. The lack of educational opportunities for girls has also been highlighted in previous studies and surveys as another critical development focus. While these are real problems for many Solomon Island women, real change can never be effective or meaningful for the local people through formal policy approaches alone. Putting a man in prison for the crime of wife beating is like band-aiding a big wound. It may earn some points for those fighting against VAW, but it will go a long way when there is attitudinal shift among men and women. In much of the Pacific, change of attitudes towards women as equal partners and who can also be leaders (and towards anything for that matter), begins within the circles of the informal tok storis (conversational) sessions and daily interactions among local people. This is why attention to local level women's groups and NGO activities is very important.

The work of the Temporary Special Measure Working Group is a good example of community level operation that is also directly linked to policy level. The Group works to both raise awareness (use of media, lobbying with MPs etc) but also tries to influence parliamentary perspectives on women's leadership. This was the main activity related to women that happened at the time while this research was undertaken.

Despite the fact that Samoa is often hailed as the model for the Pacific in this regard, the problems of violence against women and incest cases against young girls, still exist. Day after day one reads in the paper or hears over the radio about crimes against girls and women. The establishment of the new NGOs 'Victim Support Group' and 'Faataua le Ola' (Value Life), in the last four years reflects the increase of illegal practices against women. These new civil groups – alongside the Ministry of Health and Ministry of Education, the National Council of Women and the YWCA – drive the campaign against domestic violence bringing about more awareness at the local level, working with both men and women towards a shift of attitudes towards women's and men's roles as equal partners in development.

Thus while it appears that all is improving at the upper levels, this does not indicate a similar pattern at the broader societal level. Policy change at/from the top becomes much more effective and meaningful for society as a whole when attitudinal change also happens at the community and village level. In the Solomon Islands, the call for serious attention to improved educational opportunities for girls in particular has never been stronger. Not only has there been keen advocacy by international women's groups and aid donors such as UNIFEM, but the unyielding stand of the local women themselves is indication that change is inevitable. Almost a decade ago, prominent Solomon Island woman leader and scholar, Alice Pollard (2000: 16) argued

> ...with the greater involvement of women in education and employment and increasing male acceptance of female participation in areas traditionally denied to them, the old division of labour based on gender will gradually be undermined. Solomon Islands society is in the process of adapting to a new system of economic relationships that are based on cash. Accordingly, new social, political and cultural values are slowly being defined, to which these Solomon Islands women (and men) will have to adjust. In short, change is inevitable, however much some women and men seek to cling to old ways and traditional ideas.

The potential of women's leadership as an indicator for improved women's status and means towards gender equality in Pacific societies extends beyond simply increasing the number of women in top government positions. It may be a formal measure, but it is one that sends a clear message to institutional and social agents about gender inequalities. Attention to women's leadership in government is a recognition that women and men are not playing on a level field. And it raises the profile of women's struggles for greater representation in decision-making positions. But all this must translate to the language and perceptions of the rest of society – at the village and community levels where some extreme examples of crime against women and girls and practices reflecting gender inequalities still exist.

References

Liki, A. 2010. 'Women leaders in Solomon Islands Public Service: A personal and scholarly reflection'. State Society and Governance in Melanesia Discussion Paper 2010/1. Canberra: The Australian National University. Avaliable at http://ips.cap.anu.edu.au/ssgm/papers/discussion_papers/2010_01_liki.pdf

Maetala, R., and A. Pollard. 2009. 'Turning the tide: celebrating women's history in the Solomon Islands: 1948-2009', in A. Pollard and M. Waring (eds) *Being the First: Storis Blong Oloketa Mere Lo Solomon Aelan*. Honiara and Auckland: RAMSI and Pacific Pacific Media Centre, AUT: 8-33

Pollard, A. 2000. *Givers of Wisdom, Labourers without Gain – Essays on Women in Solomon Islands*. Suva: Institute of Pacific Studies, USP.

Zubrinich, K., and Haley, N. 2009. 'Experiencing the Public Sector: Pacific Women's Perspectives'. State Society and Governance in Melanesia Research Paper. Prepared for AusAID. Canberra: The Australian National University. Avaliable at http://ips.cap.anu.edu.au/ssgm/papers/research/SSGM_Public_Sector.pdf

11. Young People Creating the Future Today: Youth Development in the Pacific

Rose Maebiru

Les jeunes qui aujourd'hui créent l'avenir : L'évolution des jeunes dans le Pacifique

Quand il s'agit de l'évolution des jeunes, les pays du Pacifique ont besoin de changer de modèle. La période pendant laquelle on se tournait vers les sports et le divertissements en tant qu'activités en vue du développement de la jeunesse est révolue. Les questions des jeunes sont complexes et présentent de nombreux aspects ; elles exigent une réflexion et des approches innovantes. Il faut considérer et traiter les jeunes et les problèmes de la jeunesse non pas comme une question d'aide sociale mais comme une question de développement national. Les secteurs public et privé peuvent tous les deux tirer des avantages s'ils impliquent les jeunes en tant que participants au développement du pays, et les jeunes ont quelque chose à apporter. La croissance annuelle de 2,2% prévue pour la population jeune dans la région exige de la créativité et de l'innovation dans les méthodes de travail avec les jeunes gens et les jeunes femmes pour surmonter des questions comme l'accès à une éducation de qualité pour tous, le chômage, les modes de vie et les comportements malsains, les conflits et la violence, les qualités de dirigeant, la participation à l'activité politique et l'inégalité des sexes. Cet article examine les stratégies adoptées par divers pays du Pacifique pour traiter du développement de leurs jeunes, en particulier les politiques nationales de la jeunesse en vue de donner des conseils et orienter le développement des jeunes. L'article se concentre sur le Plan Pacifique, sur la Stratégie de la jeunesse Pacifique 2010 et sur d'autres initiatives dédiées au développement des jeunes pour analyser les efforts des organisations régionales, des partenaires du développement, des donateurs et d'autres agences qui soutiennent le développement des jeunes qui tentent de reconnaître le besoin d'élargir les choix d'investissement dans le potentiel et le développement des jeunes comme ressource pour l'avenir et conclut que l'on peut faire davantage pour la jeunesse du Pacifique par le biais de partenariats efficaces et par la promotion d'une approche multisectorielle.

From Issues to Policies and Action: Youth Development in the Pacific Region

The projections of an annual growth rate of 2.2 per cent of the youth population in the region will continue to demand creative and innovative ways of working with young women and men to overcome issues of accessing integrated and quality education, unemployment, unhealthy lifestyles and behaviours, conflict and violence, leadership and participation, gender inequality to name a few.

The Pacific region has come a long way in its endeavours to unleashing the potential of young women and men to become leaders and custodians of our societies. With a mean age of 21 years for most Pacific island countries, the region has a huge resource at its disposal to address national and regional issues. However, for the most part, young people are viewed as 'problems' rather than solutions; a view that is detrimental to youth development itself.

Countries in the Pacific have embarked on several strategies to address the development of their young people, one of which is the development of national youth polices to provide guidance and direction for youth development. These 'paper commitments' often lack political will, resources and capacity to realise the policy goals and targets, fuelling discontent, alienation and a sense of hopelessness among young people. The frustrations of young people are evident in unfortunate events such as political and social upheavals that have occurred in some countries where young people were engaged in armed conflict, violence and other anti-social actions. These actions have drawn attention to the plight of young people in the context of national development and rebuilding. In more recent years more regional and international assistances are geared towards youth development, which is slowly putting more focus on addressing some of the institutional and structural weaknesses that hinder the implementation of the national youth policies. These efforts are slowly breaking the cycle of producing policies without actions. However, political will to support the expansion and sustainability of these changes is still minimal.

The development of national capacity to develop evidence based youth development policies and plans, implementation, coordination and monitoring are essential to ensuring that services and opportunities are equally and equitably accessed by young people in rural and urban areas. While these responsibilities fall within the mandate of the government, very little is being done to ensure that these capacities are built and supported. In some countries, the capacity does exist however, inadequate resources are allocated to utilise the opportunities.

This next section briefly touches on a strategy that sets the stage for effective implementation of national and regional commitments and mandates, recognising that youth is not a sector but a cross-cutting matter that requires input from various sectors. This section also briefly highlights regional commitments and plans for youth development in the region by our leaders.

Establishing Partnerships to Progress: Youth Development in the Pacific

Achieving More for Pacific Youth through Effective Partnerships and the Promotion of a Multi-sectoral Approach

Regional organisations, development partners, donors and other agencies supporting youth development have recognised the need to widen options for investing in the potential and development of young people as a resource for the future. Youth development encompasses the inclusion of young people in all aspects of national development – economic, political, cultural and social – and requires an emphasis on developing young people so that they can fully participate in national efforts to increase economic growth, achieve good governance, maintain and improve security and stability and achieve sustainable development.

Investing in young people can draw long-term benefits for countries and territories in the Pacific region and is a less expensive option to addressing issues such as youth violence and crime, mental health, teenage pregnancy and HIV/STI infections which are a few of the growing and serious challenges facing young people in the Pacific today. Examples from the Caribbean region show that the region could increase its GDP by 1 per cent by lowering unemployment and by achieving higher enrolment in tertiary education, which could bring more than 2 per cent increase in the region's GDP growth as a result of the higher earning potential of university graduates on the labor market.

The Pacific region has not been able to generate such analysis, and solid research and analysis on the benefits of focused investment in youth development over the long term at both national and regional level can assist with bringing high level attention and resources to the table for progress. What is also clear is no single agency can support the full range of development options inclusive of programmes and services needed to ensure that young people are given the opportunity and experience to become responsible and productive individuals. A coordinated multi-sectoral approach can assist; based on sound evidence and analysis that involves countries and agencies in a collaborative planning, implementation and monitoring process. This process should cover and involve: social services, sports and creative arts agencies, educational institutions, representatives of the employment sector, health service providers, private and public sectors agencies, policymakers, communities and young people.

The Pacific Plan, Pacific Youth Strategy 2010 and Youth Development Initiatives

Youth development is a strategic objective of the Pacific Plan and the Pacific Youth Strategy 2010 provides a solid framework on which to develop and mobilise multi-sectoral support for the development of young people at both national and regional level. However, limited available resources, weak economies and competing national and regional priorities; together with the huge challenge of promoting ownership and progressing coordination in the youth sector has hampered efforts to progress these youth commitments. At the same time, PICTs' young populations continue to grow putting pressure on already inadequate and weak services and the challenges mentioned earlier continue to expand. Current commitments and efforts need to be re-examined, consolidated with renewed approaches tried and resources up-scaled.

Pacific Plan Initiatives:

Initiative 9.1: Enhance Advocacy for and Coordination of Youth Programmes and Monitor the Status of Youth

This refers to the implementation of the Pacific Youth Strategy 2010 which was designed to promote, coordinate and monitor youth development in the region. Currently, SPC is conducting a review of the strategy in partnership with UNICEF Pacific and in consultation with other development partners, donors, financing institutions and SPC member countries and territories. This review and consultative process will contribute to the development of the next Pacific Youth Strategy which this time round will aim for stronger regional and country ownership; provide a solid framework on which to base a multi-sectoral strategy and implementation plan will require coordination, collaboration and joint approaches and programmes – both at regional and national level. This time round it is hoped that the emphasis on consultation and country and development partner ownership will result in more support and resources being directed to implementation.

Initiative 15.4: Establish Volunteer Schemes and Other Forms of Regional Exchanges and Sharing of Services and Expertise for Regional Capacity Building

There is huge capacity to implement this initiative both in country but in particular across the region as there are many good examples of innovative and sustainable youth development programmes that can be shared and duplicated through a structured multi-sectoral approach and increased resources. A proposal that was designed by the SPC's Human Development Programme as part of this initiative is the Pacific Regional Volunteer Scheme. The scheme was designed in consultation with member countries and other regional youth agencies in 2005/2005; however it has not been implemented due to a lack of financial commitment and resources. The main purpose and objectives of the scheme are: contribute to building the skills of young people in the Pacific, provide career related opportunities and sharing of services and expertise regionally. The expected impact over the long term is to have skills exchange and skills development opportunities for young Pacific Islanders and promoting regional cooperation and integration.

Pacific Youth Strategy 2010

As mentioned above, the Pacific Youth Strategy 2010 was endorsed by Youth Ministers in 2005 and was recognised as the regional road map for youth development. Like other regional strategies, this strategy will remain a paper commitment if there are no resources and support for its implementation. The results of the review of this strategy will reveal the gaps, challenges and success stories, which will help to shape the future youth development strategies.

Conclusion

Countries in the Pacific need a paradigm shift when it comes to addressing youth development. Gone are the days when we look at sports and entertainment as youth development activities. Youth issues are complex and multi-facet and require innovative thinking and approaches. Youth and youth issues need to be addressed as a national development matter and not merely as a welfare issue. Both private and public sectors can benefit from involving young people as contributors to national development and young people have something to offer. Youth development is a win-win situation.

12. Tourism Issues in the Pacific

Susana Taua'a

Les problèmes du tourisme dans le Pacifique

Cet article met en lumière quelques problèmes réels perçus concernant le tourisme dans la région. On constate trois grands domaines qui affectent ce secteur : le domaine social, économique et environnemental. La nature et le caractère de ce secteur dans le Pacifique sont également définis en fonction de ces trois sphères d'influence. La clé pour comprendre le tourisme dans la région est la reconnaissance du fait qu'à la fois le secteur et son contexte, mondial et régional, traversent une période de transition profonde. On a besoin de comprendre les mutations qui se produisent et les raisons de ces mutations afin que le secteur puisse être mieux géré et mieux planifié. Il existe des questions plus larges qui affectent ou qui sont affectées par le tourisme : les migrations internes, l'émigration, la complexité du foncier, le sexe, la gestion de l'information, la restructuration du secteur du transport aérien, le rôle des ONG, la capacité de mettre sur pied les ressources humaines, l'usage des institutions tertiaires régionales comme l'USP (l'Université du Pacifique Sud) et des organismes comme le SPREP et la CPS (Communauté du Pacifique Sud). L'article présente une étude des tendances en matière de tourisme dans la région en mettant l'accent sur les effets économique, social et environnemental, avant de proposer le potentiel du modèle fale de plage samoane comme modèle pour gérer quelques-uns des effets social, économique et environnemental du tourisme dans la région.

Introduction

This paper attempts to highlight some real and perceived issues concerning tourism in the region. There are three broad areas in which the industry has impacted strongly: social, economic and environmental. The nature and character of the industry in the Pacific is also defined in terms of these three spheres of influence. The key to understanding tourism in the region is a recognition that both the industry and its context, global and regional, are in a state of profound transition. There is a need to understand the changes taking place and the reasons for these changes so that the industry can be better managed and planned. There are broader issues that impact or are impacted upon by tourism: internal migration, emigration, land tenure complexities, gender, information management, airline restructuring, the role of NGOs, human resource capacity building, use of regional tertiary institutions such as USP and bodies such as SPREP and SPC.

Tourism in the region is created in those places where the natural environments are unsuitable for farming or forestry – beaches feature strongly – or where there are no valuable minerals. Basically, there are two futures for tourism in the region, the product can be exploited and used up as in a mined out mineral resource, or it can be managed sustainably (Hall and Kearsley 2001; Cleverdon and Milne 2003).

The tourism industry in the Pacific has the capacity to return long-term benefits, but to be able to do this and remain sustainable it needs to satisfy four criteria:

- It must be financial viable and provide real rates of return for investors (local and overseas) and provide worthwhile jobs for its workforce
- It must provide continuing visitor satisfaction. Bad experiences and declining satisfaction levels are rapidly communicated (as in a series of stray dogs attacking tourists in Samoa)
- It should be recognised that while the resources for tourism have often been thought of as the natural environment, many tourists are increasingly drawn to people's cultures (hence the festivals – teuila, hibiscus, heilala) and ways of life which are just as vulnerable
- Tourism must be based upon a supportive host community, very important with the beach fale operation in Samoa.

None of these four criteria operate in isolation, for instance community support is enhanced by the visible flow of dollars and jobs into the local areas although material benefits are often fragmentary and diverse that making such benefits visible is a difficult task. In the same way, without careful resource management, locals may find favourite popular picnic spots and beaches crowded and commodified as tourist 'experiences'. Resource strategies must be developed so that they benefit locals as well as visitors. After all, satisfied visitors are far more likely to interact with locals than are tourists who feel resented or exploited.

Regional Tourism Trends

There are three types of tourism to the region: business tourism, visiting friends and relatives (this is the most common form in Samoa), and holiday/ leisure tourism. There are also other forms but of a lesser degree of importance such as adventure tourism (surfing/bungy jumping) and special interest tourism (eco-tourism, sports). There has also been a 'new' form of tourism emerging since the 1990s that appeals to the experienced and well educated traveller who is looking for much more than just the sun or to gaze at culture. This is a market that's complicated, individual and sophisticated tastes are made possible by advanced information technology and communication – e-commerce and internet booking. It is characterised by variety, diversity, participation and individual flexibility (Poon 1993). It is a customised form of tourism to suit the consumer and the experiences sought are most likely to be much more diverse with a focus on quality environmental experiences, and 'authentic' settings and societies. For example these types of tourists do not seek standard hotels, they patronise backpacking accommodation, bed and breakfast lodgings and beach fale stays. This new form of tourism is an off-shoot of the development of the tourism industry in the Caribbean. It is important for the Pacific in the sense that the product is locally owned and therefore more authentic compared to standardised mass tourism which focuses on large destination resorts, group travels and scheduled tours. This new wave of tourism demands a particular set of products and services, so destinations must provide the facilities and experiences in line with the consumer aspirations. The issue is whether the small island states can do it in a sustainable manner.

The competitive nature of the industry is manifested in the segmentation of destinations in the region into four groups, based on the number of visitor arrivals and source markets (Cleverdon and Milne 2003). Fiji, French Polynesia, New Caledonia and Palau have visitor flows of 100,000+ people a year from Europe, Japan, Australia, New Zealand and North America. The Cook Islands, PNG, Samoa and Tonga have around 30,000-70,000 visitors a year mainly from New Zealand and Australia, and benefit from the long-haul flight services by Air New Zealand and hopefully by Air Pacific in the case of Samoa. The third group (the Federated States of Micronesia and Vanuatu) experiences similar numbers of visitors as the second group and also mainly from the same markets (Australia and New Zealand). American Samoa, Tuvalu, Niue, Nauru, Marshall Islands, Kiribati and Solomon Islands make up the fourth group with modest levels of visitor arrivals due to access constraints, limited airline flights from originating points, leading to high costs of hotel operation and minimising the level of demand.

In addition, the organisation and spatial allocation of capital and tourists in the region is also segmented and unevenly spread, highlighting the core-periphery nature of the industry with Fiji, Tahiti and New Caledonia making up the core while the rest are peripheral destinations. Tourism in the region can be defined and analysed in relationship to issues of economic restructuring, globalisation, and post-Fordist modes of production (Hall 1994; Shaw and Williams 2004) where the region is commodified as an 'experience' – a place characterised by a relaxed lifestyle where one is released from the stress of everyday life – to be consumed.

There is competition for the same product, characterised by aggressive marketing campaigns amongst the South Pacific Tourism Organisation (SPTO) member countries. The web advertising of the region is surreal, almost fraudulent: the 'exotic melting pot cultures and fascinating lifestyles of Fiji', the 'pristine aqua-marine waters of Samoa', the 'sugary-white magical beaches' of Tahiti, the 'spectacular marine life and timeless Tuvalu' and 'the strict observance of the Sabbath and the strong influence of the church provide a fascinating experiences for tourists' in Tonga (SPTO Country Report). These claims conceal the environmental, economic, social and governance problems confronting the region. They are marketed as 'premium' destinations based on quality, safety, and their unique and diverse cultures. Product differentiation must take into account the great diversities in the culture, size, resources, private sector, and the different needs of SPTO countries.

We know for a fact that the economies of the island states are driven by tourism, and virtually all governments in the region have identified the industry as a priority sector for future economic growth through foreign direct investment, so I am not going to dwell on this except to cite some examples to illustrate the point. The SPTO suggests target revenue for the region from tourism of US$2 billion per annum by 2010. If this is achieved tourism would be the largest contributor to 'Pillar 1' of the Pacific Plan (OSTA 2008:20). In Fiji, tourism was 25.6 per cent of GDP in 2009 and is expected to increase to 27.8 per cent in 2019, providing 91,000 jobs – or 23.5 per cent of total employment (World Travel and Tourism Council). In Samoa, tourism has boomed since 2005 and in 2007 visitor flow exceeded the 100,000 mark (but that was due to the South Pacific games – a one-off special interest tourism event). Tourism contributed 25 per cent of GDP in Samoa in 2006 (Human Development Report 2006). In Palau, tourism accounts for 67 per cent of GDP, and in the Cook Islands, 50 per cent of GDP. In 2007, strong visitor growth was recorded in Papua New Guinea (+34 per cent), Solomon islands (+19.7 per cent), Vanuatu (+19.3 per cent), Tonga (+16.7 per cent) and Kiribati (6.9 per cent) (South Pacific Tourism Organisation: 19). Growth was driven by increased cheap air services (for example, Polyblue, a no-frills service) and destination marketing. In Samoa, the category of Visiting Friends and Relatives (VFR) made up 51 per cent of total visits in 2006 (Ministry of Finance 2007). In terms of volume, Samoa has the highest proportion of VFR visitors (35-40 per cent) in the region, followed by Tonga (33 per cent), Fiji (19 per cent) and Cook Islands (4 per cent) (Kavesi 2000). In Tonga, tourism contributes 12.2 per cent of GDP and 10.5 per cent of total employment in 2009 (World Travel and Tourism).

Developing a regional cruise shipping strategy to strengthen regional cooperation and integration (Pacific Island Forum Auckland Declaration 2004) based on the cruise tourism experiences of Fiji, Kiribati (as a remote new destination), PNG and Vanuatu would only serve to highlight the differences in size, population and resource endowments. In order to develop cruise ship tourism we need to promote the region's cultural richness and natural beauty. The issues identified in the cruise ship strategy for action are based on the four beacons approach which are: 1) shore excursions and land based activities; 2) marine infrastructure and support services; 3) institutional management and cooperative frameworks; and 4) cruise destination marketing and promotion (South Pacific Cruise Shipping Development Strategy 2007:3). Samoa attempted to boost cruise ship visits and went all the way to Europe to promote Samoa as a possible destination and reported an increase from eight to twenty visits per year. In comparison, Port Vila gets 60 visits per year. Old ports have been rebuilt, turned into international ports in the past 12 months and have yet to receive cruise ship visits. Overall, the region is rated highest for friendliness of the locals (1.57, where one is excellent and five is poor), and lowest for safety/medical facilities (3.6) and port cleanliness (3.57) (Regional Cruise Shipping Strategy 2007:22).

As mentioned earlier, tourism is in a state of transition throughout the world, with the Pacific no exception. The industry is emerging as one of the few industries that can supply jobs, profits and growth. So it is essential that tourism should thrive and grow in ways that do not jeopardise its own future wellbeing, nor impose unacceptable pressures on the environment or society – that is, it must be sustainable, not only in itself, but also in terms of its wider context. As development practitioners, we can devise models of the broad parameters of sustainable tourism for the individual states in the region, but I am uncertain whether all stakeholders – the industry, host communities, visitors and resource managers – see sustainability in the same light. Commitment to sustainable tourism in the Pacific Islands is not always translated into practice (Harrison 2004:13). Table 1 shows the results of a 2007 survey of 30 members of the tourism industry in Samoa, randomly selected from a number of sources such as the operators of beach fales, hotel and tour operators and administrators, which reveals some attitudes towards sustainability and associated issues in Samoa.

Table 5: Knowledge/Idea of Sustainable Tourism

Extent of knowledge	No. of responses	Percentage
A great deal	2	7%
Quite a bit	3	10%
Moderate	6	20%
Very little	7	23%
None	9	30%
No response	3	10%

Source: Research Project for Environmental Geography, National University of Samoa 2009.

One in three respondents did not give an answer, so it is not surprising that many people felt they needed to know more about sustainable tourism. Over 50 per cent said that they felt they needed to know more. Some of the respondents' comments about issues pertaining to sustainable practices within the tourism industry reflected the lack of understanding and awareness about sustainable tourism, for instance:

> We needed to clear the big trees near the fales because there is too much rubbish from the leaves, and adds to breeding grounds for mosquitoes which is bad for business (26 year old female, April 2009).

> I grew up here in Lalomanu, and our family have lived here for hundred years, and yes there are some changes to the beach face but it has always been like that in the past, the sea, beach, land is part of our culture and will remain when we are gone (60 year old male, April 2009).

Social Impacts

Governments of the region are focussing on the macro-economic impacts and potential for growth of tourism to trickle down to the poor and marginalised communities. This is all very well, but it needs to be incorporated into the tourism agenda as an additional policy objective (Kennedy and Dornan 2009).

Tourism is more often than not made the scapegoat for the social ills in the region. Prostitution, cultural change and environmental deterioration are not necessarily a result of tourism. The mass media and other socio-economic developments are also responsible if not sole contributors.

Crowding (which is the negative perception of the numbers of groups or individuals in a particular setting) is not a measure of density although it reflects it, but it is an indicator that social carrying capacities have been breached (Hall and Kearsley 2001). A commonly used measure of crowding in the region's tourism sites is the concept of *encounter norms* – that is, the number of groups, families or individuals that a person meets in a given setting. The beach fale context in Samoa is a good example to illustrate this perceptual construct, particularly over the festive season and public holidays such as Children's Sunday where parents normally would treat the children for a swim and picnic at the beach.

Environmental Trends

Michael Hall and Stephen Page have written extensively on the environmental and ecological impacts of tourism on the Pacific islands including the clearing and dredging of mangroves and estuaries for resorts and golf courses and the near shore vegetation clearance for beach fale space which has accelerated coastal erosion and coastal pollution. On the other hand, tourism can contribute significantly to environmental protection and conservation through sound environmental management of tourism facilities, especially the large hotels and resorts. If it is to be sustainable in the long run, then it must incorporate the principles and practices of sustainable consumption, important for the fragile ecosystems of small islands like Samoa. Should locals/Pacific islanders reduce their ecological footprints to allow for massive uncontrolled consumption of global and regional resources in the name of tourism?

The Samoan Experience: The Beach Fale

This industry can be described as young or new. It only managed to adopt a modern approach to marketing and promotion after the two destructive cyclones in 1990 and 1991 and the taro leaf blight in 1993 that destroyed the islands' agriculture and main export earner (Twining-Ward and Twining-Ward 1998). Prior to that, the Samoan government were not too keen to develop and promote mass tourism. The 1992 -2001 Tourism Development Plan emphasised a policy of 'low volume, high yield' and an industry that was environmentally responsible and culturally sensitive. The development of tourism in the early 1990s can be described as cautious and small-scale oriented with a focus on sustainable tourism and attracting higher spending leisure tourists who require upmarket accommodation options.

Despite plans to attract higher spending tourists, the most obvious growth area in the last 15 years has been within the 'beach fale' sector which is categorised as a small-medium enterprise. A beach fale is an oval shaped hut with wooden posts supporting a thatch/corrugated iron roof, with a wooden floor, either with no walls but woven coconut leaf blinds or a tarpaulin for privacy and to protect against the elements (Scheyvens 2005).The beach fale approach to tourism for small island states such as Samoa is an example of 'best practice' tourism for various reasons:

- It is advocated as a 'pro-poor' form of development where the grass roots benefit directly from the backward and forward linkages entailed in the operation

- It provides for a 'sustainable livelihood' of rural Samoan families – rural based industry and people-centred (Haughey 2007:16). The 'sustainable livelihood' approach to development specifies that a household's livelihood depends on assets (social, human, financial, natural) at their disposal which can be harnessed to achieve a desirable/acceptable level of social-economic wellbeing for the household(s). These assets are fundamental to the establishment of beach fales in the first instance and there is adequate continuous supply of these 'factors of production' for further expansion of beach fale tourism.

- It integrates subsistence and cash-based livelihoods in that subsistence production is enhanced or encouraged by the availability of a 'market' for fish, pork, crayfish, vegetables, fruit and root crops (Rosalote, Litia, Tanu and Vacations beach fale consultations 2009).

- There are direct links with the invisible but growing 'informal economy' both in urban and rural Samoa. Previous work on the informal sector suggests strong linkages between beach fale operations and village hawking in handicrafts such as printed wraparound lava-lavas, tee shirts, woven fans and table mats, coconut and shell trinkets, and souvenirs.

- Women feature strongly in beach fale operations as owners and managers because of their organisational, hospitality and financial skills (Haughey 2007). Having women run beach fale operations empowers them socially, economically with some financial independence.

- It is an authentic way to experience the culture of the place, in this case the 'faa Samoa' and simple living. However it should be noted that beach fale operations are evolving away from simple open fales to enclosed modernised self-contained units in response to demands for privacy and comfort, which appeals to families with young children, older travellers and couples. However, 'authenticity' is a matter of degree, and the average tourist can only bear two to three days of sleeping in an open fale exposed to the elements, especially the rain, in a sandy bed, feeling oily and sticky (Haughey 2007: 53-55).

- These fale are privately (family) funded either locally or from remittances. Two beach fale owners (one on Upolu and the other in Savaii) who were interviewed stated that their cattle farm and small retail shop supported the early beginnings of their beach fale venture which started with two small fales. They have reclaimed the land and added four other fales and a small-medium sized conference room. All these extension to the business have been funded by the cattle farm, shop, bakery (which supplies other small shops with biscuits (popo and masi saina) and buns, and from children living overseas. Access to commercial bank borrowing has been difficult due to land tenure issues where 80 per cent of the land is customary owned and 98 per cent of beach fale operations in Samoa are located on customary owned land.

- Beach fale operations have a minimum impact on the environment but are very vulnerable to natural disasters. The latest earthquake on 29 September 2009 highlighted the vulnerability of beach fales to the forces of nature.

Future Trends

Beach fale tourism will continue to feature strongly in Samoa. While the latest disaster destroyed 50 per cent of beach fale operations in the country, this will only serve to improve planning and setting standards – building code, resettlement patterns, sewage disposal – to minimise loss should there be a repeat of the 29 September disaster. We need to think locally while maintaining good quality international standards in accommodation.

Given that Samoa lacks the facilities for large scale tourism, nature-based tourism (or eco-tours) can be applied to smaller states, and I am hoping that we leave the promotion and development of mass tourism such as cruise shipping to the larger states of New Caledonia, PNG, Fiji, and concentrate on beach fales and small- to medium-sized operations.

Tourism in the region is generating a range of social, economic and environmental impacts, although they vary greatly across islands, the impacts invariably manifest upon the islands communities at all stages of their respective developments. For this reason, there needs to be a longitudinal study of community attitudes to beach fale tourism, to monitor the cumulative impacts of beach fale tourism in the context of broader demographic, economic and social forces that moderate tourism on small islands and will provide some explanation for the change in community attitudes to tourism over time.

Tourism in the islands will be affected by global travel and tourism which is expected to grow more rapidly in the coming years, probably outpacing the growth of world economic output. The industry in Asia Pacific is projected to grow at 8 per cent and the South Pacific will share in this growth. But the growth of the industry will require the removal of some major internal constraints such as inadequate, low quality infrastructure, land tenure restrictions. Also, there is a demand for small island states to focus on specialty tourism to meet growing global interests for clean, green, unspoilt natural environments especially for health-conscious travellers. Lastly, the islands need to work in partnership with academic institutions, regional organisations, the private sector and the donor community to develop sustainable tourism practices. The Oceania Sustainable Tourism Alliance in collaboration with Victoria University are working with Pacific islands to 'produce a new road map for the growth of their tourism industry, a road map that sees island tourism as carbon clean' (OSTA 2008:20).

References

Cleverdon, R., and Milne, S. 2003. *Negotiating Framework For Economic Partnership Agreement Negotiations With The European Union Tourism Study*. UK/EU Brussels: Robert Cleverdon Associates.

Haughey, A. 2007. 'Beach Fale Tourism for Pro-poor Development: A Study of Expectations in Rural Samoa'. Unpublished dissertation. Lincoln University, Christchurch.

Hall, C.M., and Kearsley, G. 2001. *Tourism in New Zealand: An Introduction*. Oxford: Oxford University Press.

Hall, C.M. 1994. *Tourism and Politics: Policy, Power and Place*. Chichester: John Wiley.

Hall, C.M., and Page, S. 2006. *The Geography of Tourism and Recreation: Environment, Place and Space*. Abingdon and New York: Routledge.

Harrison, D. 2004. 'Tourism in Pacific Islands'. *Journal of Pacific Studies*. 26(1&2): 1-28.

Kennedy, K., and Dornan, D. 2009. 'An overview: tourism non-governmental organisations and poverty reduction in developing countries'. *Asia Pacific Journal of Tourism Research*. 14(2): 183–200.

Oceania Sustainable Tourism Alliance (OSTA). 2008. 'South Pacific Island Tourism: A Carbon Clean Future'. Available at: http://www.oceaniatourismalliance. net/Documents/OSTA%20Pacific%20Island%20Carbon%20Clean%20 Tourism%20Oct%202008.pdf

Poon, A. 1993. *Tourism, Technology and Competitive Strategies*. Wallingford: CABI Publishing.

Scheyvens, R. 2005. 'Growth of beach fale tourism in Samoa: the high value of low cost tourism', in C.M. Hall and S. Boyd (eds), *Nature-Based Tourism in Peripheral Areas: Development or Disaster?* Clevedon: Channel View: 173–187.

Shaw, G., and Williams, A.M. 2004. *Tourism and Tourism Spaces*. Sage, London.

Singh, T.V. 2003. 'Tourism and development: not an easy alliance', in R.N. Ghosh, M.A.B. Siddique and R. Gabbay (eds), *Tourism and Economic Development: Case Studies from the Indian Ocean Region*. Aldershot: Ashgate: 30–41.

South Pacific Tourism Organisation. 2007. *South Pacific Cruise Shipping Development Strategy*. Available at http://www.south-pacific.travel/spto/export/sites/spto/tourism_resources/cruise_shipping/south_pacific_cruise_dev_strategy.pdf

Twining-Ward, L. and Twining-Ward, T. 1998. 'Tourism Development in Samoa: Context and Constraints'. *Pacific Tourism Review*. 2: 261–71.

13. Rural Development: Back on the Agenda in the Western Pacific?

Matthew G. Allen

Le développement rural : de nouveau à l'ordre du jour dans le Pacifique occidental?

Après des décennies pendant lesquelles on l'avait négligé, le développement rural, en particulier l'agriculture, est bien de nouveau à l'ordre du jour de l'assistance mondiale au développement. Cette tendance semble se refléter dans la région du Pacifique occidental, où quelques projets de développement rural bien dotés par les donateurs ont soit été récemment lancés soit le seront bientôt. Toutefois, si le développement rural peut être de nouveau à l'ordre du jour des donateurs, il l'a toujours été pour les Mélanésiens, dont la majorité habite des zones rurales. Le développement continue à être le discours dominant qui nourrit tous les domaines de l'Etat et de la société. Il continue également à être très contesté et devient de plus en plus politisé. Avec l'engagement récent par les donateurs dans le développement rural, il serait opportun de revisiter quelques-uns des débats les plus en vue sur le développement en Mélanésie et la question clé de savoir quelle sorte de développement rural est la plus appropriée. Pour explorer ces questions, cet article puise dans une partie de la recherche récente et du travail de consultant de l'auteur en Papouasie-Nouvelle-Guinée et aux Îles Salomon.

Introduction

After decades of neglect, agriculture and rural development are very much back on the global development aid agenda. The revival of donor interest in agriculture and rural development has been enabled by broader shifts in aid priorities and delivery mechanisms, particularly the move from the structural adjustment programs of the 1980s and 1990s to the local and community-level engagement strategies that increasingly characterise contemporary aid programming. The Millennium Development Goals, the global food crisis, and the 2008 World Development Report – which had as its theme 'Agriculture for Development' – have also variously contributed to the renewed donor impetus to agriculture and rural development.

It is not my intention here to describe and analyse the extent to which these trends have been mirrored in the Pacific Islands context. Indeed, the absence of readily available disaggregated data makes it difficult to do so. Having said that, a number of recently commenced, or soon to commence, agriculture and rural development programmes in the Western Pacific would appear to provide at least anecdotal evidence for renewed donor interest in these sectors. Two such projects in Solomon Islands, for example, are the recently-commenced Rural Development Program, jointly funded by the World Bank, AusAID and the European Union; and the AusAID-funded Rural Livelihoods Program, which is at an advanced stage of project design. Similarly, donors in Papua New Guinea are increasingly engaging at the sub-national level, engagements that have significant rural development dimensions, all the more so if we are to include service delivery under the rubric of rural development as I believe we should. Importantly, donors are accompanying these local and community-level engagements with rigorous political economy analysis.

Rather than exploring the question of whether or not rural development is back on the agenda in the Western Pacific, I instead want to ask whether it has ever been off the agenda? While there may indeed be renewed donor and, in some cases, 'recipient' government interest in rural development, if one was to pose this question to a Melanesian, be a they a villager or a Member of Parliament, the response would be that rural development is, and has always been, firmly on the agenda. Development is the dominant discourse in postcolonial Melanesia and, as the vast majority of Melanesians continue to reside in rural areas, development discourse remains inescapably concerned with rural development including, importantly, the delivery of public goods and services.

In an interview on Al Jazeera in 2009, Michael Somare, Prime Minister of Papua New Guinea, denied the existence of poverty in Papua New Guinea. This statement spawned a lively discussion on the Association of Social Anthropologists of Oceania email list (known as ASAO net). The debate was peppered with words like poverty, livelihoods, food security, subsistence, exchange economies, cash economies, capitalism, culture and development. I was simultaneously struck by the extent to which these issues remain highly contested and unresolved on the one hand, and by how little some of us have learned from the story thus far on the other. Romanticism about idealised traditional lifestyles, characterised by subsistence abundance and social and ecological harmony, persists even amongst those who purport to have expert knowledge on these matters. The debate eventually and inevitably settled around the time-honoured dialectic of tradition and modernity, and to the similarly perennial question of what type of development is appropriate for rural Melanesia?

That is the question I explore in this short essay. What type of development is appropriate for rural Melanesia? While this is obviously a question that

Melanesians themselves are best placed to answer, bearing in mind that their perspectives are by no means unitary or homogenous, I proceed from the position that informed outsiders, 'outlanders' to borrow Margaret Jolly's term, also have a valid voice and role in the debate. However, rather than attempting to offer a definitive answer to this question, I instead intend to frame it by discussing a number of other questions which contextualise and enrich the discussion, and provide some support for the tentative conclusions that are offered.

These questions include: How has development played out in Melanesia? What does it look like? What has been the role of the state? To what extent has rural development become politicised? How much agency have local people had in forging their own development trajectories? I will base my observations on a number of diverse activities I have been undertaking over the past two years: teaching an undergraduate course on conflict and development in Melanesia; undertaking an analysis of the political economy of rural service delivery in Papua New Guinea; and preparing a research proposal to investigate the socio-economic dimensions of smallholder oil palm production in Solomon Islands.

Theoretical Matters

First I change lexicon in order to delve briefly into matters theoretical and, in particular, to locate my discussion and approach within the development studies literature. Most readers will be familiar with the successive phases and perspectives in development theory: from modernisation through to structuralism (encompassing dependency and world-system theory), then to poststructuralism and, most recently, to postdevelopment which of course is strongly informed by postmodernism.

Many contemporary development studies scholars agree that development has not seen the universal disintegration of culture and traditional societies in the face of capitalist modernisation that was posited by modernisation theorists. Similarly, developing countries of the so-called periphery have not been permanently subjugated as providers of labour to be exploited by the capital-intensive core, as theorised by the structuralists. And postdevelopment and postmodernism, with what geographer John Connell describes as their 'comprehensive yet totally intellectual assault on the foundations of modernism' have, Connell continues, 'largely failed to shake off the perceived virtues of modernity, whether in villages or parliaments, in boardrooms or international institutions' (Connell 2007:122). Governments need to raise revenue to provide public goods and perform essential functions. People in rural communities want to earn money to pay for school fees, kerosene, clothes, soap, and imported food. Postdevelopment's pronouncement of the end of capitalism clearly seems premature.

Where, then, does Melanesia fit in this theoretical schema? Poststructuralists — those who see the contours of development in terms of hybridity and syncretism — appear to have much to offer in the context of rural Melanesia. This perspective enables us to account for the persistence and 'robustness of indigenous economic and cultural forms' (Curry and Koczberski 1998:31). It enables us to consider social and cultural logics, as well as purely economic ones, as salient shapers of place-based development outcomes and trajectories. It implicitly emphasises the social embeddedness of economic activity and decision-making.[1]

Social Embeddedness

Economic geographer George Curry applies a social embeddedness framework to his analysis of the relationships between smallholder palm oil production and the local gift-exchange economy in West New Britain Province of Papua New Guinea. He employs palm oil production data, interviews conducted with smallholders, and ethnographic observations to demonstrate that the timing and extent of smallholder engagement with the cash economy is significantly determined by the level of activity in the indigenous exchange economy, which in turn is underpinned by the need to maintain social relations and group identity (Curry 2003:412-418).

Similar patterns and relationships are seen in the ways in which labour is organised and mobilised to produce palm oil (which is often along kinship lines), and in the practice of trade stores extending loans and credit to enable smallholders to respond to unanticipated requirements for gift-exchange, such as funerals. Curry (1999) and fellow geographer Glenn Banks (1999) reported similar findings in their studies of trade stores in parts of East Sepik Province and the Highlands respectively. Preliminary investigations into smallholders' engagements with a commercial oil palm operation on Guadalcanal in Solomon Islanders indicate that similar processes are also at play there (Fraenkel et al. 2010:70-71).

Curry argues that the West New Britain palm oil example demonstrates how smallholders' engagements with one another and with an ostensibly capitalist economic activity are transformed through 'place-based practices', in this case gift-exchange and its importance in maintaining social relations, to create a hybrid modernity that 'bears little resemblance to the idealised notions of market economic relationships and the economically rational, utility maximising individual' (Curry 2003:406).

---

1 There is expanding body of literature that addresses the social embeddedness of economic activity and decision-making, both internationally (see Zukin and DiMaggio 1990 for an overview) and in the particular case of Papua New Guinea (see for example Gregory 1982; Banks 1999; Curry 1999, 2003, 2005).

Importantly, the social embeddedness framework provides a robust critique of the Marxist inspired structuralist perspectives applied by earlier scholars of Papua New Guinea's development trajectory of whom Amarshi, Good and Mortimer (1979) and Thompson and MacWilliam (1992) are exemplars. These researchers shared a conceptualisation of capitalism as a monolithic, hegemonic and homogenising force and argued that the penetration of global capitalism would inevitably 'result in the destruction of non-capitalist societies and their infrastructure' (Curry 2003:407). Poststructuralist perspectives such as that offered by Curry (2003) and Connell (2007) are of considerable analytical importance for our purposes as they emphasise the importance of hybridity, syncretism, agency, and the influence of culture:

> In this view socially and culturally constructed place becomes important for shaping patterns of interaction at the local level. Agency is therefore recognized, and the assumption of a hegemonic capitalism therefore undermined (Curry 2003:408).

> Capitalist forces thus played out in different cultural universes as did all other alien introductions such as Christianity, cricket, clocks and law (Connell 2007:124-125).

Extractive Resource Industries

I change tack now to consider the local development discourses surrounding large-scale extractive resource industries, especially mining and logging. Why have so many rural communities throughout PNG and Solomon Islands allowed these activities to occur on their land in spite of their demonstrable ability to cause severe environmental and social harm? For Filer and MacIntyre, writing in regard to mining in PNG the answer lies, at least partly, in the failed 'promise that wealth generated by mining would strengthen the state and increase its capacity to improve services across the nation…' (Filer and MacIntyre 2006:227). A collection of essays on mining in PNG edited by Filer and MacIntyre reveals:

> the ways that mining, in spite of the problems it generates, appears to be a sure way that local people can gain employment, business opportunities, roads, hospitals, and schools – the development that their government has been unable to deliver…there is sufficient evidence of relative wealth and advantage to feed aspiration among those who have no mine and nostalgia among those whose mine has closed (2006:224).

Of course communities are by no means united nor unified in their views on extractive resource projects. One need only look as a far as Russel Hawkin's documentary Since the Company Came or Martin Maden's more recent Crater

Mountain Story to see just how locally-contested and divisive such projects can be. In some instance these competing local perspectives map onto broader epistemological contestations manifest as competing visions for development. For example, in the only detailed study to date of the social impacts of commercial logging in a particular locality in Solomon Islands, Kolombangarra, Ian Scales identifies:

> a fractionation of local society into groups competing for 'large scale' or 'small scale' forest resource development. The crosscutting social differentiation drives conflict between 'entrepreneurial landowners' and 'traditionalist smallholders' over forest resources and generates competing island-level political associations (Scales 2003:iv).

In other instances the localised contestation over extractive resource projects takes on salient gender dimensions. Frequently it is women who articulate the greatest opposition to mining and commercial logging activities, more so perhaps in matrilineal societies such as Bougainville, Guadalcanal and Western Solomons.

The Politicisation of State Development Funds

I return now to Filer's and MacIntyre's point about communities' enthusiasm for mining and logging being driven by the failure or inability of the state to provide services. Ironically, the failure of state service delivery has been used to justify the increasing politicisation of the state development budgets, most notably in Papua New Guinea and Solomon Islands. Here I am talking about the so-called slush funds, the District and Provincial Support Grants and, more recently, the District Services Improvement Program in Papua New Guinea; and the Rural Constituency Development Fund in Solomon Islands.

Supporters of such funds argue that they were initially devised as a useful way of capitalising on MPs' intimate knowledge of their electorates and bypassing bureaucratic bottlenecks to fund critical infrastructure projects to the benefit of the whole electorate (Ketan 2007:8-14). However, in the case of Papua New Guinea, the history of constituency development funds is perhaps best seen in the context of so-called decentralisation reforms. The 1995 Organic Law on Provincial Governments and Local Level Governments (OLPGLLG) and subsequent amendments can be interpreted as a successful attempt by national level politicians, particularly Open MPs, firstly to remove their competitors in the form of elected provincial representatives, and then to gradually increase the volume of resources directly channelled into the district level over which they have developed significant de facto and de jure control.

Described by one informed commentator as 'a kind of decentralisation race to the bottom' (Whimp 2009:3), a string of amendments to the OLPGLLG have seen the establishment of district-level committees over which Open MPs have significant control; the removal of Regional MPs from these committees; and, most recently, the removal of Local Level Government (LLG) presidents from provincial assemblies arguably providing Open MPs with more power and leverage vis a vis provincial governors.[2] Alongside these developments was the increase in District Support Grants, but not Provincial Support Grants, to a maximum of K1.5 million for each Open MP in 1999 (though we must also note the bearing that the machinations of parliamentary politics have had on the capricious nature of these allocations); and, most recently, the dramatic increase in the District Services Improvement Program grant to K4 million, K6 million and K4 million per district in 2007, 2008 and 2009 appropriations.

De facto arrangements have included the deliberate marginalisation of LLG presidents, and even District Administrators, from district level decision-making processes, meaning that the significant amount of funds now being channelled through the districts can be, and are being, used for pork-barrel politics (see Allen and Hasnain 2010:16-17). This comes at the cost of good service delivery outcomes not only because projects are targeted at MPs' voter strongholds at the expense of the wider electorate, but also because there is a strong emphasis on capital investments made with scant regard to provincial, district, LLG or ward planning processes and, therefore, to on-going operational funding.

Importantly these developments have not been driven by the dictates of 'rational actor' political economy alone. Like the economic behaviour described earlier in relation to hybrid forms of modernity, political behaviour in postcolonial Melanesia is also significantly determined by social and cultural logics. Elected representatives and public servants at all levels of government continue to be enmeshed in social networks of reciprocity and obligation (see, in particular, Morgan 2005). Their kinship groups, which in the case of elected representatives are often coterminous with their political support bases, expect them to distribute and share whatever resources they can access.

This hybridity is not restricted to the behaviour of MPs and government officials; it characterises state institutions throughout postcolonial Melanesia. Reviewing the literature on the relationships between local political cultures and the formal state in Melanesia, much of which is concerned with Papua New Guinea, Morgan concludes that 'pre-existing social forms pervade the state at almost every level' (Morgan 2005:4). Indeed, there is widespread support in the

---

2   The Papua New Guinea Supreme Court has recently ruled the 2006 amendment to be unconstitutional, which would appear to pave the way for LLG presidents to be reinstated to Provincial Assemblies (*National*, 7 June 2010).

literature for the proposition that the introduced state in Papua New Guinea has become thoroughly indigenised (Gordon and Meggitt 1985, Standish 1992, Ketan 2000, Morgan 2005).

Conclusion

While rural development may be back on the agenda for donors, it has never been off the agenda for the predominantly rural inhabitants of Melanesia. It is a discourse that remains enmeshed in historical and contemporary imaginings of the state – 'the government' – as a provider of services and public goods. Indeed it is the failure of state to provide services and generate economic opportunities that arguably informs Melanesians' desire to host extractive resource projects, even amongst communities which have directly experienced the catastrophic social and environmental impacts of such projects. Ironically, the failure of state service delivery has also been used to justify the increasing politicisation of development budgets, at least in Papua New Guinea and Solomon Islands, thereby further undermining the equitable allocation of public goods.

In this short essay, I have argued that social and cultural logics, as well as economic ones, have shaped the ways in which development, and development discourses, have played out in postcolonial Melanesia. The cases examined have highlighted the dangers inherent in the bifurcation and dichotomisation that continues to characterise much of policy and even scholarly discourse about development in Melanesia: modern versus traditional; rural versus urban; informal versus informal. Such bifurcation is counterproductive at best. Hybridity as it has been elucidated here is best seen as total and complete merging: the emergence of new and complete socio-economic forms which are a 'vibrant blend of modern and pre-modern, of capitalist and pre-capitalist phenomena, where the boundaries are continually shifting and indistinct' (Curry and Koczberski 1998:48).

What, then, is the most appropriate form of development for rural Melanesia? I re-emphasise that this is a question which Melanesians are best placed to answer as demonstrated eloquently by Solomon Islander scholar David Gegeo's exposition of the West Kwara'ae (a region of Malaita) philosophy of gwaumauri'anga, meaning the 'good life' (1998:75). The philosophy encapsulates a holistic approach to 'rural development' which caters for spiritual, psychological and physical needs – in addition to economic goals – and is firmly anchored in indigenous knowledge (Gegeo 1998:73-74). Gegeo contrasts this philosophy with government approaches to development which villagers describe as 'a one-sided vision'. Villagers believe that this disjuncture has led to the inevitable failure of official rural development projects in the region. The philosophy of gwaumauri'anga is echoed in the Papua New Guinea Tok Pisin phrase 'gutpela sindoan', perhaps also best translated as a highly localised conception of the 'good life'.

These conceptions underscore the salience of local epistemologies of development, of the dialectics of people and nature, and of the connections between land and identity. They also point to the growing recognition that Melanesians' engagements with capitalist economies are inflected to serve place-based socio-economic and cultural goals as they seek to achieve a meaningful blend of modernity and tradition. The forgoing discussion has thrown up some implications for development practice. Having applied a social embeddedness framework to his analysis of smallholder oil palm producers' engagements with the cash economy in Papua New Guinea, Curry (2003) offers two such implications which warrant restating here. First, modes of production and marketing should be flexible enough to respond to the demands of the gift-exchange economy. Second, development interventions should be conscious of the ways in which surpluses can be appropriated by the exchange economy. This appropriation is more problematic in the case of ventures that require high levels of operating capital.

References

Allen, M.G., and Hasnain, Z. (2010). 'Power, pork and patronage: decentralisation and the politicisation of the development budget in Papua New Guinea'. *Commonwealth Journal of Local Governance*. 6: 7-31.

Amarshi, K., Good, K. and Mortimer, R. 1979. *Development and Dependency. The Political Economy of Papua New Guinea*. Melbourne: Oxford University Press.

Banks, G. 1999. 'Business as usual', in C. Filer (ed.), *Dilemmas of Development: The Social and Economic Impact of the Porgera Gold Mine*. Canberra: Research School of Pacific and Asian Studies, The Australian National University.

Connell, J. 2007. 'Islands, idyll and the detours of development'. *Singapore Journal of Tropical Geography*. 28(2): 116-135.

Curry, G. 1999. 'Market, Social Embeddedness and Precapitalist Societies: the Case of Village Tradestores in Papua New Guinea'. *Geoforum*. 30(3): 285-98.

Curry, G. 2003. Moving Beyond Postdevelopment: Facilitating Indigenous Alternatives for 'Development'. Economic Geography. 79(4):405-423.

Curry, G. 2005. 'Doing 'Business' in Papua New Guinea: The social embeddedness of small business enterprises'. *Journal of Small Business and Entrepreneurship*. 18(2): 231-246.

Curry, G., and Koczberksi, G. 1998. 'Migration and circulation as a way of life for the Wosera Abelam of Papua New Guinea'. *Asia Pacific Viewpoint*. 39(1): 29-52.

Filer, C., and Macintyre, M. 2006. 'Grass Roots and Deep Holes: Community Responses to Mining in Melanesia'. *The Contemporary Pacific*. 18(2): 215-231.

Fraenkel. J, Allen, M.G. and Brock, H. (2010). 'The Resumption of Palm Oil Production on Guadalcanal's Northern Plains'. *Pacific Economic Bulletin*. 25(1): 64-75.

Gegeo, D.W. 1998. 'Indigenous Knowledge and Empowerment: Rural Development Examined from Within'. *The Contemporary Pacific*. 10(2): 289-315.

Gordon, R., and Meggitt, M. 1985. *Law and Order in the New Guinea Highlands*. Hanover: University Press New England.

Gregory, C.A. 1982. *Gifts and Commodities*. London: Academic Press.

Jolly, M. 2007. 'Imagining Oceania: Indigenous and Foreign Representations of a Sea of Islands'. *The Contemporary Pacific*. 19(2): 508-545.

Ketan, J. 2000. 'Leadership and Political Culture', in M.A. Rynkiewich and R. Seib (eds), *Politics in Papua New Guinea: Continuities, Changes and Challenges*. Goroka: The Melanesia Institute.

Ketan, J. 2007. 'The Use and Abuse of Electoral Development Funds and their Impact on Electoral Politics and Governance in Papua New Guinea'. CDI Policy Papers on Political Governance 2007/2. Canberra: Centre for Democratic Institutions, The Australian National University.

Morgan, M. 2005. 'Cultures of Dominance: Institutional and Cultural Influences on Parliamentary Politics in Melanesia'. State Society and Governance in Melanesia Discussion Paper 2005/2. Canberra: Research School of Pacific and Asian Studies, The Australian National University.

Scales, I. A. 2003. 'The Social Forest: Landowners, Development Conflict and the State in Solomon Islands'. Unpublished Ph.D. thesis. Canberra: The Australian National University.

Standish, B. 1992. 'Simbu Paths to Power: Political Change and Cultural Continuity in the Papua New Guinea Highlands'. Unpublished PhD Thesis. The Australian National University.

Thompson, H. and MacWilliam, S. 1992. *The Political Economy of Papua New Guinea*. Manilla: Journal of Contemporary Asia Publishers.

Whimp, K. 2009. 'If we had funding…Implementing fiscal decentralisation in Papua New Guinea'. Unpublished thesis proposal, February 2009.

Zukin, S. and DiMaggio, P. (eds.). *1990. Structures of Capital: the Social Organization of the Economy*. Cambridge: Cambridge University Press.

Oceania and its Wider Setting

14. Regionalism: Performance and Promise

Henry Ivarature

Le régionalisme – réalisations et espoirs

Cet article examine les réalisations et la promesse du régionalisme dans le Pacifique en considérant les accords commerciaux et économiques, la fourniture de services et les facilités de soutien (appelées également le développement sectoriel), les réactions politiques et en matière de sécurité et le Conseil des organisations régionales dans le Pacifique (CROP) en mettant l'accent sur le Forum des Îles du Pacifique et la promesse d'une plus grande intégration et d'une plus grande coopération régionales par le biais du Plan Pacifique. Cette question des réalisations et des promesses pour le régionalisme appelle des réponses variées, l'une d'elles étant que les résultats de l'énergie globale dépensée en vue de l'intégration régionale sont quelque peu mitigés. On n'a pas obtenu les rendements attendus de cette intégration régionale. Par conséquent, cela vaut-il la peine d'investir ? En outre, les résultats du régionalisme, quelle que soit la façon dont on le définit, ont besoin d'être examinés et mis à la disposition de tous ceux qui ont un intérêt à la question afin qu'ils soient en mesure de les juger. Une autre proposition est le besoin d'un examen plus approfondi du régionalisme. Quelles sont les réalisations de ce régionalisme ? Quels sont les difficultés et les défis auxquels il doit faire face ? Quelles en sont les réussites ? Quelles en sont les perspectives et les promesses ? Cet article retrace l'évolution du régionalisme dans le Pacifique et présente une réponse personnelle au défi qui consiste à le construire et le promouvoir tel qu'il s'articule dans le Plan Pacifique.

Introduction

From the outset, some qualifications are necessary. As a regional public servant involved in coordinating the implementation of some initiatives in the Pacific Plan, this chapter may be biased towards regional integration. The topic suggests several things. One is that the overall energy put into regional integration has been somewhat mixed. The perceived returns on investment in regional integration have not been delivered. Therefore, is it really worth the trouble in investment? Moreover, the performance of regionalism, however that is defined, needs to be examined and laid out for all stakeholders to assess. What has regionalism achieved? What are the challenges and difficulties? What are the successes? What are the prospects and what are the promises?

Regionalism as it is defined by the Pacific Islands Forum will be revisited after a review of the regional governance architecture. But from the outset, several publications on regionalism should be acknowledged in contributing to the discourse and might also help to share perspectives on the subject. These include the publication edited by Graham (2008) on models of regional governance, Bryant-Tokalau and Frazer (2006) on redefining the Pacific, the article by Freitag (2006) on regional integration in the South Pacific, and Fry (2005) on the regional governance infrastructure. Reviewing these works bring out the importance of the subject as well as its complications and dynamics. Fry's paper is notable for its analysis of the evolving phases of pooled regional governance, overlapping in different time periods covering different issues.[1]

For this discussions, regionalism will be considered under the following headings: trade and economic arrangements; service delivery and support facilities (also referred to as sectoral development); political and security responses; Council of Regional Organisations in the Pacific (CROP) with a specific focus on the Pacific Islands Forum; and the promise of greater regional integration and cooperation through the Pacific Plan. The performance of and promise for regionalism should speak for itself.

Regional Trade and Economic Arrangements

Many trade arrangements have been entered into by many independent Pacific Island states for many different developmental objectives. These include the belief that economic growth would be stimulated, jobs and employment opportunities would be created, and the national economies would diversify and grow. Often it is the challenge to the abilities of Pacific states to generate revenue to support public expenditure away from the traditional tariff-based revenue generation and the subsequent exposure of national industries to international competition which generates much scepticism about trade arrangements. Concessions to these concerns have often been addressed through trade preference arrangements but have over the years been gradually negotiated away to free trade agreements.

---

1   Fry (2005) describes five main phases, beginning with comprehensive regional integration (1971-74), overlapping and advancing with sectoral integration (1971-1978), moving with increased collective diplomacy (1979-90), and intertwined with regional security community (1984-89) and the harmonisation of national policies (1994-2003).

Early trade preference arrangements for Pacific states include those granted by the United Kingdom in the mid-1960s when former colonies joined the European Economic Community and later incorporated with Africa, Caribbean and the Pacific states as well as the Generalised System of Preference (GSP) under the United Nations Conference on Trade and Development (UNCTAD) and General Agreement on Tariffs and Trade (GATT) in 1971. Initially, the Pacific states entered these agreements individually as they became independent self-governing states and were followed by others. Fiji, Samoa and Tonga entered Lomé in 1975 and other Pacific states entered into the series of Lomé agreements in 1979, 1984, 1990 and later the broader Cotonou Agreement (1975) – the flagship of the ACP-EU development cooperation. The EPAs which are under negotiation, involving individual states and groups of countries will replace the Cotonou agreement. Only Fiji and Papua New Guinea have signed onto Interim EPAs on Trade in Goods Agreement as both need to maintain market access to the EU, especially for sugar and tuna respectively. Currently, Fiji's sugar preference is suspended as part of the EU sanctions following the military coup, placing at stake approximately 26 per cent of its total export earnings.

Aside from the developmental objectives, the need to export their raw materials to sustain national economies inadvertently brought Pacific states into the broader arena of globalised and regional trade and economic arrangements. The inherent risks, threats, challenges and benefits are all an integral part of this process. Trade agreements however provide the broad governance framework under which trading parties agree to conduct commercial exchanges, investment and trade in goods and services.

Other notable trade arrangements with an economic growth agenda initiated at the bilateral level have been entered into between Pacific states with Australia and New Zealand, and between Pacific states. Some bilateral agreements interface with other regional agreements. For example, the Papua New Guinea-Australia Trade and Commercial Relations Agreements (PACTRA) was complemented by the South Pacific Trade and Economic Cooperation Agreement (SPARTECA) in 1980 at the Leaders meeting in Kiribati and which was later incorporated into PACTRA. Trade between the 14 Forum countries is limited, estimated at only 2 per cent of their total trade (Dearden 2008). The Melanesian Spearhead Group (MSG) and the Pacific Island Countries Trade Agreement (PICTA) are amongst the most notable examples of reciprocal and non-reciprocal trade agreements between and amongst Pacific Island countries. The former was initiated and put into place by leaders of the three Melanesian states – Papua New Guinea, the Solomon Islands and Vanuatu in 1993 and Fiji later in 1998. The agreement commits MSG members to liberalise trade over 8 years from 2005.

Unlike the MSG trade agreement, PICTA essentially laid the basis for a free trade agreement and economic integration through the Pacific Islands with its region-wide arrangement. It was signed by 14 Pacific Island states[2] along with the Pacific Agreement on Closer Economic Relations (PACER), with Australia and New Zealand in 2001. Reviewed through the Forum Trade Ministers Meetings which is held once a year, PACER sought 'to provide the 'stepping stone' to allow Forum Island Countries to gradually become part of a single regional market and integrate into the international economy'. While tariffs were scheduled to be reduced to zero by 2010 and 2012 for different Pacific Island states, exemptions and protection of certain industries exist. PICTA is broad minded in that it recognises other trade agreements of its members such as the Cotonou agreement, SPARTECA and the Compact of Free Association.

The recent trade and economic integration agreement with Forum countries, PACER Plus, is anticipated to assist in 'furthering regional integration and helping to create opportunities for economic growth and prosperity in Forum Countries, including employment'. Some observers, notably NGOs are not convinced and believe the prospects for some Forum Island countries are not good. Others contend that PACER and PACER Plus attempt to offer the Forum Island region the real prospects for economic integration. To help overcome Fiji's 'isolation', Leaders in 2009 agreed that the Fiji military regime would not participate in the PACER Plus negotiations but Fiji officials would be briefed following each negotiation meeting and who would also convey Fiji's concerns.

For the northern Pacific the Micronesian Presidents' Summit is another sub-regional political platform for Micronesian leadership to provide a collective sub-regional voice on a range of issues affecting their region as well as to develop a collective position and direction. Similar to the Pacific Islands Forum and MSG, outcomes of the Micronesian Presidents' Summit are issued at the end of their meetings. The Federated States of Micronesia, the Republic of Marshall Islands and the Republic of Palau operate under a Compact of Free Association with the United States which ends in 2023. Trade arrangements, especially exports to the United States are an integral component of the Compact arrangement. The Compact arrangement, aside from providing a broad framework for economic development and assistance, self-government and national defence and security, provides these Island states privileged immigration access to the United States. Monetary aid to the Federated States of Micronesia is approximately US$90 million, about US$60 million a year for the Republic of the Marshall Islands and about US$450 million over a period of 15 years for the Republic of Palau under the Compact arrangement. Concessions for this arrangement include permitting the United States to deploy troops, undertake military exercises and test fire missiles until 2066 with an option to extend it to 2086. Claims arising out of

---

2   All the Forum Island Countries, except for Australia and New Zealand signed this agreement.

US nuclear test at Bikini and Enewetak Atolls are deemed to be settled. These Island states are restrained from acting contrary to the security and defence agreements.

Some Pacific states (Fiji, Papua New Guinea, Samoa, Solomon Islands and Tonga) have joined the successor of GATT, the World Trade Organization (1995) which has stronger enforcement powers as well as the challenges of multilateral trading system. Papua New Guinea aside from Australia and New Zealand is the only Pacific state that is a member of the Asia Pacific Economic Cooperation (APEC) which also advocates trade liberalisation and the gradual reduction of barriers to trade.

Trade and economic arrangements set out the conduct of trading countries within a legally enforceable framework which, aside from trade in goods and services, and as articulated in PACER, 'provide a framework for cooperation over time to the development of a single regional market'. Essentially, the new regional trade arrangements, like earlier ones, make this inevitable but for Pacific states to explore alternative revenue strategies. Substantial opposition is expected given the narrow economic and revenue base for many small island states with growing public sector costs without a correlating increase in public revenue.

Like trade and economic arrangements, a new regional effort endorsed by Forum Leaders in 2009 is the Cairns Compact on Strengthening Development Coordination which in many respects complements regional effort at improving and coordinating development outcomes, assist Pacific states address global financial and economic impacts and strengthen the long-term economic resilience of the region. The Compact is currently being worked on.

Council of Regional Organisations in the Pacific (CROP)

CROP was formerly known as the South Pacific Organisations Coordination Committee. It was replaced with the CROP in 1988. Before the implementation of the Regional Institutional Framework (RIF) there were 11 agencies each with different roles and functions, and with their own governance structures in serving the region. Chaired by the Secretary General of the Pacific Islands Forum Secretariat, it 'exists to ensure that regional organisations pursue their collective aim of achieving sustainable development in the Pacific Island Countries in the most effective and efficient manner' and that this can be achieved 'through coordinated and cooperative action'. CROP is the vehicle for the formulation and dissemination of the regional strategy on development priorities and exists to provide services to Pacific people. Striving to ensure that regional organisations service the needs of the people of the Pacific Islands is an ongoing consideration of Leaders of the Pacific Islands Forum. The RIF which has been underway since 2007 not only reduces the number of regional organisations but seeks to minimise duplication of functions and to reduce wastage of regional effort.

Member organisations of the CROP based outside Fiji are the Forum Fisheries Agency (1979) situated in Honiara, Solomon Islands, the Pacific Islands Development Programme (1980) based in Honolulu, Hawaii, and the Samoa-based South Pacific Regional Environmental Programme (SPREP) established in 1980. The SPC is headquartered in Noumea, New Caledonia with a branch in Fiji. New branches are being set up in the region. The rest of the CROP are based in Fiji. Education service providers include the USP (1986), the Fiji School of Medicine (1885) and the South Pacific Board of Education Assessment (1980). Investment and infrastructure enhancing service providers are the Pacific Power Association and South-Pacific.travel. Technical service providers include the South Pacific Applied Geoscience Programme (SOPAC) established in 1972 and which is now absorbed into SPC.

The Secretariat of the Pacific Community and the Pacific Islands Forum

Perhaps the two most pivotal regional organisations are the Secretariat of the Pacific Community and the Pacific Islands Forum. The Secretariat of the Pacific Community was established in 1947 as the South Pacific Commission by Great Britain, France, the United States, Australia and New Zealand. It is the oldest technical organisation delivering specialised services covering land and human resources, agriculture, health and demographic statistics to 22 Pacific Island territories.

The Pacific Islands Forum is considered as the regional body that sets the Pacific region's political and economic policy agenda. It is made up of 16 sovereign independent Pacific States[3] and has been around since August 1971. Forum Observers include Tokelau, Wallis and Futuna, the Commonwealth, the Asian Development Bank and Timor Leste as a Special Observer. Its creation was initiated by Pacific Island leaders, in particular the late Ratu Sir Kamisese Mara of Fiji, as an informal regional forum with for Pacific states to discuss issues of politics, trade and services and as vehicle to register its voice on regional and

---

3   Members of the Pacific Islands Forum are Australia, Cook Islands, Federated States of Micronesia, Fiji, Kiribati, Nauru, New Zealand, Niue, Palau, Papua New Guinea, Marshall Islands, Samoa, Solomon Islands, Tuvalu, Tonga and Vanuatu.

international issues that affected the region. Over the years, it has grown to take a formal structure. In 2005, Leaders adopted the new Agreement Establishing the Pacific Islands Forum as an intergovernmental organisation at international law (see also Spillane 2008). The Agreement also updates the Forum's purpose and functions to reflect the vision and direction taken under the Pacific Plan. As a way of facilitating regional cooperation and integration Leaders agreed to broaden the Forum's membership by establishing new associate and observer membership categories (Pacific Islands Forum Secretariat 2005).

Basically, the Forum has no formal rules governing its operations or the conduct of its meetings. The agenda is based on reports from the Secretariat and related regional organisations and committees, ministerial meetings as well as from members. Decisions by the Leaders are reached by consensus and outlined in a Forum Communiqué from which policies are developed and work programmes are prepared. The Head of Government of the host country is the Chair of the Forum until the next meeting.

The administrative arm of the Forum is the Pacific Islands Forum Secretariat, based in Suva, Fiji. It acts as the Secretariat for Forum related events, implements decisions by Leaders, facilitates the delivery of development assistance to member states, and undertakes the political and legal mandates of Forum Meetings. The Secretariat is headed by the Secretary General. The Forum Officials Committee (made up of representatives from all Forum governments) is the governing body for the Secretariat and oversees its activities. The Secretary General is also the permanent Chair of the Council of Regional Organisations in the Pacific (CROP) that brings together the eleven main regional organisations in the Pacific region. The Pacific Plan Action Committee (PPAC) made up of officials from all Forum member countries which is also chaired by the Secretary General oversights the implementation of the Pacific Plan.

The formation of the Forum was the expression of many things, one of which was certainly about how Pacific Islands states, then making their preparations for independence, sought to address the trade and economic challenges posed by remoteness, smallness, isolation and resource limitations – issues which the Pacific Plan is currently grappling with today. It was and is about functional regional cooperation some of which has been discussed above. The list of topics considered by the leaders over the years includes the establishment of the FFA, regional shipping, regional civil aviation, trade agreements and marketing, the environment, the USP and relations with a range of international organisations and the admission of new members.

Regional Service Delivery and Support Facilities

Regional approaches to overcoming capacity limitations in service delivery and support at a national level is perhaps an area where the greatest gains have been recorded. Benefits to the region have flowed from tertiary education, transport, shipping, telecommunications, fisheries, environment and investment support. Since its establishment in 1968, the University of the South Pacific (USP) whose main campus is situated in Suva, Fiji has contributed significantly to the human development needs of many Pacific Islands states in the areas of science and technology, law and politics, economics, accounting, education and others. The USP has campuses in Kiribati, Tonga, Samoa, Tuvalu, Solomon Islands, and a school in Vanuatu offering degrees in law. Partly to harmonise educational standards across the region, the South Pacific Board for Education Assessment was created in 1980 but under the Regional Institutional Framework (RIF) aimed at re-aligning regional organisation, it will merge into the Secretariat of the Pacific Community (SPC).

In order to provide shipping services in the region, the Pacific Forum Line (PFL) was established in 1977. Its fleet of vessels service ports linking Australia and New Zealand and the Pacific Islands. Twelve Forum member governments own PFL. Air Pacific, Fiji's national airline evolved in the 1960s through the joint collaboration of Great Britain, Australia, New Zealand and Fiji was designed to tackle the challenges of long distances which separated many Pacific Islands. Unlike the USP, support for Air Pacific did not go far enough as other Pacific states relinquished their shareholding to establish, albeit with mixed results, their own national airlines, leaving Fiji to develop Air Pacific. To overcome the air services problem and to liberalise the aviation market in the Pacific, Cook Islands, Nauru, Samoa, Tonga and Vanuatu signed the Pacific Islands Air Services Agreement (PIASA). The aviation sector however remains vulnerable to global fuel and energy crisis, including financial setbacks.

The establishment of the Forum Fisheries Agency (FFA) in 1979 to support the management of the Pacific region's biggest fisheries resources and maximise the returns on its harvest of fish on a sustainable scale on behalf of Pacific states is considered a success story (Tarte 2006). FAA assists its members negotiate the sale of fishing licenses to countries like Japan, Taiwan, Korea and the United States. It also undertakes monitoring and surveillance programs against illegal fishing and works closely with the SPC on scientific programs and with the Pacific Islands Forum Secretariat on trade and investment matters.

Technical assistance on environmental management and climate change is provided by the South Pacific Regional Environmental Programme (SPREP) which was established in 1973. Geoscience matters covering mineral exploration, petroleum, water management and community natural disaster and risk management is provided by the South Pacific Applied Geoscience Commission (SOPAC), established in 1972. Under the current RIF process, some of the work of SOPAC will merge with the SPC and the SPREP.

In terms of investment development several service delivery vehicles offer that support. In harnessing the tourism potential of the region, the South Pacific Tourism Organisation now renamed as 'south-pacific.travel' was established to promote and market the potential of the Pacific as a tourist destination. In 2007, the Pacific Islands Private Sector Organisation (PIPSO) was created to support private sector organisations in the region. The Oceania Customs Organisations (OCO) based in Suva, Fiji offers support to Pacific states to help monitor and audit imports as well as the movement of goods, including contrabands and to maximise the returns in revenue for governments as well as to protect national consumers.

Other regional organisations that provide technical and advisory support on security related matters include the Pacific Islands Police Conference based in Wellington, New Zealand, the Transnational Crime Unit and the Pacific Immigration Directors Conference. New challenges which have harnessed a collective regional voice in the international fora include climate change and related environmental issues as well as the global financial crisis which not only test the vulnerability of small islands in the region but also the ability of regional organisations to response to these challenges.

In response to the global energy crisis, and in response to the Leaders' directive, increasing effort is being made to draw more Pacific Islands countries to sign onto the Forum's regional initiative on bulk petroleum procurement. So far, only Nauru, Tuvalu and the Cook Islands signed. Other Forum countries are expected to sign up after consulting their governments. The idea of the bulk purchasing of fuel to save small island states money has been on the agenda of Pacific meetings for years. The global crisis and increasing price of fuel and which forced the Marshall Islands to declare a state of emergency, beckons more Pacific Islands to seriously consider the Agreement. The bulk procurement project essentially promotes the idea of a single market and economy in the Pacific - towards the creation of a single Pacific market where this is seen as a potentially important strategic response to overcome the issues of market smallness and isolation needs to be considered thoroughly given it benefits for the region. Its main rationale in response to the recent crisis in the petroleum market in the Pacific should expand into other possibilities through the strength presented by a single market. The possibilities for developing a coordinated regional strategy or package for the Pacific region in readiness for the impact of the global financial crisis therefore should not be undervalued. Certainly, the potential of the Pacific's regional architecture to respond to critical regional and global crisis remains to be fully realiased, including the opportunities available through multilateral arrangements.

Political and Security Responses

Forum Leaders in the opening section of the vision statement of the Pacific Plan 'believe that the Pacific can, should and will be a region of peace, harmony, security and economic prosperity, so that all of its people can lead free and worthwhile lives'. Except for the separatist rebellion in Santo, Vanuatu, the region enjoyed a relatively quiet and peaceful transition to Independence. In recent years, however, the demise of parliamentary democracy and the rule of law in Fiji which has experienced four military coups in under 30 years, the 10-year long civil conflict on the island of Bougainville in Papua New Guinea in the late 1980s to the early 1990s, the political and ethnic tensions in the Solomon Islands in the early 2000s and the riots in Tonga in 2006, reminds the region of the costs of internal threats to the welfare of the people and governance.

The Biketawa Declaration

Noting the important need to play a role, a regional mechanism – the Biketawa Declaration – was endorsed by Leaders in 2000. The Declaration is essentially a guiding tool which seeks to develop a collective and coordinated regional response to national conflicts and crisis in the region but which at the same time recognises the principle of non-interference in the domestic affairs of its members. The Declaration was invoked in 2003 where a police-led operation restored law and order, supported by regional peacekeepers, and a programme of assistance strengthened the justice system, restored the economy and basic services in the Solomon Islands. The intervention now known as the Regional Assistance Mission to the Solomon Islands (RAMSI) received the full support and endorsement of the Solomon Islands and all Forum members. This was a significant milestone for the Forum in regional cooperation.

The Biketawa Declaration was again invoked in 2004 on Nauru's request in response to the economic crisis and the threats posed to its national security and stability. Both scenarios were different. For the Solomon Islands, it involved the restoration of law and order, economic recovery, governance rehabilitation with recovery projected to be achieved in the long-term. It also includes a rebuilding of trust, setting aside and reconciling differences and re-forging relationships between different communities and amongst the different ethnic groups. As has been witnessed from other conflicts, in Bougainville and more recently, riots in

Tonga, the wound and scars of internal conflicts need the benefit of time to heal. For Nauru, however, the problem was financial and economic mismanagement needing a long-term task of rebuilding and reforming its economy. The spirit of cooperation, consultations and partnership between RAMSI and the Solomon Islands has matured over the years leading to the conclusion of the Solomon Islands Government – RAMSI Partnership Framework in 2009. It has also attracted the interest from other governments to be part of the regional effort. The success of the Pacific Regional Assistance to Nauru (PRAN) and the effort of the Nauru government has restored Nauru on a path to sustainable economic recovery and development. PRAN ended in 2009 although ongoing economic, social, infrastructure, and development challenges continue to receive the commitment of support from Forum members of its reform agenda.

The situation in Fiji however has presented the Biketawa Declaration with yet another test of its versatility and ability. Given recent comments that the Biketawa Declaration has failed with regard to Fiji, and is therefore ineffective and should be abandoned, it is imperative to shed light on the regional effort on Fiji, at least from the Forum's perspective. At the request of Fiji, several consultative mechanisms were established to try and resolve the impasse between the Government and the military since 2007. These mechanisms included an Eminent Persons Group which reported to the Forum Foreign Affairs Ministers meeting in Port Vila, Vanuatu in 2007 and later in Auckland in 2008, the Ministerial Contact Group, and the dialogue process between Fiji and other Forum members through the Forum-Fiji Joint Working Group; and a Special Forum Leaders' Meeting in Port Moresby, Papua New Guinea in 2009. The Fiji-Forum Joint Working Group under the Chair of Papua New Guinea, and comprising senior officials from Australia, Micronesia, Fiji, Kiribati, Nauru, New Zealand, Marshall Islands and Tuvalu, held a total of 35 meetings between 2007 and early 2009. Aside from discussing the standing issues such as the restoration of civilian rule, upholding the 1997 Constitution, and the cessation of human rights abuses, the Fiji-Forum Joint Working Group had oversight over the report of the independent technical assessment of an election timetable for Fiji and of the coordination of donor assistance for the census and election process. Reporting to the Eminent Persons Group, the Ministerial Contact Group, the Forum Foreign Ministers through to Forum Leaders, this Fiji-Forum Joint Working Group maintained the "bridge" with Fiji and kept discussions alive and active for a return to parliamentary democracy. Essentially, an uncooperative and less politically discerning leadership remain a major barrier to early restoration of parliamentary democracy for Fiji, and thus deny the potential for conflict resolution in the Biketawa Declaration.[4]

---

4   The independent technical assessment report of an election timetable for Fiji found that from a technical point of view, a parliamentary election was feasible in the first quarter of 2009, or earlier in November 2008.

On 1 May 2009 Fiji was suspended from the Forum. Fiji briefly returned to re-engage with Forum members through the Forum-Fiji Joint Working Group but this has since fallen through although not officially abandoned. Seeking to remain engaged with Fiji on an ongoing basis has been of paramount importance to the Forum and the Biketawa Declaration. Essentially, it was the state of crisis in Fiji and the Solomon Islands in 2000, which led the Forum to adopt the Biketawa Declaration, mainly because the Forum needed a mechanism to deal with such a crisis, and more importantly, there was a political consensus in the region to create one. The Declaration also saw a clear shift in the region's attitude to serious crises in the region, compared to its response to the 1987 coups in Fiji. The Declaration contains guiding principles and provides measures for a regional response to help a Forum member, which is in need of urgent assistance. The Declaration should also be seen in the spirit of regionalism as promoted by the Pacific Plan but also mindful of and sensitive to sovereignty. Engagement through diplomacy underpins the Biketawa Declaration to build the bridges through ongoing dialogue – irrespective of time.

It is therefore perhaps presumptuous to view the Biketawa Declaration to be endowed with the versatility and utility of application to all manner of conflict and crisis across the region. Further, it is also erroneous to visualise the Biketawa Declaration as having an unlimited reservoir of magical powers to resolve, to provide answers to and to fix (including offering successful regional responses) every national conflict and crisis. Such an observation is over-simplistic and reflects a poor understanding, as well as disregard and appreciation for the complex socio-political, socio-cultural and socio-economic environment from which the conflicts and crisis arise. To write-off and to discard the Biketawa Declaration because it is has been unable to assist Fiji through the challenges that it has encountered is both short-sighted and foolish. It is short-sighted because denies other Forum member states the opportunity to draw on members' collective resources during their times of strife. It is foolish because its absence does not afford others in the region a mechanism for a collective regional response to problems. Rather, the Biketawa Declaration is only a mechanism, a guiding tool now available to the region with the capability to provide a collective regional response to crisis. It would however be more constructive to assess the strengths and limitations of the Biketawa Declaration and to suggest ways it could be made to be more effective. However out of three situations of crisis that the Biketawa Declaration was invoked; two have been constructive. One perhaps is complicated.

Regional Integration and Cooperation: Regionalism

The decision of Forum Leaders in 2004 to strengthen regional cooperation and integration and endorsed in 2005 through the Pacific Plan for Strengthening Regional Cooperation and Integration is an ambitious undertaking on regionalism in the region. The Plan which has a general timeframe of 10 years seeks to enhance and stimulate economic growth, sustainable development, good governance and security, by attempting to channel the development effort all regional organisations, donors and development partners through a single plan.

The Pacific Plan Action Committee (PPAC) has oversight over the implementation of the Pacific Plan. In recent years, the decision-making process has been streamlined to bring CROP into the PPAC process to provide regional direction and collectively implement the decisions of Leaders. Key regional ministerial meetings comprising of relevant ministers from the Forum countries that deal with regional matters beyond the Pacific Plan and which also feed into the annual Forum Leaders' meetings and which also implement Forum decisions include the Forum Economic Ministers Meetings[5] and the Forum Trade Ministers Meetings. The Forum Foreign Ministers Meeting is activated to deal with crisis issues under the Biketawa Declaration with educational matters handled by the Forum Education Ministers.

Strengthening regional cooperation and integration in the Pacific as it is proposed by Forum Leaders involves exploring three concepts of regionalism. The first is about cooperation and how this is allowed to happen. It involves setting up the process for dialogue and processes between governments. The second is provision of good and services at the regional level. This is about freeing governments from managing some service because it is economically advantageous to pool resources and expertise, and minimise wastage, reduce costs of services but increase the coverage of beneficiaries. Where diseconomies of isolation significantly affect logistical issues in service delivery, one solution would be to deliver the service through a sub-regional or a grouping of a few countries. If it added value to the national effort, even better! And where resource constraints are always going to be problem, consideration in favour for regionalism is sensible.

---

5   Endorsed by the Forum in 1999 as integral to supporting national economic development strategies, FEMM advises the Forum on issues of economic management and development, structural adjustment, identifies sectoral opportunities for region-wide approach to development. Ad hoc Forum ministerial meetings such as trade, aviation and communication were sanctioned by FEMM.

Regionalism is not about replacing or taking over national policies and programs. Rather, it seeks to support and complement them. For example, management of services under a regional initiative may be moved to a regional mechanism but not policy-making. This may seem contradictory, as many regional initiatives pool services into a regional body, away from the oversight of national governments. Sovereignty is enhanced as national governments have regional bodies implement their policy decisions (in effect, as service providers). Shifting service provision to regional mechanisms allows national governments to utilise national resources on core activities and priorities, thereby conserving resources on services that could otherwise be provided regionally.

The third is regional integration. This is about reducing market barriers. Physical barriers include land and sea borders and technical barriers include quarantine protocols, import taxes, immigration and border control. The general benefits include improved access to business and to consumers, increased economies of scale, competitive and affordable prices and increased choice of good and service. The examples of regionalism outlined above are currently being delivered by the regional governance architecture. It is already happening in the Pacific. In general, the existing regional governance infrastructure appears to support approaches that overcome capacity limitations in service delivery at the national level, and approaches that increase and expand economic opportunities through market integration.

For example, where Pacific states have existing ombudsman offices, the regional initiative is expected to add value to the work of the national ombudsman. It is not about replacing a national ombudsman with a regional ombudsman. Similarly, where audit services are under stress, a regional support mechanism would complement the national effort. Both ombudsman and audit initiatives are already providing support to the national effort. It is about mechanisms that also support and complement the national effort. In essence, a regional approach would be worthy of consideration where it strengthened, built and enhanced work at the national level.

Conclusions: What Do These Experiences Tell Us About the Prospects and Promise for Regionalism?

This paper is an attempt at putting together a large regional jigsaw puzzle that exists under the banner of regional integration and cooperation into manageable headings and perspectives. Obviously, if the question were posed to different stakeholders it would generate different perspectives given its complexity.

Certainly, the recipients or those for whom regionalism is intended such as the governments of the Pacific Islands and the people to whom initiatives and activities at the regional level are targeted, may paint a different picture.

However, the present regional governance architecture could be viewed as the building blocks upon which the experiences that are gained, the challenges that are confronted and tackled, the human and institutional capacity that is built and the knowledge that is acquired are laid. Such a foundation may later lead to a more ideal regionalism which some observers and commentators of regionalism want the Pacific to achieve; that is free movement of people, goods and services, common currency, shared economic policy, and a more coherent polity.

The current experiences however seem to suggest a region working its own regional governance architecture, perhaps sometimes in isolation from each other but somehow connected, that is nonetheless relevant to its perceived needs. The Pacific Plan, while ambitious in timeframe and purpose, does attempt to harmonise regional effort under the ownership of one umbrella. It seems to caution against imitating or copying other models from elsewhere, including the leap forward to what the Plan aspires. Several possible explanations have been put forward with respect to the model's limitations (Fong Toy 2006). One explanation is that the current forms and levels of regional cooperation are not really ready for the challenge of regionalism. Another is that the fundamental shift in thinking and approach to regionalism needs to be made. Yet another thought is an inability to really visualise the true enormity of regionalism – that is, the vision of Forum Leaders versus the ability of the officials to grapple with it. In response to regional and global challenges, the region is working within its current arrangements to service its people. Whatever the shortcomings, at least all of these regional governance infrastructures are well-founded and hold the potential to help the Pacific find its own authentic model.

The region does not need to look for a better and wholesome articulation of the vision for the Pacific. It was endorsed in 2005 in Papua New Guinea when the Pacific Plan was launched. The Pacific leadership which initiated the development and establishment of some of the political and economic institutions to promote both sub-regionalism and regionalism, is not short of potential to drive better regionalism.

Nonetheless, the experience from the region seems to suggest that delivery of services by service delivery organisations such as tertiary education, fisheries, and crisis interventions (such as RAMSI) appear to have greater credibility compared to areas of regional economic integration which seem to pit Pacific states against each other. Effort needs to be focused on arrangements that harness the diversity of the region in union.

References

Fong Toy, A. 2006. 'The Pacific Islands Forum and Regional Cooperation', in J. Bryant-Tokalau and I. Frazer (eds). *Redefining the Pacific? Regionalism Past, Present and Future*. Aldershot: Ashgate: 33-42.

Bryant-Tokalau, J., and Frazer, I. 2006. (eds). *Redefining the Pacific? Regionalism Past, Present and Future*. Aldershot: Ashgate.

Dearden, S.J.H. 2008. 'The Interim Pacific Economic Partnership Agreement'. European Development Policy Study Group Discussion Paper (DP36). Available at http://edpsg.org/Documents/DP36.doc

Freitag, S. 2006. 'Vision or Friction? Prospects of Regional Integration in the South Pacific'. *Issue Analysis*. 76 (25 October). The Centre for Independent Studies. Available at http://www.cis.org.au/images/stories/issue-analysis/ia76.pdf

Fry, G. 2005. "Pacific Integration and regional governance. 'Pooled regional governance' in the island Pacific? Lessons from history". *Pacific Economic Bulletin*. 20(3): 111-119.

Graham, K. (ed.). 2008. *Models for regional governance for the Pacific*. Canterbury University Press: Christchurch.

Pacific Islands Forum Secretariat. 2005. *The Pacific Plan for strengthening Regional Cooperation and Integration*. Suva: Pacific Islands Forum Secretariat.

Pacific Islands Forum Secretariat. 2005. *Thirty-sixth Pacific Islands Forum Communiqué*. Papua New Guinea, 25-27 October 2005. Suva: Pacific Islands Forum Secretariat.

Spillane, S. 2008. 'The Pacific Plan 2006-15: Legal Implications for regionalism', in K. Graham (ed.). *Models of Regional Governance for the Pacific*. Canterbury University Press: Christchurch: 72-82.

Tarte, S. 2006. 'Managing Tuna Fisheries in the Pacific: A Regional Success Story?', in J. Bryant-Tokalau and I. Frazer (eds), *Redefining the Pacific? Regionalism Past, Present and Future*. Aldershot: Ashgate: 89-100.

15. How Relevant are European Models of Government to Pacific Island States?

Jon Fraenkel

Les modèles européens de gouvernance sont-ils pertinents pour les Etats du Pacifique insulaire?

Dans tout le Pacifique insulaire, des modèles de gouvernance originaires d'autres parties du monde sont souvent présentés comme des solutions aux problèmes locaux, que la situation problématique soit réelle ou simplement perçue comme telle. Cependant, les enjeux autour de la construction de l'Etat ou de la nation ne sont plus, au 21e siècle, les mêmes que ceux posés aux 19e et 20e siècles. Si les modèles européens eurent une grande influence durant l'époque coloniale, leur héritage post-colonial fut mitigé: l'influence continua d'être forte pour le législatif et la gouvernance, mais la variation dans les adaptations fut plus grande que ce qu'on imagine souvent. Maintenant que les Etats insulaires abordent leur troisième, quatrième ou parfois cinquième décennie dans leur indépendance, l'influence des modèles européens s'est encore dissipée davantage, et de nouvelles influences sont apparues. Des modèles de gouvernance venus d'ailleurs et des institutions importées-- quand les circonstances sont inhabituelles-- ont joué un rôle significatif et positif, parfois de manière imprévue. Mais ceux qui appellent à ces changements feraient bien de ne pas se cantonner à de grands principes internationaux et devraient plutôt ancrer leurs arguments dans une prise en compte du contexte local, de façon détaillée et en profondeur.

Around the Pacific Islands region, one often hears models of government from elsewhere extolled as solutions to various perceived or real political problems. Models of institutions back home are frequently carried around in the back of the heads of diplomats, seconded advisors and well-paid consultants from overseas and depicted as solutions to every political difficulty in the Pacific.

I was at a workshop organised by Papua New Guinea's Commission on the Integrity of Political Parties and Candidates a few weeks ago in Gaire, outside Port Moresby. This was aimed at discussing feasible alternatives in the wake of a July 2010 decision ruling unconstitutional a law aimed at tying MPs to particular Prime Ministers and lessening the incidence of 'no confidence' motions. As those of you who know the country well will be aware, the parliament has been plagued by incessant 'no confidence' votes, long adjournments to avoid challenges to incumbent governments and usages of cash and ministerial portfolio handouts to hold together fragile coalitions. At that meeting, a UNDP representative insisted that a European (or Latin American)-style list proportional representation system would resolve all these difficulties of party loyalty, despite much contrary evidence. Despite the efforts of many with years of experience in the many twists and turns of Papua New Guinea politics, no one could convince her that these problems would not be resolved simply by tweaking the electoral rules.

It is an all-too frequent kind of error: both in analysis and recommendation. One often hears Pacific chiefly systems described as 'feudal' drawing on the European historical experience, for example, without much attention to studying forms of tribute or labour service if these exist at all (and they usually don't). At embassy or high commission garden parties, you regularly hear European, Australian or American history drawn upon to explain how islands should travel on the rocky road towards democracy. Interesting – perhaps sometimes, but usually misleading as regards the kind of issues faced by small island polities in the 21st century.

This is certainly not an exclusively European penchant. More unofficially than officially, Australians in the Pacific regularly emphasise the virtues of preferential voting systems (as used both for federal and state level governments), and that regional influence has obviously been important in the adoption of such systems both in Fiji and Papua New Guinea. A few years ago, as Fiji wrestled with the problems of handling *mandatory* power-sharing between highly polarised political adversaries, I recall New Zealand advisors emphasising their own unique qualifications in handling coalition governments (heedless of the massive differences between voluntary and mandatory power-sharing).

On Europe day over the last decade around the islands, diplomats frequently point to the Treaty of Rome and the European Union as a viable model for Pacific regionalism. Yet the 'German question" that loomed so large in late 19th and early 20th century European history, and so influenced the initial steps towards European unification, has no meaningful or likely parallel in the Pacific Islands. The Pacific Islands are, for the most part, separated by vast sea areas, and do not have a history of states forged through warfare that closely resembles the European experience. The recent spat between Tonga and Fiji over the Minerva Reef hardly resembles the controversies over Alsace-Lorraine in the 1870s or the 1937-8 German Sudetenland. The gains from trade and capital flows witnessed by a Europe without borders are scarcely likely to be replicated in Oceania, where island countries have little to trade with each other and little capital to export.

If European regionalism provides an intriguing model of government, it would surely rather be inclusive of Australia and New Zealand, which dominate so much of the trade at least to the South Pacific island countries. For here one might consider how European regionalism tied together stronger and weaker economies: Germany and northern Europe together with historically weaker economies like Ireland, Portugal and parts of the Southern Mediterranean. The cost of such arrangements, including permitting access for labour to Australasia, would probably be far less than that incurred by the stronger economies of northern Europe. After all, there is little likelihood that a bankrupt Tonga or Tuvalu (should that arise) will put as much pressure on the vitality of the financial system as Greece, Ireland or Portugal do on that of contemporary Europe.

Warning against unthinking transplantations, of course, is not an argument against all comparisons, or useful lessons drawn from different parts of the world. It is only to counsel against poorly thought-through recommendations, disregarding the vast differences between European, North American and Pacific settings. Even within the region, partly due to the experience of Christianisation, there is often a perception that Pacific peoples are fated to tread a similar path to Europeans, North Americans or Australasians. Amongst Europeans deployed on brief employment contracts in the Pacific Islands, there is an understandable urge to reach for the familiar, the known and the proven workable.

In universities, also, states in other parts of the world are often understood through the European lens, or measured by their correspondence to European perceptions of what constitutes an effective or viable state. They are defined as something *other* than European states. They are not Westphalian states. They are not Max Weber's 'rational-legal bureaucratic' states. They are not states like those European institutions splendidly studied by Charles Tilly (1990), where war built revenues and peace built institutions of accountability and democracy, though such tax-raising states regularly figure in the donor literature as a suitable model for elsewhere. Jeffrey Herbst's excellent study of the way the African experience of warfare and state-building differs from that in Europe provides a useful example of the kind of theorising about the state that might be attempted for the Pacific Islands (Herbst 2000).

Perhaps one way to address the question of the relevance of European models of governance in the present or future tense is to first consider their relevance in the past. In this paper, I focus mainly on the South Pacific, where the principle colonial influences were European, or by extension, Australasian, whereas in the northern Pacific the key influences (eventually) became American.

European models of government have influenced the past and still influence the present of many Pacific Island states. Most obviously, the French territories of New Caledonia, French Polynesia and Wallis and Futuna not only have Francophone systems of law, but still participate in elections to the National Assembly in Paris and for the French President. In some cases, departures from French influences have proved critical for political settlements. For example, New Caledonia's Noumea Accord entailed such a breach with French legal doctrine that it required a constitutional amendment and a referendum in France.

While the former British territories are all de-colonised (bar tiny Pitcairn Island), the English system of common law remains in operation in varying ways in the former colonies. Westminster systems were left in both in former British territories, and in countries where the colonial power had been Australia or New Zealand – although often with more consultation about the shape of post-colonial arrangements than is commonly recognised by those who critique the 'imposition' of Westminster on island territories. In Solomon Islands, for example, the British experimented with a 'Governing Council' system alleged to be more suitable for a 'Melanesian' context, but it was ambitious politician Solomon Mamaloni that urged adoption of a full-scale Westminster system with a 'Prime Minister' and 'cabinet', a Leader of the Opposition and, curiously, even a 'leader' of the independent members of parliament. In Papua New Guinea and Kiribati too, there was more local-level discussion about the modification of inherited institutions than is commonly realised. Too much is often blamed on the 'Westminster' legacy by Pacific commentators, partly due to rosy-eyed claims about a propensity to consensus inherent in Pacific cultures.

In the New Hebrides (Vanuatu), the electoral system adopted at independence – the single non-transferable vote – was a compromise between the British and French authorities designed to ensure that the Anglophone majority did not win all the seats in parliament. That system exists nowhere in Europe, but today only for the lower house in Afghanistan (having been dropped in Japan, Taiwan, South Korea and, recently, Jordan). The electoral system of Nauru also has no parallels to anything currently in use in Europe, but resembles the system invented by French 19th century mathematician Jean Charles De Borda. It is a preferential system, but with a second preference counted as worth 0.5, a third as 0.33 and so on, and all preferences immediately tallied to get a result. Known in Nauru as the Dowdell system, it is in fact named after the Irishman in government at independence who devised it. In Kiribati (the former British Gilbert Islands), a unique presidential system was adopted at independence that bears no resemblance to anything elsewhere in the world (let alone Europe). The President is directly elected, but constrained to form a cabinet from within parliament. The nominees for a presidential election are decided by parliament, and, particularly unusually, the President can be ousted by a parliamentary 'no confidence' vote, but in such cases there is an immediate dissolution of parliament. Designed to ensure presidential support in parliament, the system has worked reasonably well since independence (as compared to neighbouring Tuvalu and Nauru, which have both experienced numerous no confidence votes and regular changes of government).

Going back further, the Pacific Islands can count some very odd experiences with European models of government. It was Pope Leo XIII in Rome who was called upon to deliberate on the division of Micronesia in 1885 between Spain and Germany. Tonga's monarchy has commonly been described as an 'absolutist' system typifying an extremely hierarchical variant of the Polynesian chiefly system. In fact, it was an adaptation to European styles of monarchic rule codified in the 1875 constitution in an effort to resist the influence of European colonisers. Samoa found itself under a tripartite 'condominium' or 'Tridominium' in 1889, run together by the United States, Germany and Britain, but with key appointments made, rather bizarrely, by the King of Sweden. The New Hebrides (Vanuatu) also found itself with a European 'Condominium' (agreed as part of the Anglo-French *entente cordiale* in 1906) – an arrangement much later famously described rather as rather more 'pandemonium' than 'condominium' by Vanuatu's first post-independence Prime Minister Walter Lini.

Of course, the models of government suitable for Pacific colonists were not at all those favoured, or conceded, back at home. Usually, there was initially no elected representation. In Fiji, for example, for the first 25 years of colonial rule Governor Sir Arthur Gordon and his successors ran the show, though with a native administration – a state within a state – sometimes described as a precursor to Lord Lugard's 'indirect rule' arrangements in Nigeria. Only in the early years of the 20th century were local Europeans and Fijians granted nominees on the Legislative Council. Only in 1929 were the descendants of Indian indentured labourers granted elected representation, and then only on communal rolls regarded as symptomatic of colonial oppression by Mahatma Ghandi and many amongst the Fiji Indian leaders. Ethnic Fijians did not get the vote until 1963, and by then stark divisions as regards what could be expected from constitutional democracy were well-ingrained. In Solomon Islands, it was only after the Maasina Ruru uprising of the 1940s that the British colonists experimented with local-level governments. It was in the French territories – New Caledonia and French Polynesia – that extension of the franchise and territorial assembles emerged first, and with these political parties. In the British territories, democracy – after a fashion – emerged only very late in the colonial era, and even then at first under a continuing official majority.

That said, the forms of colonial rule witnessed in the Pacific Islands, if we exclude the early Spanish adventures, were very different to those that would have been experienced if the Pacific had been carved up in the 17th or 18th centuries. By the second half of the 19th century, colonial adventures were characterised by what Jane Samson (1998) calls 'imperial benevolence'. Fiji's colonisation in 1874 was partly triggered by the activities of unruly white settlers in Levuka, and also by the desire to control the trade in indentured labourers that had reached the New Hebrides, Solomon Islands and even island New Guinea. Oddly, both British rule in Fiji and German rule in Samoa entailed a 'protectionist' apparatus that restricted employment on plantations and sought to control, minimise or abolish alienation of native lands. Tonga's monarchic system survived despite a very loose form of colonial control, while the monarchies in Hawaii and Tahiti (if monarchy that can be called) were abolished – the former as a result of the Pacific's first coup d'état by American settlers in 1893. In most of the British territories, the most cost-effective forms of colonial government were thought to allow the continuation of local forms of government (where possible), even if – to raise money – much *de facto* control was conceded to big companies like the CSR, Lever Brothers, Carpenters, and Burns Philp among others.

For much of the Pacific, the colonial influence remained small for the first half century or so. The location of colonial capitals on small offshore islands, like Tulagi in Solomon Islands, Jaluit in the German Marshall Islands or Ovalau (Levuka) in Fiji was testimony to restricted influence on the larger and more populous islands. There was a problem of control. Most Pacific islanders, particularly in Melanesia, continued to reside in rural areas with little or no contact with threadbare colonial administrations, which were required to finance their own operations (there was usually no 'aid' and where there were loans these had to be raised on the private money markets). The Edwardian era was a brief golden age for the colonial plantation economies, boosted by rising world prices and still favourable possibilities for importing indentured labour from India, China or Java, but by 1914 the world was plunged into a new era of economic uncertainty. Indentured labourers were no longer recruited from India for Fiji after 1916, and the troubled recruitment of Chinese for Samoan plantations had also halted. The global depression in commodity prices of the 1920s was reinforced by a broader collapse in the World economy during 1929-32, although the forms of protection adopted in response paradoxically assisted Fiji's sugar industry while the approach of war fuelled demand for New Caledonian nickel.

The Pacific War, when it came, was not only a final nail in the coffin of the European-owned plantation system, but also damaged the political authority of European colonialism. Americans in unprecedented numbers – far greater than the pre-war number of European colonists – spread across that thick Oceanic line of resistance to the Japanese advance connecting Hawaii to Australia. They paid higher wages, and brought numerous new influences. With the end of that war, forms of quasi-'colonial' rule also changed, with the advent of United Nations Trust territories in Micronesia (and building on the earlier arrangements under the League of Nations for Western Samoa, Nauru and New Guinea). That notion of trusteeship, and administration oriented towards development and eventual independence, further undermined the moral certainties of the colonial era.

Western Samoa was the first to de-colonise in 1962, and when it did so it adopted arrangements very different to those of its 'trustee' power, New Zealand. Only *matai* (chiefs or family heads) could vote or stand for parliament, an arrangement much criticised by some, but recognised by a visiting U.N. team as 'democracy in two stages', i.e., accommodating traditional methods of leadership selection through the *matai*-only franchise. That arrangement was partially changed in 1991, when the franchise was opened to all citizens, although it remains the case that candidates must be *matai*. Those who criticise that system as 'undemocratic' are often unaware that there were already 35,000 *matai* titles in the early 1990s (according to the records at the Land and Titles office), and there will be many more now. Far from being a tradition-bound government, Samoa is probably one of the most reform-oriented countries in the world – few states could change what side of the road their cars drive on and shift the dateline eastwards so as to enter the same time-zone as its major trading partners. By most measures, Samoa probably has the most robust of the island governments – with a single party in office for nearly 30 years (with one brief exception) and is carefully (and healthily) resistant to the imposition of outside models.

For Fiji, which became independent in 1970, the new arrangements bore the colonial imprint. There was a British-style Westminster parliamentary system, together with an upper house (called the Senate) and a first-past-the-post electoral system, but there were also communal electoral rolls that separated 'Fijians', 'Indians' and 'general' voters, and the Great Council of Chiefs played an important role with regard to Senate selection. The dangers inherent in that deeply divided polity, and in those choices of institutional arrangements, were already evident before independence, and were highlighted again by the Street Commission report of 1975, which recommended the abolition of communal rolls and introduction of a system of proportional representation. A constitutional crisis in April 1977, and coups in 1987 and 2000, in each case followed the election of governments largely drawing on the votes of the Fiji Indian population (slightly larger than the indigenous Fijian population from 1944-1987). The extraordinary political settlement reached in 1997 between ethnic Fijian and Fiji Indian political leaders did not survive the pressures generated by the first election under the new arrangements in 1999 (when the country elected its first ever Prime Minister of Indian descent, Mahendra Chaudhry). The coup of 2000 unleashed a new set of destabilising forces, with the military seizing power yet again in December 2006 but this time promising a 'coup to end all coups' in the name of multi-racialism, good governance and anti-corruption. Four and a half years later, military rule remains in place, but the promises of 2006-7 have been thoroughly breached.

None of the other Pacific countries was faced with the problem of designing political institutions capable of withstanding deep bipolar divisions like those in Fiji with the partial exception of New Caledonia. There the division between pro- and anti-independentists brought the territory to the brink of civil warfare in the mid-1980s, although ethnicity was never as coterminous with political party affiliation in the way that it was in Fiji. The 1988 Matignon and 1998 Noumea Accords, agreed between leaders of the largely Kanak-backed FLNKS and the largely (but not exclusively) settler backed RPCR entailed in the latter case (i) regional autonomy, (ii) power-sharing (or 'collegial') cabinet and (iii) an agreement to put off the vote on independence until 2014-19. As previously mentioned, much about the Noumea Accord entailed a departure from constitutional arrangements long deemed sacrosanct in France. As the deadline approaches, many are fearful of resorting to a polarising vote on independence. Others are canvassing further shifts in once unshakeable Gaullist doctrines for the French overseas territories, and considering the possibility of 'free association' arrangements such as those between New Zealand and Niue and the Cook Islands, or between the USA and the Republic of the Marshall Islands, Federated States of Micronesia and Palau.

Resolving secessionist disputes by agreement on a delayed vote on independence was also a critical element of the arrangements reached to bring to an end a decade of low intensity civil warfare on the island of Bougainville. [The only other country in the world to have agreed such arrangements is Sudan, now about to reach the point of separation]. In Bougainville, now an autonomous region of Papua New Guinea, a unique presidential system was adopted, with many constraints on cabinet formation designed to accommodate the demands of women, former militants and the different regions. A vote on independence is due between 2015-20, but with nothing resembling the buckets of French aid that have poured into largely Kanak areas in the northern and Loyalty Islands provinces of New Caledonia. Continuing trouble in the south of Bougainville, and the weak revenue stream of the government still located in the north, have encouraged politicians to consider re-opening the large Panguna copper mine.

New Caledonia's mandatory power-sharing arrangements have so far proved much more successful than similar arrangements in Fiji. In New Caledonia, a 'collegial' executive bringing together pro-independence and loyalist parties has been formed after elections in 1999, 2004 and 2009, although breakdowns have been frequent recently. Fiji's arrangements, which were poorly grafted at the last moment onto a Westminster-based 1997 constitution, proved much less successful. The first government elected under those rules in 1999 successfully excluded the largest ethnic Fijian party (measured by share of the vote), while the second government elected in 2001 excluded the largest Indian backed party from cabinet (and consequently was judged to be in breach of the constitution).

When a government was finally forged that obeyed the power-sharing rules in May 2006, it was overthrown only seven months later by a military coup. Fiji's arrangements were heavily influenced by the experience in South Africa during the transition from Apartheid. Power-sharing arrangements for deeply divided polities (including South Africa) have been heavily canvassed by University of California political scientist Professor Arend Lijphart (1977): the origins of his 'consociational' model go back to continental European democracies like the Netherlands, Belgium, Switzerland and Austria.

In this chapter I have tried to answer the question of 'how relevant are European models?' largely in the past tense: 'How relevant have European models been?' Almost by definition, European models were highly influential during the colonial era, though Europeans rarely ruled subject peoples as they ruled their own peoples. The post-colonial legacy was mixed; influences were obvious on systems of law and government, but flexibility was greater than often imagined. As the island states enter their third, fourth or fifth decade since independence, that influence has waned further, while other influences have grown. In many ways, the Asian or African history may provide the more useful lessons, even if the Pacific Islands' experience differs markedly also from those regions. Issues of state- and nation-building in the 21st century are not the same as those faced in the 19th or early 20th centuries, not least as the Melanesian experience clearly shows, due to the impact on state formation of large resource-extractive mining or logging interests.

Nowadays, simple transplantations are usually the least successful. Lifting models of government from one part of the world to another is a hazardous exercise: institutions can operate very differently in different contexts. The problems are different, the issues often unfamiliar and the proposed solutions commonly half-baked. Even amongst the European models of government, the variety is extraordinary, and those from one European country are often unfamiliar with forms of government in another.

Nevertheless, a comparative lens is often useful, but only on the basis of a rich understanding of the specific tensions witnessed within the Pacific region. When Tonga, as it did ahead of the first ever elections to a majority popularly elected parliament in November 2010, considers adopting a single transferable vote system, it helps to know something about the operation of that system in Ireland and Northern Ireland and Malta (even if only to reject that option, as the Tongan government –rightly I believe – did). When Papua New Guinea (or for that matter French Polynesia) struggles with floor-crossing and 'no confidence' votes, it helps to know something about how France dealt with those problems in the 1950s when a strong presidential system was adopted, even if a highly majoritarian presidential system would create major problems in a hyperfractionalised and extremely heterogeneous polity like PNG.

This is not to urge some rampant exceptionalism or resistance to foreign models. Fiji's coup leader Frank Bainimarama oddly combines a perverse embrace of western models of 'good governance' in his struggle with Fijian traditionalists and a rejection of imported models of democracy as unsuitable. He urges that ethnic cleavages, weak development and corruption are to be resolved by military dictatorship, though we know from the experience in Africa, Latin America and even parts of Europe that this is false, and that such divisions are better handled by strengthening democratic institutions.

Nor are transplantations always failures. The French law on parity, for example, aimed at increased women's representation but has had a restricted impact on mainland France, where elections to the National Assembly use a single member district system. Transplanted to the Pacific territories of New Caledonia and French Polynesia, it has had a major impact because these use a list proportional representation system for elections to territorial assemblies, and because both have well-established party systems. As a result, both New Caledonia and French Polynesia have close to 50 per cent women's representation, uniquely across the Pacific Islands. The story of how local women's organisations and aspiring female politicians handled these exported changes in law has yet to be fully told.

Both models from elsewhere and imported institutions can thus – in unusual circumstances – play significant and positive roles, sometimes in unexpected ways, but in general those urging such reforms or changes would do wisely to avoid grandstanding on international principle, and instead to base arguments on a deep and rich appreciation of the local contexts.

References

Herbst, J. 2000. *States and Power in Africa: Comparative Lessons in Authority and Control*. Princeton: Princeton University Press.

Lijphart, A. 1977. *Democracy in Plural Societies: a Comparative Exploration*. New Haven: Yale University Press.

Samson, J. 1998. *Imperial Benevolence: Making British Authority in the Pacific Islands*. Honolulu: University of Hawaii Press .

Tilly, C. 1990. *Coercion, Capital, and European States, AD 990-1990*. Cambridge, Mass.: Blackwell.

16. Regional Security and the Major Powers: An Overview

James Bunce

La sécurité régionale et les grandes puissances : vue d'ensemble

Depuis les années 1980, la région du Pacifique Sud a connu un niveau de plus en plus élevé d'instabilité. Cet article présente une vue d'ensemble de l'état actuel de la sécurité régionale dans le Pacifique Sud en examinant le rôle des grandes puissances extérieures dans la promotion de la stabilité à la fois au sein des Etats de la région et en promouvant la sécurité régionale de façon plus large (ou l'inverse, selon le cas). Plutôt que de présenter une vue d'ensemble complète de l'état de la stabilité de la région, l'article examine la crise actuelle à Fidji et le rôle de trois grandes puissances extérieures, à savoir la Chine, l'Australie et les Etats-Unis. Si d'autres grandes puissances extérieures jouent un rôle vraiment important en matière de sécurité régionale dans le Pacifique Sud, cet article met un accent particulier sur la Chine en tant qu'acteur relativement récent et sur l'Australie, dont l'approche vis-à-vis de la région a connu un changement important au cours de ces dernières années. On examinera également le rôle des Etats-Unis, qui se réduit, et l'on conclura sur le fait qu'en dépit de très nombreux exemples d'instabilité interne dans plusieurs Etats du Pacifique Sud, l'état actuel de la sécurité régionale permet quelque espoir.

Introduction

The South Pacific region has experienced an increasing level of instability in the years since the 1980s. This paper provides an overview of the current state of regional security in the South Pacific region. It does so by examining the role of the major external powers in fostering stability both within regional states, and in promoting security in a wider regional sense (or not, as the case may be). It does not seek to present a comprehensive overview of the state of regional stability though – that is significantly beyond the scope of this paper. Instead, this paper will examine the current crisis in the key state of Fiji, and the role of three major external powers; China, Australia and the United States.[1] While

---

1   Editors' Note: For reasons of brevity Dr Bunce's analysis of regional security in the South Pacific has focused on the roles of three of the major powers active in the Oceanic region – China, Australia and the United

other major external powers do play an important role in South Pacific regional security, this paper will place particular emphasis on China, as it is a relatively new regional player; and Australia, which has seen its approach to the region undergo significant change in the last several years. The US's diminishing role will also be examined, as the perceived US withdrawal from the South Pacific deserves some attention.

Before conducting this overview, it is necessary to discuss exactly what regional security is, and what has the potential to both diminish it. This paper will draw on both old and new conceptions of what enhances and diminishes regional security. Furthermore, it is assumed that there is no imminent threat to the territorial integrity or sovereignty of any South Pacific state. In the absence of such a threat, regional security in Oceania has two facets: internal instability and the effects of external actors' activities. The following list presents a checklist of factors that diminish regional security in the South Pacific and is drawn from a checklist devised by David Hegarty (1987), with only minor adjustments. Diminished security results from:

- Increases in threats and use of force
- Major power rivalry
- Alterations in the balance of power
- Internal instability leading to increased influence for external non-state actors or potentially hostile state actors
- The discovery or placement of new strategic assets

To a degree, all of them are either possible, or are currently happening. Concerns about superpower rivalry escalating in the region may seem to have gone with the Cold War, but according to some commentators, major power contests may be returning. China's increasing role in the region has led to some quite alarmist conclusions. Internal stability is another increasingly common factor that diminishes regional security, but this is offset somewhat by the recent Australian and New Zealand tendency to take a more proactive role in assisting the region to maintain stability. There are some issues with the reasoning behind this more proactive role, particularly the linking of failed states and terrorism, but nonetheless the result has largely enhanced regional security. The wider

States. It is important to note that both France and New Zealand are also significant players with respect to the South Pacific's international and regional security. While France's legitimacy as a Pacific regional power had been contested for decades, that situation changed considerably in the 1990s following the cessation of French nuclear testing in French Polynesia and the settling of the political process in New Caledonia via the Matignon and Noumea Accords of 1988 and 1998 respectively. France is widely accepted as a regional defence and security player being a founding member of the FRANZ Agreement designed largely to assist in natural disaster emergencies in the South Pacific. It is also involved with the ANZUS members in a cooperative framework arrangement on Pacific security and stability issues known as the 'Quadrilateral Defence Forum'. We thank Hélène Goiran for this additional information.

balance of power in the Pacific has been shifting in recent years, and there is potential for major conflict inherent in this shift. As US power declines relative to that of China, there is a possibility it could result in increased major power competition for influence. This is also related to strategic assets in the region, as both China (in terms of strategic resources) and the US (in terms of its Pacific Fleet) have important strategic interests in the region. This paper begins with a discussion of the implications for regional security of the coup regime in Fiji, before moving on to discuss how Australia conceives of (and its role in support of) regional security. It then moves on to examine China's growing role in the region, and its implications for regional security. The paper concludes with a brief discussion of the perceived US withdrawal from the region.

Fiji

Since December 2006 the Republic of Fiji has been under a military government. The details and events that led up to and occurred subsequent to the 6 December coup are dealt with elsewhere in this volume, and need not be discussed here. Suffice to say, the military leader Commodore Frank Bainimarama has exhibited no desire to back down and allow elections. After promising in 2007 to hold elections by March 2009, and when it became clear in early 2009 that no preparations were being made, Bainimarama's reasons for the 'Fijian military intervention' switched from the earlier justifications to fixing Fiji's 'sick electoral process' before any election is held. In January 2009, a leaders' meeting of the Pacific Islands Forum was convened, with Bainimarama sending in his stead interim Attorney-General Aiyaz Sayed-Khaiyum. An ultimatum was issued to Bainimarama's government by the Forum leaders: announce an election to be held before the end of 2009 by 1 May or face suspension from the PIF (Toohey 2009: 11).

In April 2009 a panel of judges found Bainimarama's coup unconstitutional; Bainimarama's response was to sack the judiciary, re-appoint himself prime minister, and abolish the constitution. He further announced that no elections would be held until September 2014 after significant constitutional and electoral reform had been carried out. Since, Fiji has been suspended from both the PIF and the Commonwealth. Currently, the military regime is censoring the local media, and after the arrest and expulsion of the Australian Broadcasting Corporation's Sean Dorney, international reporting of events in Fiji has been minimal. Amnesty International has released a report on human rights in Fiji, which condemns the situation in Fiji, and claims that due to the actions of Bainimarama and President Iloilo, rule of law in Fiji has been effectively undermined (Amnesty International 2009).

While there has been no significant violence, the situation in Fiji is still very serious. One of the largest states in the region, and traditionally one of the most stable, has been under the control of a military government for nearly three years, and it looks as though it will be for another five years yet. This is Fiji's fourth coup in 20 years, and it can be argued that a 'coup culture' seems to be developing. This is a concern for the whole region, as well as Australia, and this concern has been reflected in Fiji's suspension from multilateral institutions like the PIF. Jenny Hayward-Jones painted a pessimistic picture of the direction the economic situation in Fiji could take, arguing that an economic meltdown in Fiji could cause a 'regional meltdown' (Hayward-Jones 2009: 5). Needless to say, this kind of economic turmoil would have dire consequences for regional security.

The implications of the Fiji military regime for regional security go much further than the economic implications. It is significant that no initiative taken by regional or global organisations has had any real effect on the situation in Fiji. As mentioned, Fiji is currently suspended from the PIF and the Commonwealth, and Bainimarama has recently complained to the United Nations that unnamed 'big powers of the South Pacific' have 'used their extensive diplomatic and financial resources to deny Fiji to participate in new peacekeeping operations', which are a very important source of foreign exchange earnings for Fiji (Nicholson 2009: 6).

Furthermore, if the extensive constitutional and electoral reform in Fiji is carried out under a military government, which it looks like it will, future stability in Fiji will be jeopardised. Any such reforms carried out under a military government will have legitimacy issues in the long term, and it sets a precedent that could potentially be followed by future Fijian military leaders: that is, if you do not like the constitution or the electoral system, stage a coup and fix it. This does not herald well for the future state of regional security, if one of the leading states of the region can fall under military control and remain so for nearly a decade. There is very little, if anything, that Australia and other major powers in the region can do about it either – so far no method has proven even partially successful. Fiji is the least aid dependent country in the South Pacific, so withholding aid would not seem to be an effective tool. In any case, China has provided substantial aid to the regime in Fiji since the coup, so even were the economic situation to get worse; there is an alternative source of funding for Bainimarama which places no political conditions on aid recipients. Military intervention is unthinkable – given that the regime is a military one, it is a reasonable assumption that any military intervention would be opposed, and it is impossible to imagine anything being worse for regional security than a war between two or more states in the region. This is not good for the regional security outlook, as it shows that there is very little that outside interests can do to influence the situation in Fiji, which is the least aid-reliant, and the least reliant on outside powers generally, of the South Pacific states.

Australia

In the 2000 Australian Defence White Paper, it states that, after the defence of the Australian continent itself:

> [Australia's] second strategic objective is to help foster the stability, integrity and cohesion of our immediate neighbourhood, which we share with Indonesia, New Zealand, Papua New Guinea, East Timor and the island countries of the Southwest Pacific. (Department of Defence 2000: 30-31)

This statement came one year after the Australian-led intervention in East Timor to stop the violence that resulted after a vote in the former Indonesian province which resulted in almost 80 per cent of East Timorese choosing independence over continued association with Indonesia. This intervention was a significant break from the past in terms of Australian policy. Since this, and the Australian-led RAMSI intervention of 2003, Australia has taken on a much more proactive role in the South Pacific region, and this role does not look like diminishing. This section of the paper will give a brief outline of Australia's involvement in the region since 2006, as well as discussing the 2009 Defence White Paper, Force 2030.

In 2006 Australia made three deployments to neighbouring countries in support of regional security broadly defined. In April, it sent troops and police to boost the ability of RAMSI to deal with riots and unrest in Honiara. Then in late May, troops and police were sent to East Timor to assist in stopping riots, ethnic fighting, as well as a breakdown of law and order. In November, and along with New Zealand, troops and police were sent to Tonga, after pro-democracy protests turned violent. Along with its commitments to the wars in Iraq and Afghanistan, this was the highest operational tempo experienced by the Australian Defence Force (ADF) since the Vietnam War.

Force 2030 expresses the interest Australia holds in regional security in much the same, although much more focused, terms as the 2000 White Paper:

> After ensuring the defence of Australia from direct attack, the second priority task for the ADF is to contribute to security and stability in the South Pacific and East Timor. This involves conducting military operations...providing disaster relief and humanitarian assistance, and on occasion by way of stabilisation interventions...(Department of Defence 2009: 54)

While all Australian Defence White Papers contemplate a degree of engagement, Force 2030 was the first to formalise this as a direct and sophisticated component of the calculation of strategic interests (Beazley interview). Prime Minister Kevin Rudd outlined why this was such an important task for Australia to undertake in 2008. He talked about Australia having a long-term commitment to helping resolve conflict in East Timor and Solomon Islands, as there is a real risk of 'fragile states disrupting stability and prosperity' in the region, not to mention the humanitarian implications. To ignore these kinds of problems 'runs the risk of refugee outflows to neighbouring states', and a 'wide range of economic, diplomatic, and security initiatives' should be put into play to achieve regional security (Rudd 2008).

It must be remembered that the only time Australian territory has been directly threatened by a hostile power was during World War Two, when Australia was (arguably) threatened with invasion by Japan, or at least enforced strategic isolation. During that time, Australian and US military forces defeated Japan in several key battles, which (again arguably) saved Australia from this threat. These battles occurred in the Coral Sea, Papua New Guinea and Solomon Islands, and never on Australian soil. This has left a noticeable mark on the minds of those who study and make strategic and defence policy in Australia, and has meant that the South Pacific occupies a special place in Australian considerations of its own security. A central tenet of this is that other potentially hostile powers must be denied a foothold in South Pacific states – strategic denial. Essentially, strategic denial involves Australia seeking to deny other external players an influential role in key states in the South Pacific region (at least as far as they relate to Australian security interests) – namely Papua New Guinea, Solomon Islands, Fiji and Vanuatu, as well as East Timor. This strategic denial reached its peak in the Cold War period, when fears over Soviet fishing fleet activities in the region verged on hysteria, and there was always a potential South Pacific Cuba lurking, just waiting to provide a springboard for nefarious influences in neighbouring states. Since the terrorist attacks on the World Trade Centre and the Pentagon of 2001, non-state actors have come to dominate this list of potential threats.

One of the central theses driving the new Australian interventionism since the 2003 RAMSI intervention has been what is generally called the Petri dish scenario. This was first developed in a paper authored by Australian academic Elsina Wainwright for the Australian Strategic Policy Institute about the crisis in Solomon Islands (Australian Strategic Policy Institute 2003). This was released shortly before Australian policy towards the crisis in Solomon Islands that simmered between 1998 and 2003 changed from one of non-intervention, to a so-called deep intervention, involving troops, police and public servants. The Petri dish scenario holds that, should instability in Australia's neighbours lead to a situation where rule of law breaks down, and national governments are effectively unable to control their territory, the likely result would be a failed state. These potential failed states could then become a Petri dish, where all sorts of nasty things like transnational criminals and terrorist groups could live and flourish, and pose threats to neighbouring states. Commentators like Kabutaulaka have linked this with the US-led war on terror, which led discussions of security within the US alliance framework to shift from inter- and intra-state conflicts to the threat posed by non-state organisations (Kabutaulaka 2005). The links between the Petri dish thesis and Australian interventionism are also still characterised by the strategy of denial traditionally employed by Australia in its relationship with South Pacific states.

It is important to note that all the interventions carried out by Australia have been at the request of regional government, approved by the main regional multilateral institution (the PIF), and thus have been entirely consensual. That has not prevented some commentators from seeing some overarching design in Australia's activities in the South Pacific. Journalist John Pilger goes as far as to say that Australia is administering a 'hidden empire' that 'stretches from the Aboriginal slums of Sydney to the South Pacific' (Pilger 2008). While this may have been a more reasonable conclusion in the days of the 'deputy sheriff', where Australia was seen to act (and indeed saw itself) as the deputy of the US, events since 2003 have seen the Australian role shift. This paper argues that, in fact, commentators arguing that Australia is implementing some far-reaching plan are far too generous to Australia, and that events are controlling Australian policy, rather than the policy even attempting to control events.

A very important facet of Australian policy towards regional security and capacity building in particular has been the increasingly large role in the various Australian interventions that has been played by the Australian Federal Police (AFP) through its International Deployment Group (IDG). The development of the IDG since its inception in February 2004 has been a valuable and useful policy tool for Australia in its attempts to enhance regional security. Its rationale is 'to provide a formal capacity for the Commonwealth [federal] Government [of Australia] to deploy police offshore with the objective of contributing to regional and international stability and security through the delivery of law enforcement interventions and capacity building programs' (McFarlane 2007: 99). Currently, elements of the IDG are deployed in Solomon Islands, East Timor, Vanuatu, Tonga and Nauru. In Solomon Islands, the IDG personnel forms part of the Participating Police Force, itself a facet of RAMSI, and the focus of their efforts is improving the capacity of the Solomon Islands Police Force. In Vanuatu and Nauru, again the focus is on capacity building within local police forces (Australian Federal Police website). Interestingly, an AFP presence in Papua New Guinea was expelled by the government in May 2004 due to a legal challenge, but it seems that both Australia and Papua New Guinea are working towards establishing a new strategic agreement whereby the AFP could find itself deployed to Papua New Guinea again to strengthen 'the institutional resilience of the Royal Papua New Guinea Constabulary' (Banham 2009).

This role, combining peace operations with capacity building within regional police forces, is important, especially given the way that Australia defines its approach to regional security. As was discussed above, Australia's approach to these issues is defined by two concepts – strategic denial and the Petri dish scenario. Thus its approach to regional security tends to focus on developing strong national states, so that these states can implement the rule of law, thus preventing non-state actors who profit from lawless environments, and rely on them to function effectively and project their activities into neighbouring states, a foothold in the region. What we are seeing from Australia is the development of a three-pronged regional security strategy. The first focuses on military deployments to establish a peaceful environment in which local governments can control their territory. The second builds the capacity of local law enforcement agencies to establish and maintain the rule of law. And the third, as witnessed in the RAMSI intervention, focuses on building other institutions of state, in the hope that instability can be avoided to begin with if regional governments are more effective economic and financial managers. Whether or not the strategy is effective remains to be seen.

The regional security guarantor role that Australia plays does still complement US policies in a wider regional sense, but it also brings significant benefits for regional states. In times of crisis, whether resulting from political instability or natural disaster, regional states can call on Australia to deploy its significant military and humanitarian capabilities to assist. Australia also provides substantial aid to the South Pacific region – it is the largest single donor. In 2008-9, total aid to PIF member states was around A$1 billion, and this is set to increase in 2009-10. It also has the largest number of diplomatic missions in the region. Many Australian businesses hold significant investments in South Pacific countries, particularly in resource development and extraction. The security guarantor role does serve Australian interests primarily, but, while some states in the region may complain about Australia's heavy-handed approach, or its desire to drive political and economic reform in key states like Papua New Guinea, there are no other real alternatives to Australia when it comes to this key security role. There is no other power with the military and economic capabilities to play this role, especially when one considers the relative withdrawal of the United States from the region.

China

In the last several years, the People's Republic of China has been moving towards significantly increasing its role and profile in the South Pacific region. It has shown a genuine interest in the region, in terms of development aid and assistance, commercial engagement, and in the growing ethnic Chinese community in the region. This section of the paper will examine these three areas of growing Chinese influence in the region, and their impact on regional security.

To begin this discussion however, it is necessary to look at China's rise in the wider regional and global contexts, so as to put this discussion into perspective. Since undergoing economic reforms in the 1980s, China has experienced massive economic growth, and a commensurate increase in its national wealth. With this increase in wealth, has also come an increase in international influence, as China seeks to take its place as a responsible stakeholder in the international system. This has involved a normalisation of its international relations, which experienced considerable tension in the period from the Communist Party defeating the Nationalists and proclaiming the People's Republic in 1949, to the late-1970s.

Accompanying this increase in Chinese power has been a debate amongst scholars as to whether a rising China constitutes a threat, or an opportunity. In other words, will China work towards using its power to upset or uphold the current international status quo? Which one it will choose depends on whether China decides that is has more to gain from challenging the United States' military supremacy, or from peaceful coexistence. This has its inverse as well – it also depends on whether the United States decides to accommodate China's rise, or to contest it.

Insofar as the threat/opportunity debate applies to the South Pacific region, there seem to be two contending schools of thought that broadly align with the positions outlined above. One side argues that Chinese engagement in the region provides a valuable development and economic opportunity (Zhang 2007), while the other contends that China's engagement is intended to serve the purpose of both sidelining Taiwan and undermining 'ties between Pacific island nations and regional powers such as the United States, Australia and Japan' (Windybank 2005; see also Henderson and Reilly 2003). Let us now assess these claims, so as to arrive at a conclusion about China's role in the region.

China's aid to some states in the region has been increasing over the last several years, an increase which has received much attention from academics and commentators in both Australia and the United States (see Lunn and Vaughan 2007). In 2006, during a visit to Fiji, Chinese Premier Wen Jiabao told Pacific leaders that China was 'ready to provide assistance without any political strings attached' (Dobell 2007). During this visit, as part of the first China-Pacific Islands Countries Economic Development and Cooperation Forum, Premier Wen announced a new aid package worth US$375 million over three years, mostly in the form of concessional loans. Chinese development assistance is in fact administered by the Ministry of Commerce, and takes two main forms. Firstly there are concessional loans, which are usually used for large infrastructure projects, and are offered with significant interest-free periods and low interest rates. This makes up the majority of the development aid administered over the last several years. Apart from this, China offers debt relief, grants, technical assistance and scholarships. The scale of the aid program is difficult to determine, but Fergus Hanson of the Lowy Institute has produced some excellent data. Firstly though it is important to note that China only offers aid to countries with a One China policy, and thus the states in the region that recognise Taiwan diplomatically cannot access Chinese assistance.

In 2005, Hanson estimates that China's aid program to the 14 Pacific Islands Forum members totalled around $US33 million. He estimated that this increased to $US78 million in 2006, and $US293 million in 2007. The figure for 2007 is somewhat inflated by a $160 million soft loan to Fiji, which is being disbursed over several years and which led to this spike in the figure (Hanson 2008: 11-14). Hanson later revised the estimate for 2007 in light of this, with the revised figure of $100-150 million. Hanson's figure for 2008 is $100 million, and this takes into account disbursements of the loan to Fiji (Hanson 2009: 3). This makes China a significant player in terms of development assistance to the region – again according to Hanson - one of the top three. So it seems that China is well on track to provide the US$375 million it announced in 2006, heralding the arrival of a new, and major, player in South Pacific politics. A large portion of the assistance has gone towards building some major infrastructure items, such as the new Parliament House in Vanuatu, and the Fiji National Stadium in Suva.

Much of this development aid has been aimed directly at reversing diplomatic recognition of Taiwan. This competition has been going on since Taiwan lost its seat in the United Nations in 1971, and takes the form of vying with mainland China for diplomatic recognition by other countries. This is considered to be Taiwan's 'international space' by the government in Taipei, and it has been shrinking since 2000, sharpening the contest. One of the main battlegrounds of this contest has been the South Pacific. Six South Pacific states currently recognise Taiwan: Kiribati, Marshall Islands, Nauru, Palau, Solomon Islands and Tuvalu.

Three brief example of how this contest manifests itself can be found in Kiribati, Tuvalu and Solomon Islands. It was alleged during the 2003 elections in Kiribati that China and Taiwan were bankrolling candidates. Indeed, when the part-ethnic Chinese Anote Tong subsequently won the election, he quickly switched diplomatic recognition to Taiwan, reversing a twenty year One China policy. In nearby Tuvalu, Chinese diplomats claimed that Taiwanese money was behind an August 2003 no-confidence vote in Prime Minister Saufatu Sopoanga, who had apparently flown to Beijing to switch recognition (Skehan 2004). The alleged role of Taiwanese money in the 2006 election in Solomon Islands and the subsequent burning of Chinatown in Honiara is another example of the relationship this diplomatic contest has to regional security, but there is good news. Since the election in Taiwan of President Ma Ying-jeou in March 2008 there has been a diplomatic thaw, and a tacit understanding has developed between Taiwan and China that they would not attempt to encourage Pacific Island countries to change their diplomatic recognition (Callick 2009). Indeed, since Ma's election in May 2008, of twenty-eight nations which recognise Taiwan, not a single one has changed recognition, despite several states in Central America apparently intending to do so. In the absence of this diplomatic competition, it seems more likely that China can play a positive role in fostering regional security, as most instances of instability relating to China and Taiwan's respective aid programs eventuated because of the diplomatic rivalry.

Development assistance is not the only area in which China has significantly increased its role in the South Pacific. Its diplomatic influence is increasing, with some commentators saying that 'it is now accepted routine that the first official overseas visit by a new head of government in the region is made to Beijing, not to Canberra' (Henderson and Reilly 2003: 95). It has been estimated in Australia that China now has the most diplomats in the region as well as substantial economic investments. There are more than 3000 Chinese (both state and private) owned businesses registered, with investments estimated at US\$ 1 billion (yang 2009). Chinese trade with the region has undergone a huge increase – between 2004 and 2005 alone it increased from US\$530 million to \$838 million – and has been largely focused on securing resources needed to drive China's economic boom (Zhang 2007: 370). By 2006 this had increased to US\$1.2 billion (Yang 2009: 3). Alongside this has been an increase in the number of ethnic Chinese living in the South Pacific, and while there are no reliable figures, Ron Crocombe estimates there are some 80,000 (Dobell 2007: 6-7). It is uncertain, however, just how many have arrived recently, and how many have been in the South Pacific for years, if not generations. This is because there has been a Chinese presence in the South Pacific since at least the 1800s, and Chinese traders may have been visiting the region for much longer still.

China has a strong interest in regional security, along with the other major external actors active in the South Pacific. China's significant economic investments rely in internal stability, as the situation with the Ramu nickel mine in Papua New Guinea shows. In May 2009, fights between Papua New Guinean and Chinese workers at the Chinese-owned Ramu nickel refinery sparked riots and looting across Papua New Guinea, and resulted in the shooting of at least four looters, as well as calls by local activists to 'celebrate 2010 New Year with bonfires of all Asian-owned shops all around the country' (Roberts 2009). If China seeks to continue extracting resources necessary to fuel its economic growth from states in the South Pacific region, events such as this must be avoided wherever possible.

However there are important differences between the perspective China holds on regional security and that of other actors like Australia. One difference can be found in China's approach to the coup regime in Fiji. China's interests are not really engaged by events such as this in the way that Australia's interests are. While Australia has a strong interest in stable and democratic governments, China's direct interest in internal stability is primarily engaged by events such as the riots in Papua New Guinea in 2009, rather than by the existence of non-democratic governments. Furthermore, given the scale of China's aid and assistance to Fiji since the coup in 2006, it does not seem that China intends to avoid lending assistance to Bainimarama's regime in the way that the Commonwealth, Australia, New Zealand, the PIF, the European Union and most of the other major regional actors have. Still, according to the Chinese Foreign Ministry, 'China has maintained good coordination with the US, the European Union, Australia, New Zealand and other development partners in the region in safeguarding regional stability... We are willing to work jointly with all relevant parties to promote stability, development and prosperity in the region' (Callick and Kerr 2009). Overall, the Chinese role is very similar to its role in other parts of the developing world: providing development aid with no strings attached, and investing heavily in both infrastructure and resource development.

As China takes its rightful place as a legitimate international actor, it is only natural that it should play a greater role in world politics. China's interests in commerce and resources in the South Pacific will lead it to become more involved in regional affairs, as will competition for diplomatic recognition with Taiwan, should the diplomatic truce break. In large measure, the China as a threat in the South Pacific thesis relies on the assessment that the region is strategically valuable to China, which is itself subject to dispute (Yang 2009). Should China continue to avoid challenging the US militarily, and should the US continue to accommodate China's rise, there is no reason to see China as a serious threat in the South Pacific; indeed, from the perspective of many Pacific Island countries, China's engagement in the region presents a significant opportunity – what is at question now is how to capitalise on the opportunities presented.

United States

The US has a special relationship with the Freely Associated States (FAS) – namely the Federated States of Micronesia, Marshall Islands and Palau – which are essentially politically independent, but allow the US to provide for their defence amongst other things. The FAS, together with Guam and the Northern Mariana Islands 'have been regarded as a security border' by the US, and their defence is considered vital to maintaining open sea lanes of communication (SLOCs) (Lunn and Vaughan 2007: 5). Much like Australia, the US remembers well the Second World War, when its SLOCs with Australia were threatened by Japan, and Australia – vital to the US war effort in the Pacific – was nearly isolated from the US. Furthermore, the US presence in Oceania helped it to bolster its security posture during the Cold War.

The US has been winding down its role in the South Pacific steadily since the end of the Cold War. It has been closed embassies in Solomon Islands and Samoa, aid posts in Papua New Guinea and Fiji, and has wound back its provision of educational assistance in the form of scholarships. At the military level though, the US is looking to expand its presence. Secretary of Defence Robert Gates said in May 2009 that the US was 'actually increasing our military presence [in the central and western Pacific], with new air, naval and marine assets based… in Guam' ('Gates Delivers Keynote Address to Open Asia Security Conference' 2009). Indeed, over the next several years the US intends to spend A$18 billion on turning the island of Guam into what the generals are calling an 'unsinkable aircraft carrier' ('Guam: Tip of the Spear' 2007). This, however, is directed squarely at China, and is intended as a warning about China's activities in the Taiwan Strait, rather than being directed towards South Pacific regional security. That task is left to Australia – to quote Gates again, 'Australia remains a steadfast ally… we welcome Australia's new Defence White Paper reaffirming its role regionally and globally, and continue to seek ways to advance common interests together'('Gates Delivers Keynote Address to Open Asia Security Conference' 2009; author's emphasis).

Conclusion

Despite considerable instances of internal instability in several South Pacific states, the current state of regional security offers some hope. More effective mechanisms to deal with these instances are being developed and implemented by regional powers like Australia and New Zealand, alongside programs to help in preventing their occurrence in the first place. The increased Australian role has both positive and negative elements, but overall Australian interests in regional security align well with the interests of states in the region. While there has been considerable angst displayed over China's increasing role, and the relative withdrawal of the US from the region, it does not seem at this stage that it is a simple matter of China displacing or replacing the US as a major power in Oceania. Rather, it looks more likely that China is simply taking its place as a responsible stakeholder in the region, and that it is happy to work with countries in the region in pursuit of prosperity and development. Concerns about the development of a new Cold War in the region, with China and the US vying for influence has not developed, and looks unlikely to develop at this point, but this in turn depends on how China's rise in a global sense is managed by both the US, and China itself. Furthermore, China's engagement offers considerable opportunities in terms of development assistance and aid, without the sometimes onerous strings attached by donors like Australia, and international economic institutions.

References

Amnesty International. 2009. *Fiji: Paradise Lost: A Tale of Ongoing Human Rights Violations: April - July 2009.* Amnesty International Publications. Available at https://www.amnesty.org/en/library/asset/ASA18/002/2009/en/0024be13-bdd1-47d2-875a-863fff41f978/asa180022009en.pdf

Australian Federal Police website, http://www.afp.gov.au/international/IDG.html accessed 20 October 2009

Australian Strategic Policy Institute. 2003. *Our Failing Neighbour: Australia and the Future of Solomon Islands.* Canberra: ASPI Publications.

Banham, C. 2009. 'Federal Police Work on Plan for PNG Return'. *The Age* (18 September).

Beazley, K. Interview with author.

Callick, R. 2009. 'China, Taiwan end war over aid'. *The Australian* (10 August): 10.

Callick, R., and Kerr, C. 2009. 'Beijing Given Frank Bainimarama Cold Comfort'. *The Australian* (2 May).

Department of Defence. 2000. *Defence 2000: Our future defence force.* Canberra: Department of Defence.

Department of Defence. 2009. *Defending Australia in the Asia Pacific Century: Force 2030.* Canberra: Department of Defence.

Dobell, G. 2007. 'China and Taiwan in the South Pacific: Diplomatic Chess versus Political Rugby'. Policy Brief. Sydney: Lowy Institute for International Policy.

'Gates Delivers Keynote Address to Open Asia Security Conference'. 2009. *American Forces Press Service* (30 May).

'Guam: Tip of the Spear'. 2007. *Foreign Correspondent,* ABC Television (4 September).

Hanson, F. 2008. 'The Dragon Looks South'. Analysis. Sydney: Lowy Institute for International Policy.

Hanson, F. 2009. 'China: Stumbling Through the Pacific'. Policy Brief. Sydney: Lowy Institute for International Policy.

Hayward-Jones, J. 2009. 'Fiji: the Flailing State'. Policy Brief. Sydney: Lowy Institute for International Policy.

Hegarty, D. 1987.*Small State Security in the South Pacific*. Working Paper 126. Strategic and Defence Studies Centre, Australian National University, Canberra.

Henderson, J., and Reilly, B. 2003. 'Dragon in Paradise: China's Rising Star in Oceania'. *The National Interest*. 7(2): 94-104.

Kabutaulaka, T. 2005. 'Australian Foreign Policy and the RAMSI Intervention in Solomon Islands'. *The Contemporary Pacific*. 17(2): 283–308.

Lunn, T., and Vaughan, B. 2007. *The Southwest Pacific: US Interests and China's Growing Influence*. Congressional Research Service.

McFarlane, J. 2007. 'The Thin Blue Line: The Strategic Role of the Australian Federal Police'. *Security Challenges*. 3(3): 91–108.

Nicholson, B. 2009. 'Fiji Troops Excluded from UN Peacekeeping role'. *Sydney Morning Herald* (28 September).

Pilger, J. 2008. 'Australia's Hidden Empire'. *The New Stateman* (6 March).

Roberts, G. 2009. 'PNG Vow to Burn all Asian Shops'. *The Australian* (29 May): 8.

Rudd, K. 2008. *The First National Security Statement to the Australian Parliament* (4 December).

Skehan, C. 2004. 'Pawns in a Diplomatic Poker Game'. *Sydney Morning Herald* (18 December): 31.

Toohey, P. 2009. 'Pariah of the Pacific', *The Australian* (29 January).

Windybank, S. 2005. 'The China Syndrome'. *Policy*. 21(2): 28-33.

Yang, J. 2009. 'China in the South Pacific: A Strategic Threat?' *New Zealand International Review*. 34(1): 8-12.

Zhang, Y. 2007. 'China and the Emerging Regional Order in the South Pacific'. *Australian Journal of International Affairs*. 61(3): 367-381.

www.ingramcontent.com/pod-product-compliance
Lightning Source LLC
Chambersburg PA
CBHW061245270326

41928CB00041B/3418